I0901008

IMAGES
of America

MATHER FIELD

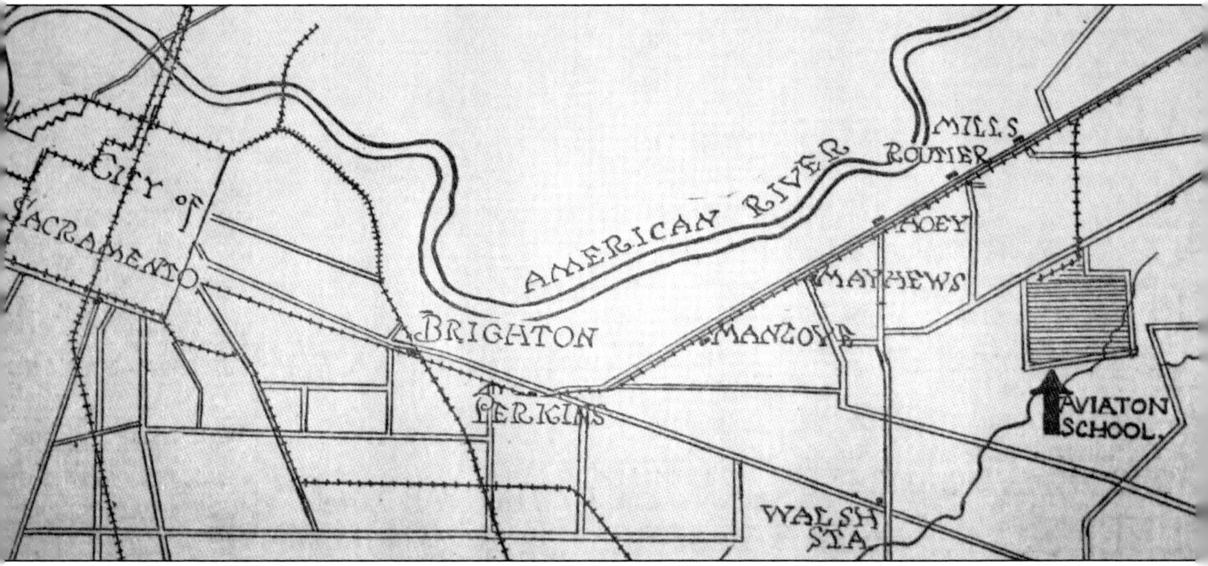

In February 1918, the *Sacramento Bee* published this map, providing coverage from Sacramento eastward to the new aviation school at Mills Station. Weather was no small factor in Sacramento winning the base. With San Diego's North Island Air Station able to train aviators in half the time it took to do the same in the less moderate climes of Texas, Sacramento had a distinct advantage in wooing Uncle Sam. (Sacramento Public Library.)

ON THE COVER: In this image taken at Mather in 1930, Air Corps aviators gather for a photograph, commemorating a record-breaking flight that reached an altitude of 30,000 feet. Clad in high-altitude suits, each man carries approximately 50 pounds of layering to counteract temperatures that dipped to 60 degrees below zero. Helmets with radio headsets were employed to coordinate high-altitude maneuvers, including dogfights and other drills that tested the mettle of America's pursuit planes. (Center for Sacramento History.)

IMAGES
of America

MATHER FIELD

Special Collections of the
Sacramento Public Library

ARCADIA
PUBLISHING

Copyright © 2011 by Special Collections of the Sacramento Public Library
ISBN 978-0-7385-8877-3

Published by Arcadia Publishing
Charleston, South Carolina

Printed in the United States of America

Library of Congress Control Number: 2011928833

For all general information, please contact Arcadia Publishing:
Telephone 843-853-2070
Fax 843-853-0044
E-mail sales@arcadiapublishing.com
For customer service and orders:
Toll-Free 1-888-313-2665

Visit us on the Internet at www.arcadiapublishing.com

Dedicated to James's son and little navigator, Liam, and Tom's grandchildren—Joel, Eli, Paul, and Sarah Padilla.

Contents

Acknowledgments

We gratefully acknowledge the contributions of the following individuals and organizations.

First, great thanks go to the Sacramento Public Library Foundation. Without their financial assistance, this project never could have taken place.

Significant contributions were also made by the following Sacramento Public Library staff: special collections archivist Amanda Graham, Central Library manager Rebecca Higgerson, technology specialist Antonio Gutierrez, library shelver William Lett, programming librarian Lori Easterwood, librarian Gerry Ward and his brother, the late John Ward. The Wards are the sons of Grant Ward, a former Mather officer and historian whose thoughtful collection and storage of base photography and ephemera was instrumental in completing this work.

Thanks also go out to Lynne Kisselburgh Mottley and Scott Davis for their anecdotal input. Both are the children of men who flew their way into history via Mather. Kay Wood, a Cold War–era teacher at Mather, Fair Oaks historian Steve Abbott, and Friends of Mather Regional Park founder Marilyn Evans all provided meaningful information. We also extend our appreciation to principal civil engineer for the Sacramento County Economic Development and Intergovernmental Affairs Department, David Norris, and senior civil engineer for the Sacramento County Department of Transportation, Refugio Razo, for their input on the development of the Mather Commerce Center.

We are also grateful to our library and archive colleagues in providing a majority of the images for this volume, in addition to those drawn from the Sacramento Public Library's (SPL) own collection. They include Sacramento's city historian, Marcia Eymann; archivists Pat Johnson, Rebecca Crowther, and Dylan McDonald of the Center for Sacramento History (CSH); and the staff of the California History Room of the California State Library (CSL). They truly are the best at what they do. Additional contributing organizations include the National Archives and Records Administration and the Smithsonian Institution's National Air and Space Museum and Archives of American Art.

Introduction

The patch of land that is now referred to as "Mather" was once tied to a pristine and lush stretch of landscape, extending eastward from the mystical confluence of the Sacramento and American Rivers to the foothills of the Sierra Nevada Range. The topography, flora, and fauna sustained the indigenous Nisenan for millennia—that is, until the discovery of gold shattered both their land and their lives. Anglo European pick-and-shovel ventures gave way to larger and more destructive means of wringing ore from the soil as rail lines delivered an infusion of permanent settlers. As the 20th century loomed, grains and grapes (both well suited to the valley's Mediterranean climate) were uneasy neighbors to a Natomas Company that fluctuated between dredging and planting the vast acreage it controlled.

In time, world events brought a federal commission to the area's de facto seat, Mills Station, in search of a site to house what was, for that time, a most revolutionary concept: a military aviation school. Seeing the venture through would be the passionate and dedicated efforts of Sacramento's chamber of commerce. To those in the county leading hardscrabble lives, the technology of flight was beyond comprehension and looked upon as unnatural, something that would be referred to as science fiction within a dozen years.

The Great War's end ushered in uncertain times for the newly established field. After the last class of pilots graduated in January 1918, the military presence slowly dwindled as hangars and other support facilities were repurposed to fire-control aircraft. In mid-1922, the Department of War placed Mather Field on inactive status, prompting a jittery and concerned chamber of commerce to contribute to the maintenance costs for the grounds and surrounding buildings. Boosts to Mather included a thrilling air circus in 1928, set to coincide with the inauguration of airmail service to the region and the 1927 appearance of aviation hero Charles Lindbergh. Perhaps Mather's most defining interwar event began in April 1930, with nearly a month of Army Air Corps maneuvers testing and showcasing new machines and technology. Congressman James M. Wilcox organized the National Air Frontier Defense Association late in 1934 with the intention of setting up bases in sections of America's borders, or frontier. The War Department took exception to the original plan, but an amended bill citing seven strategic areas requiring bases capable of maintaining at least one three-squadron group was approved and signed into law on August 12, 1935. The bases were to be located in the Northeast, Southeast, Northwest, Great Lakes, Gulf of Mexico, and Rocky Mountain regions as well as Alaska. Mather backers and promoters hoped the bill would mean rehabilitation and reinstatement of the airfield, but a new air depot built to the north of Sacramento soon to be christened McClellan Field became the government's priority.

With Japanese and German juggernauts sacking territories en masse, the Department of War opted to ease Mather back into service. The advent of World War II had watershed implications for the base, with events beginning in October 1941 that would determine much of Mather's coming fate. Again, instruction would pace the base's action, with navigator and pilot training standing as primary charges. By war's end, Mather would have the highest enrollment of any navigation school in the country, making it such that all four officers—pilot, copilot, navigator, and bombardier—on thousands of multiengine planes had potentially received their commissions at the Sacramento base. Mather, a practical cross section of American life, would also provide a bounty in the arts, music, athletics, and leadership.

While Mather and the rest of Sacramento County reveled in a hard-won peace, competing political ideologies and an accelerated growth of weapons systems brought the base into a world dominated, and perhaps even saved, by a balance-of-power geopolitics and the specter of mutually assured destruction. With the 1958 arrival of the legendary B-52, "alert pads" and "quick takeoffs" became a way of life at Mather—all within the understanding that bilateral deterrents would ensure a bilateral peace.

In 1952, Col. Sam Maddux, commander of the newly named Mather Air Force Base, described the recently created position of flight observer—an amalgam of navigator, bombardier, and radar operator—as "the man who makes the modern bomber a weapon. These highly trained specialists leave here to join the combat crews that make our Air Force such a power for peace." Made during the gear-up for a Cold War fraught with proxy conflict and extravagant defense budgets, Maddux's words speaks to the essence of an Air Force as less the aggressor and more a joint guarantor of a world kept free of nuclear cataclysm. In many ways, Maddux's comments have resonance, dovetailing with so much of what it meant (and means) to be part of the Mather experience: a sunny outpost and a self-styled "West Point of the Air" that sought to "Prepare the Man," as the Air Training Command liked to put it; and, in doing so, transformed hulks of aluminum into scepters of policy and maintaining peace.

With the passing of time, Mather shed the romance of those heady military days and formed a nexus of mixed-use progress while becoming a worldwide blueprint for a postwar community, with aggressive investment and commerce, a nationally lauded program to ease citizens into permanent housing and employment, the transformation of dilapidated housing into a veritable village on the plain, and the development of a regional medical center to tend to the ills of veterans. No less crucial are the tireless efforts of those who see Mather as a recreational spot and home to some of the American West's most unique natural spaces and habitats. Knowing the history of Mather, from jackrabbits to Jennies to jets to Jackson Properties, one will quickly see that it is indeed a place where the art of the possible was taken, implemented, and pushed into a whole new realm.

Nearly 70 years after the air training wing's arrival at Mather and almost a century after the appearance of the first Signal Corps aviators, one can see undeniably that the ethic of "preparing the man" has never left but rather has transformed itself into a practice whereby the base's stewards continue to mindfully "prepare the community." Whether concerning a stressed ecosystem, a world edging itself toward nuclear war, or a community pining for progress, Mather never seems to stop asking itself, "What are we prepared to fight for today?"

One

Preflight Mather
by Tom Tolley

The Nisenan hunted and fished the flatland between the Sacramento River and the American River for centuries before Spain and, later, Mexico claimed the California coastline and all land falling east. From the mid-1830s until the Mexican War, small groups of pioneers found their way across the country. Adaptable adventurers John Sutter and William Alexander Leidesdorff benefitted from Mexican land grants but embraced the new American presence. The military element in California played a hand in the development of a main road, and the discovery of gold on Sutter's land brought a flood of gold-seekers from around the world.

Leidesdorff died before realizing the riches on his rancho, and Sutter's wealth faded before his eyes. But many who came with the forty-niners stayed and worked the land, settling into raising crops and families. Mills visible from the main roads gave the area its name, and the first railroad in California ran through to the town of Folsom. Mining and agriculture defined Mills as gold-dredgers eventually spewed piles of rock over former fields of barley, orchards, and grapevines. Amos Catlin harnessed water and charged for the service, creating the Natomas Company, which would control the destiny of the area into the next century. Life along the rail line to Folsom was quiet, with visits to the stations scattered every few miles a welcome relief from fieldwork.

When the United States entered the First World War in 1917, the government sought suitable areas for aviation schools to train pilots for the conflict. The Sacramento Chamber of Commerce began its long association with Mills Station after a successful visit with federal commission members. The area spoke for itself, offering over 700 acres of flat ground close to a river, near a major road and rail line, and with perfect weather for flying. The deal was sealed early in 1918, and planning for the new airfield at Mills escalated into hard work in March, when the first group of laborers arrived. Aviators came to Mills Field from schools across the country, including a group from Ellington Field, Texas, where a popular flyer had died too young.

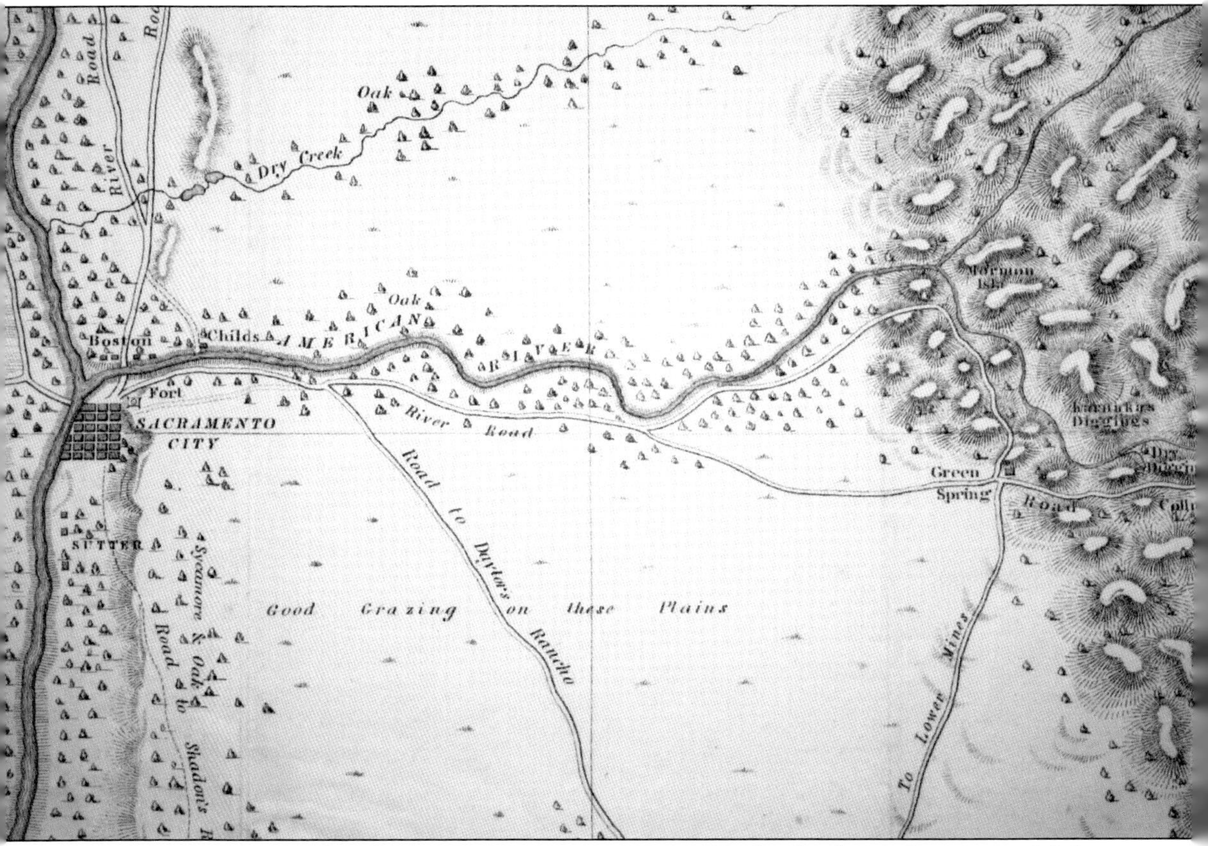

US Army topographical engineer Lt. George Horatio Derby fought in the war with Mexico before mapping what Gen. Bennet C. Riley and his troops encountered in the mining districts and the Sacramento Valley in the summer and fall of 1849. In the beginning of 1849, there were approximately 150 men in Sacramento, but within a few months of the completion of this map, they would number in the thousands, with more arriving daily. Names that do not appear on this map include Pusune, Sama, and Anape, which were communities along the rivers that were home for centuries to Nisenan tribes decimated by malaria brought with trappers in 1833. Disease took an estimated 75 percent of the Southern Maidu before the Gold Rush. Contact with rough mining parties who killed them for sport or scalped and stole their children for slaves claimed most of the others. Lieutenant Derby was one of California's first humorists. Published as "John Phoenix," his newspaper columns were gathered in book form more than 20 years after his death in 1861 at age 48. Fort Riley, Kansas, is named for General Riley. (SPL.)

The Sacramento Valley was unknown to all but a handful of Europeans in 1839 when self-styled Capt. John Sutter first set foot on land he would control for the next decade. Gregarious by nature, Sutter welcomed visitors to the fort that protected his domain and was glad to help his new neighbor William Leidesdorff establish the boundaries for the land grant bestowed on him in 1844. (SPL.)

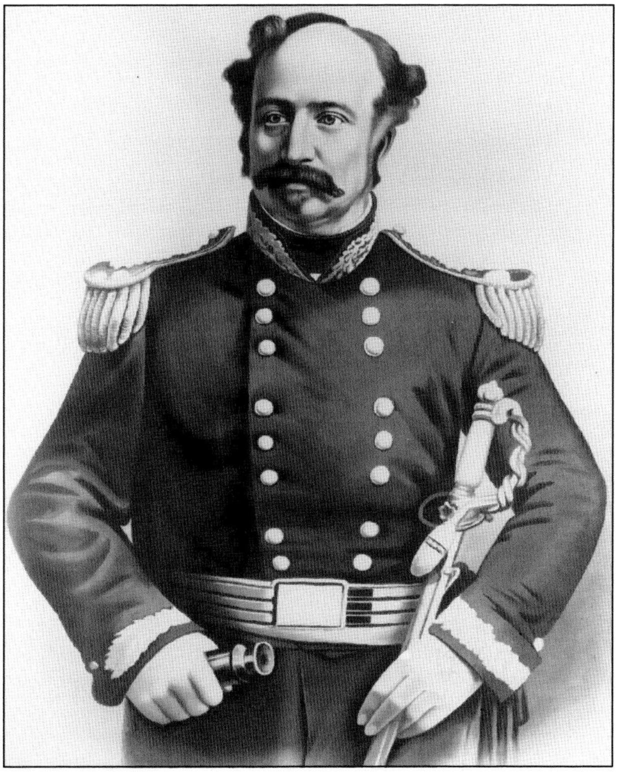

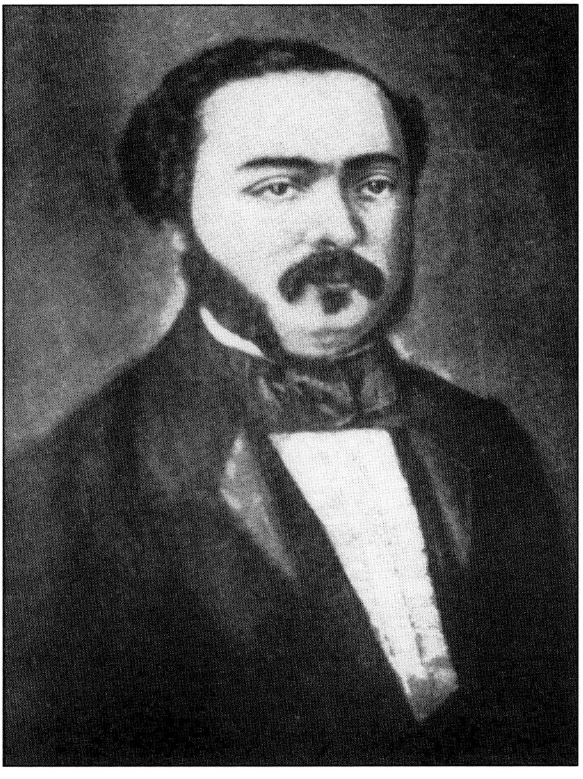

Larger-than-life William Leidesdorff was a master mariner who cut a colorful swath through early California and became a key player in the growth of San Francisco. Leidesdorff became a Mexican citizen in 1844, and he petitioned the governor "to obtain a tract of land . . . bounded by the lands of Senor Sutter . . . situated on the banks of the American River." Leidesdorff died of a brain fever in 1848, at the age of 38. (SPL.)

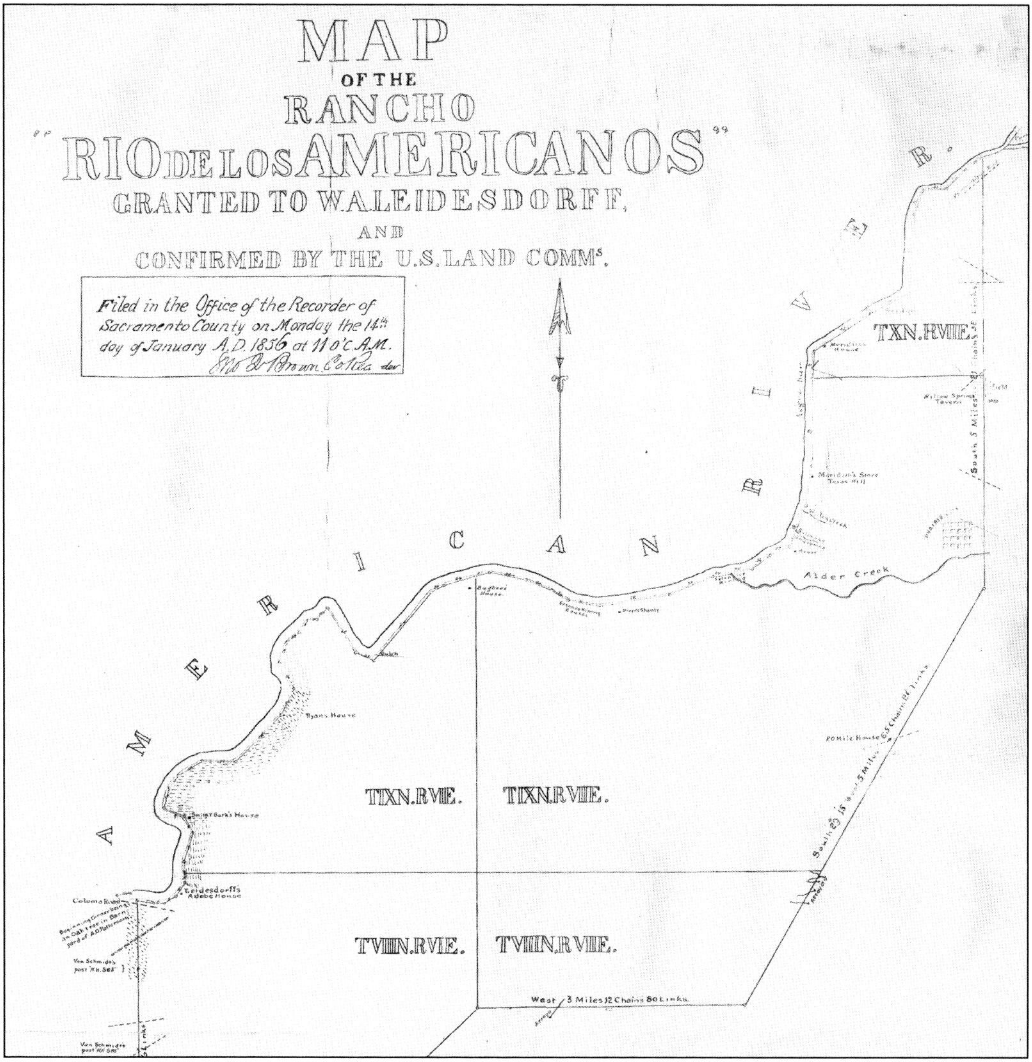

In 1848, Capt. John Sutter made a deposition concerning the fledgling Natomas Water and Mining Company and the estate of the recently deceased William Leidesdorff. Sutter explained his role in the transfer of title to the Rancho Rio de los Americanos to Leidesdorff, a process known as judicial possession. According to Sutter's diary, the event took place in January 1846. As authorized by Mexican law, Sutter and Leidesdorff rode from the eastern boundary of Sutter's New Helvetia grant near Bradshaw Road to approximately the distance specified in the grant, four leagues long and two leagues wide. The land south of the American River and east of a tree designated as the border of New Helvetia stretched past what became the town of Folsom to the *lomerías*, or low hills; but in the deposition, Sutter could not determine the exact spot on a map. Sutter stated that they rode from morning until night using no instruments for measurement. His understanding was that the ride and observation of the terrain met legal requirements for possession of the land, an old practice known as *vista de ojo*, or "view of the eye." (CSH.)

Lt. Joseph Folsom was stationed in Yerba Buena in 1848 when William Leidesdorff died. Knowing that the adventurer's mother lived on the island of St. Croix, he arranged passage and secured title to the Rancho Rio de los Americanos for $75,000 down. Folsom and his investors faced long legal wrangling over ownership of the estate, and by the time the town bearing his name was established, Folsom was dead. (SPL.)

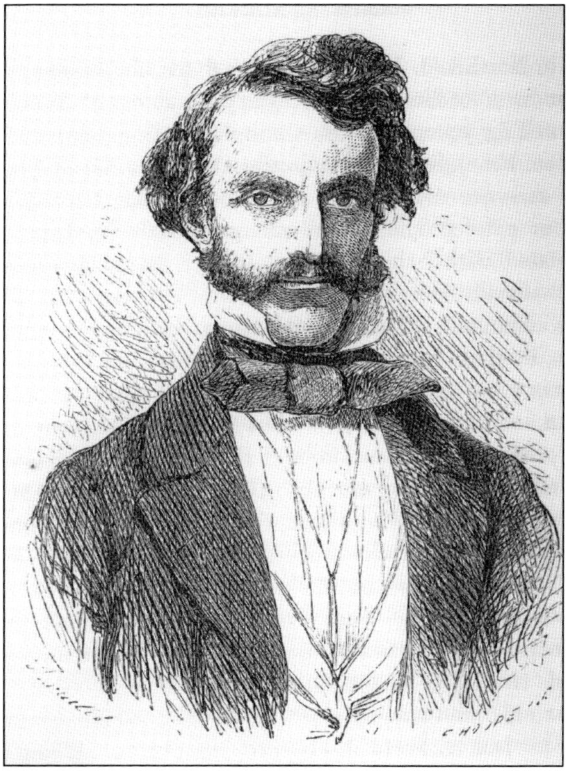

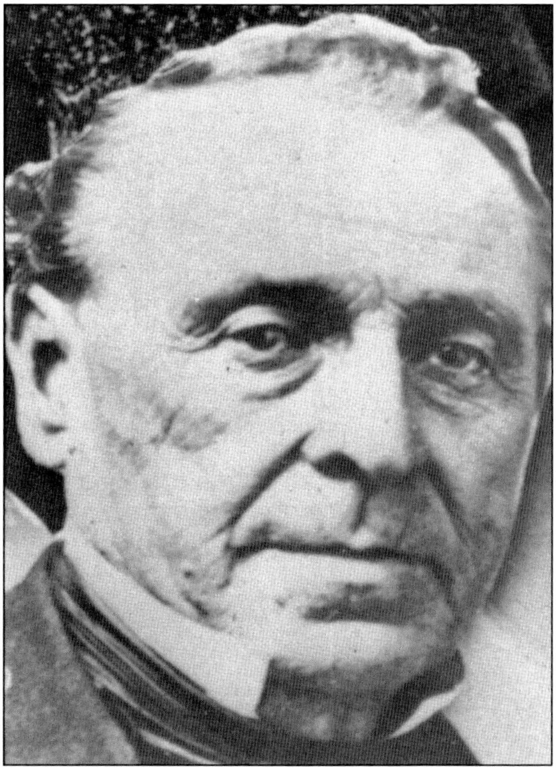

Arnold Duncan Patterson's original establishment was roughly 10 miles from Sacramento, and that designation was used to distinguish the way stations following the course of the American River. Constructed of cloth in 1849, the station near what is now Bradshaw Road became, within a year, the most popular stop along the route to the mining camps. Patterson served as sheriff, assemblyman, and justice of the peace before his station burned down in 1871. The following year, he build another station, known as Routier's, on the Folsom Road. (SPL.)

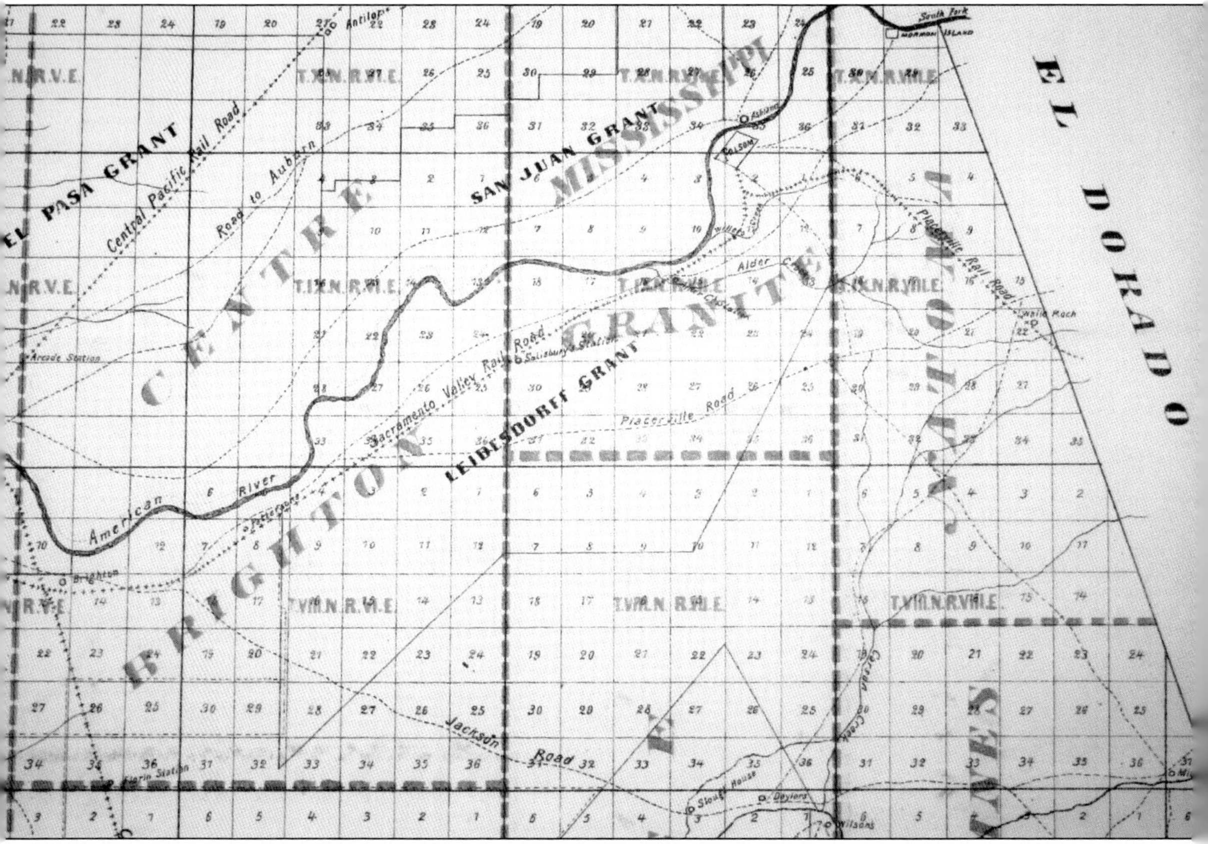

Many men and women walked and rode over Leidesdorff's land grant in search of wealth, some returning after mining and hiring their teams and wagons to new gold-seekers. Rich soil, the proximity to water, and easy access to roads leading everywhere made the area from Brighton to Mills Station and beyond attractive to settlers. The waves of men, women, wagons, and beasts came from east of the Mississippi River. Before the great California Gold Rush, the overwhelming majority of the population was content to live on less than half of America's land mass. By 1848, the newest state was Wisconsin, and travel west of the Missouri River was uncommon, though the borders of the relatively new nation now stretched from Florida swampland to sun-baked Texas. Other than a few landmarks and settled forts along the way, pioneers knew little of the trek ahead other than shared copies of the few guidebooks available at that time. Everyone was from somewhere else. Nathan Patton was born in Missouri in 1810, the year his father was killed by Indians. T.C. Perkins came from Massachusetts at 20, and James Ryan sailed from Ireland to Canada, then ventured to California in 1855. R.D. Stephens lived nine miles from Sacramento, with Nelson Shaver 10 miles away. John Studarus's orchards were 11 miles away, and John Shields farm was 13 miles down the road from Sacramento. Post offices were set along the rail route and often named for the family established in that area or the first postmaster. (SPL.)

A native of France and the namesake of a post office and historic ranch near the American River, Joseph Routier came to Sacramento in the employ of Joseph Folsom in 1853 to supervise the planting and maintenance of a vineyard and orchards on the huge Leidesdorff property. Folsom died before the various claims to the estate and conflicting surveys were resolved, but Routier purchased 120 acres and established the first orchard and vineyard on the Rancho Rio de los Americanos. (SPL.)

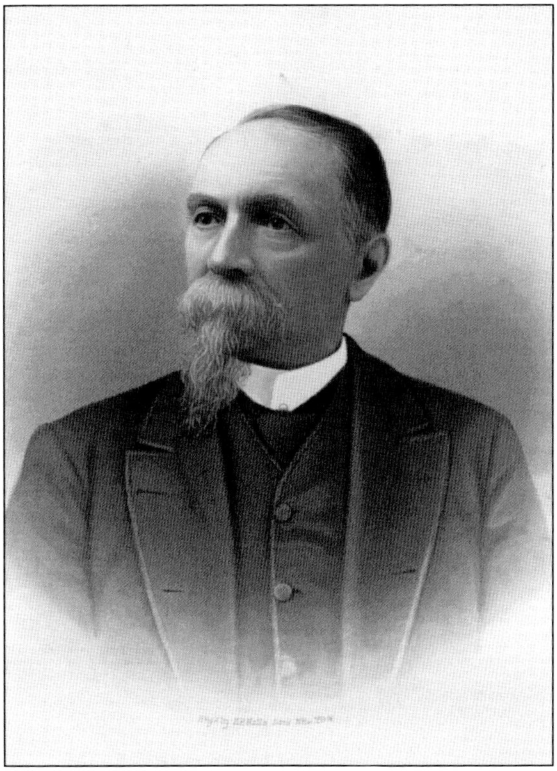

Routier and his flame Tokay grapes were widely known, as was the station built in 1871 along the Sacramento Valley Railroad and, later, Southern Pacific Company tracks. Arnold Patterson, one of the first settlers in the area, erected the station after his building burned and served as postmaster until he was 80. Routier sold his ranch in 1897, but the station bearing his name still survives as a stop along the light-rail connecting Sacramento and Folsom. (SPL.)

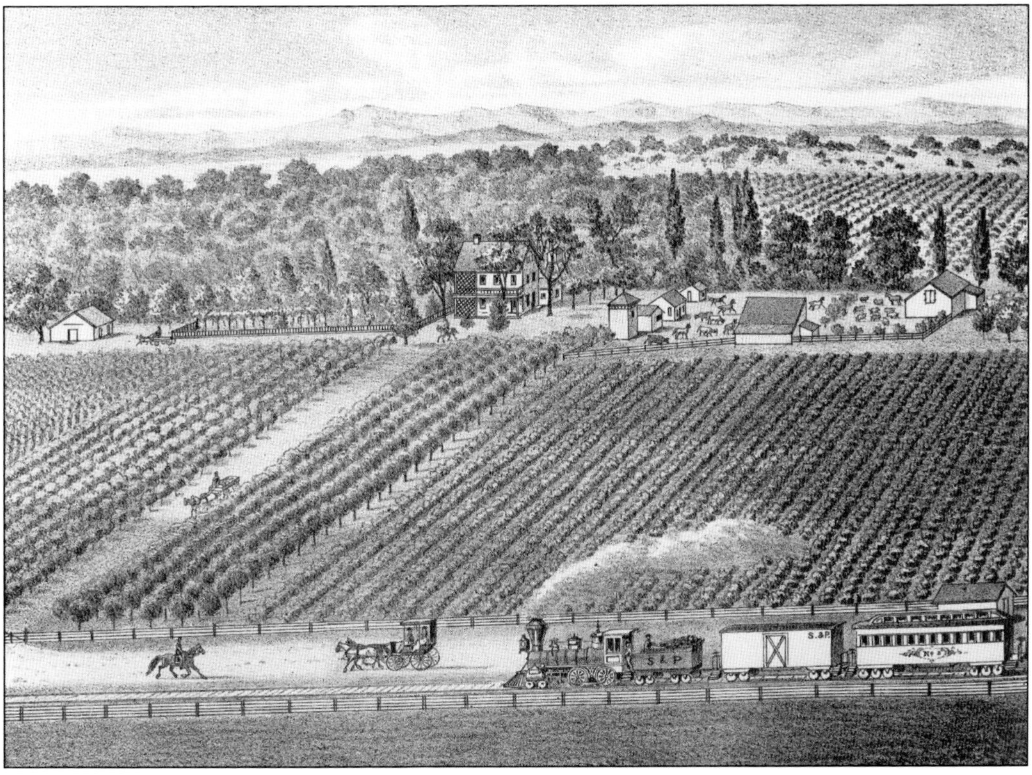

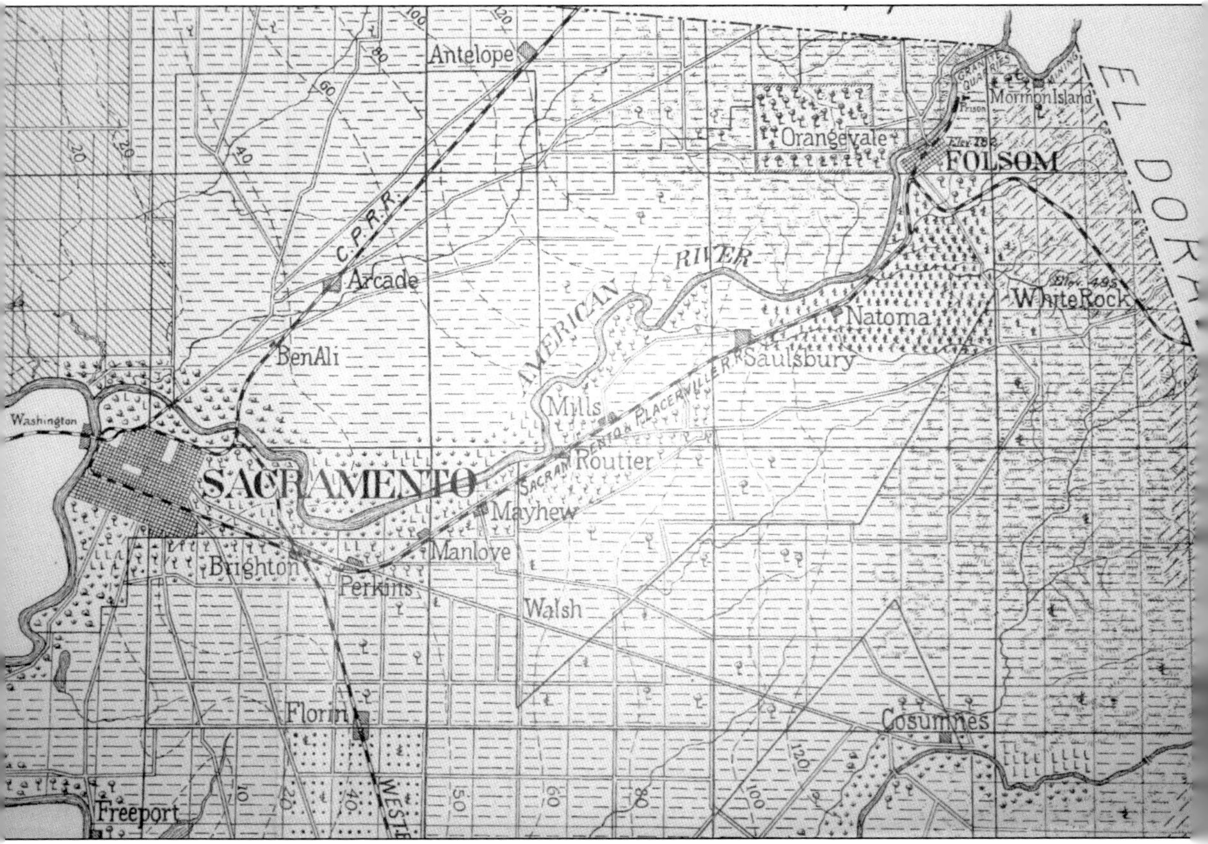

They had names like Studarus, Deterding, Kilgore, Menke, Patterson, Perkins, and Routier, and they were all immigrants headed to a new life in a new territory. Most left businesses, property, and even family behind and worked as miners, teamsters, and soldiers before putting down roots and seeds to farm the land adjacent to the American River. There were merchants and tradesmen among the men coming from the East who traveled the Placerville and Hangtown Roads. Some like James Day and Arnold Patterson built inns and way stations along the roads from Sacramento to Folsom, Coloma, Mormon Island, and outlying mining areas. The routes to the mines and goldfields in Auburn and beyond ran northeast, and the road to Sloughhouse and Jackson wove southwest, but Theodore Judah planned the path of the first railroad west of the Mississippi River to parallel the middle road directly through Leidesdorff's rancho to the town of Folsom. (SPL.)

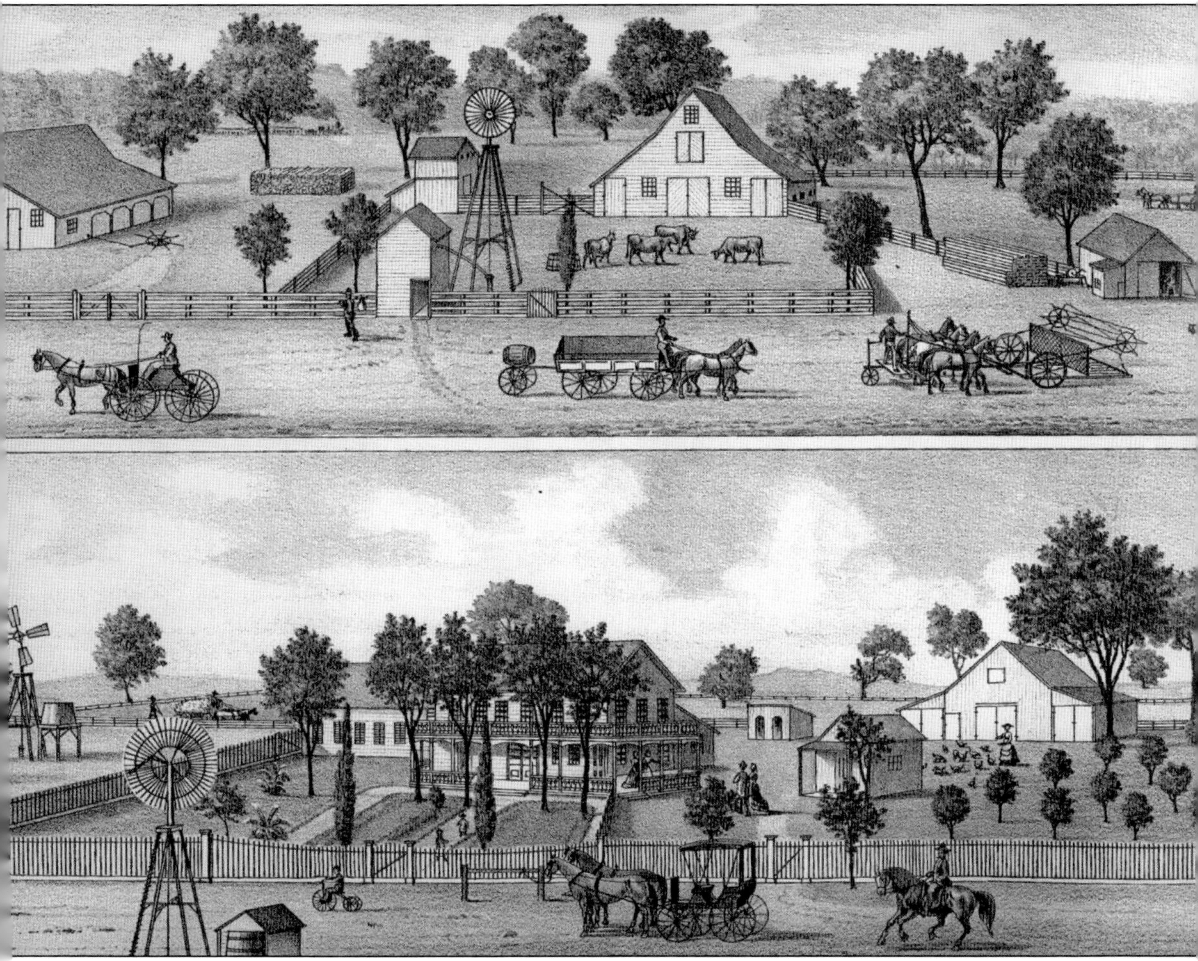

The plank road that ran from Sacramento and passed through the Carmichael Colony was never a threat to the main road that followed M Street eastward, which was the route the Pony Express would take in 1861. Roads became so congested that wagons, stagecoaches, and teams of oxen staggered their departures, putting just enough miles behind them to reach one of the way stations along the route by nightfall. Identified by their distance from the growing city of Sacramento were the 10-Mile House, 11-Mile House, 12-Mile House, and Henry Deterding's 15-Mile House on thoroughfares known at various times as the River Road/Plank Road (parts of J Street and Folsom Boulevard), Daylor Ranch Road (Jackson Road/State Route 16), and Lower Stockton Road. Most of these establishments offered board as well as meals and libations. The completion of the Sacramento Valley Railroad and subsequent rail lines coincided with the decline in prospecting and the rise of agriculture near Mills Station; and those who ran the way stations, struggling to survive, did what they could to make ends meets. In the early part of the 20th century, much of the original Leidesdorff Grant and the Granite Township were changing hands to the Natomas Company, which tore down historic structures like the 15-Mile House to dredge for minerals, continuing the cycle of exploiting the land followed by cultivating it. (SPL.)

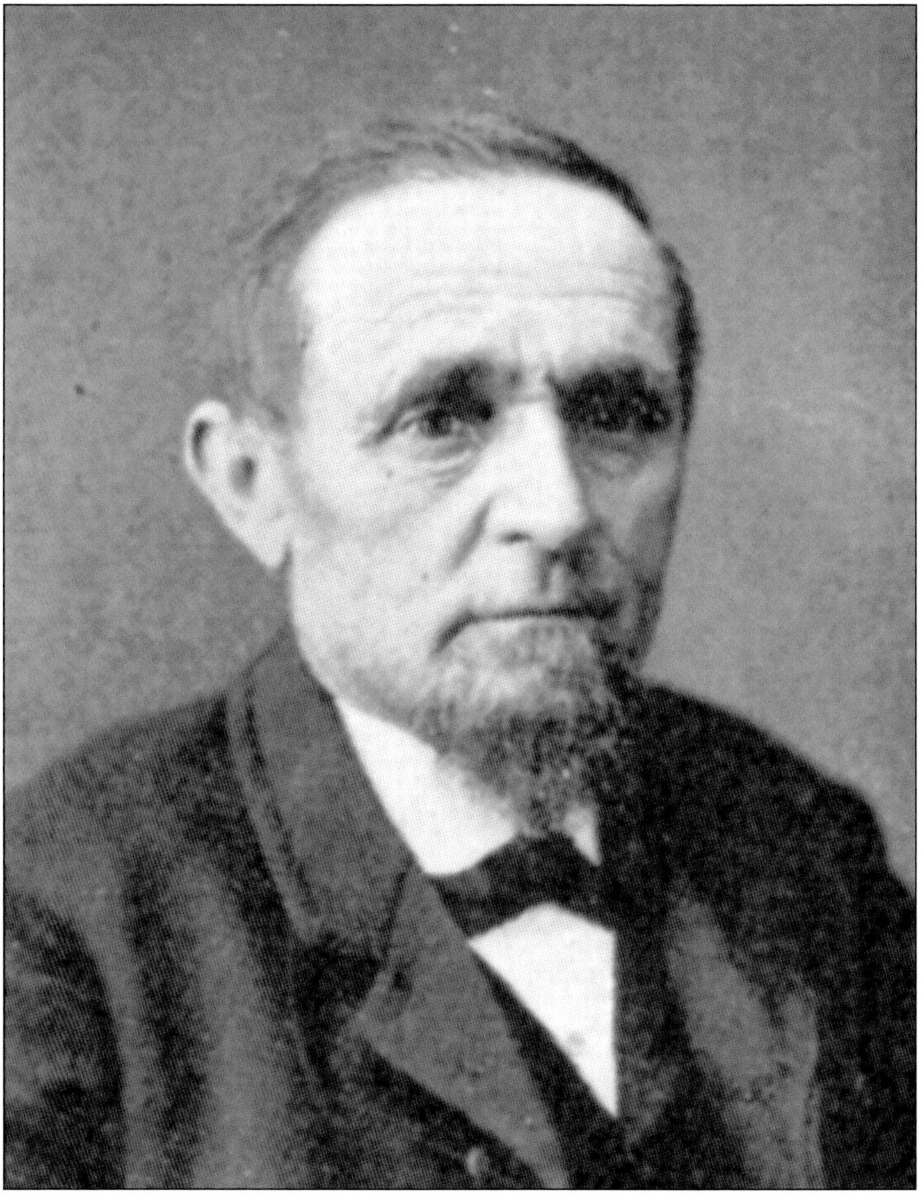

A native of Switzerland like earlier settler John A. Sutter, John B. Studarus immigrated to America in 1847. He and his family made their way in 1853 to El Dorado County, where a talent for mining provided enough funds to rent rich farmland on the American River bottom, resting on the contested Leidesdorff Grant. Studarus purchased over 330 acres in 1857. With the rise of the railways and completion of the Central Pacific Railroad, the clamor for fruit grown in the Sacramento Valley placed priorities on crops harvested from orchards and vineyards. Studarus sired more than a dozen children, many of them engaging in farming the family land. John Studarus Jr. purchased five acres at the former Hangtown crossing, popularly known as Mills since about 1870, when two flour mills built near what is now Mather Drive were landmarks along the old Brighton Turnpike Road. In 1911, Studarus built a large commercial property that served the community as dance hall, post office, grocery and hardware store, branch library, gas station, and social center. (SPL.)

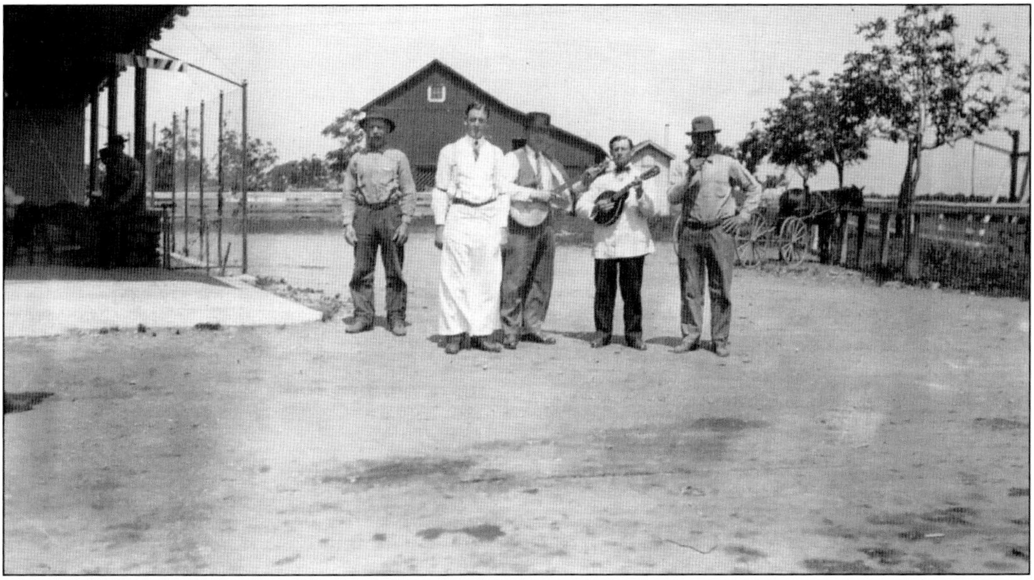

In 1914, life at Mills Station was leisurely. The station and outbuildings were still the center of activity in the area between Brighton and Folsom in the days when establishments were measured by how many miles they were from Sacramento. A handful of the barmen, waiters, deliverymen, and livery help that operated the station pose for a photograph, musical instruments in hand indicating that they doubled as entertainment to liven up the dusty depot. Posing in front of the Mills Post Office, the jaunty gentlemen astride the Indian motorcycle are harbingers of the times to come, representatives of the mechanized future that would land abruptly a mile or two away in four short years. These images came from the album of George Wissemann, a Sacramento whiskey salesman. (Both, Steve Abbott.)

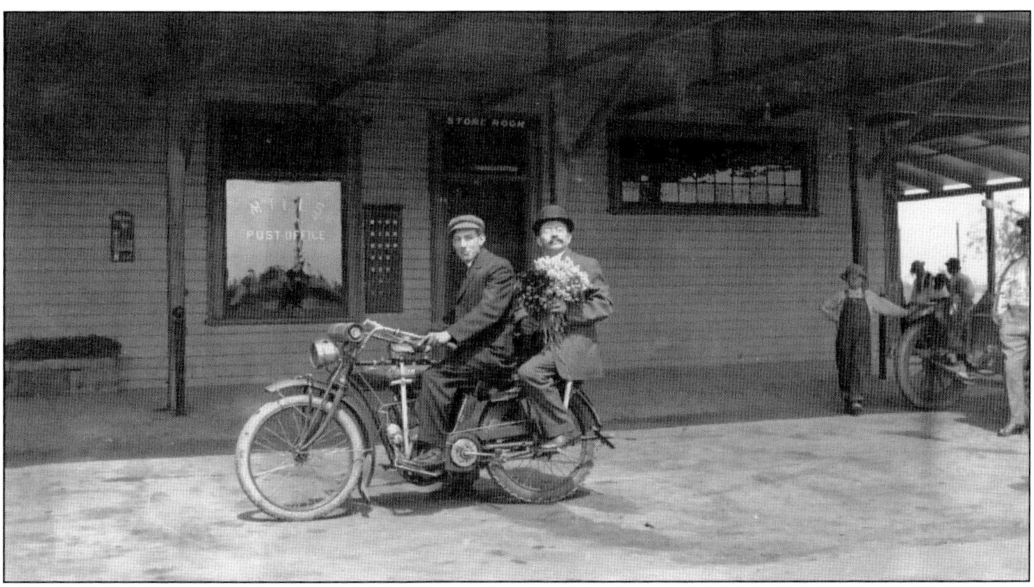

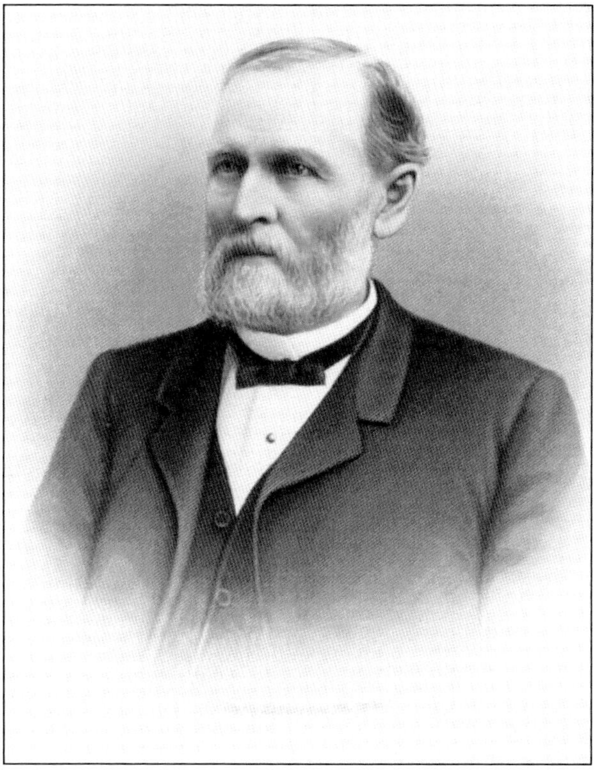

Former miners Amos P. Catlin (left) and Horatio G. Livermore knew that a supply of water was paramount to the success of any mining operation, and that knowledge led to the formation of the Natomas Water and Mining Company by Catlin around the same time that California was admitted to the Union. After leaving mining in 1865, Catlin edited the *Sacramento Union* and entered politics. A strange set of circumstances found Catlin in Washington, DC, during late 1863, testifying for two days concerning the title to Leidesdorff's vast estate. After Livermore assumed presidency of the company, his focus moved to advantages to be gained by providing water to manufacturing firms and the increased population that would take advantage of the completion of the transcontinental railroad and the deepwater route connecting Sacramento with the thriving harbor in San Francisco. (Both, SPL.)

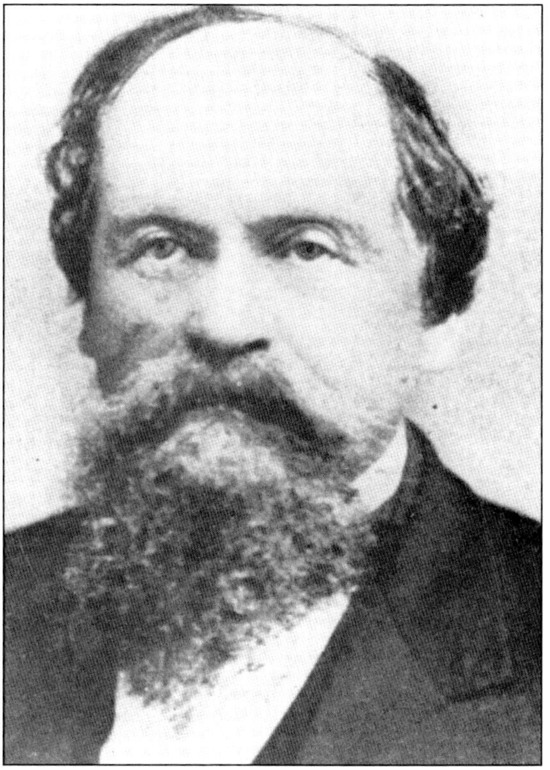

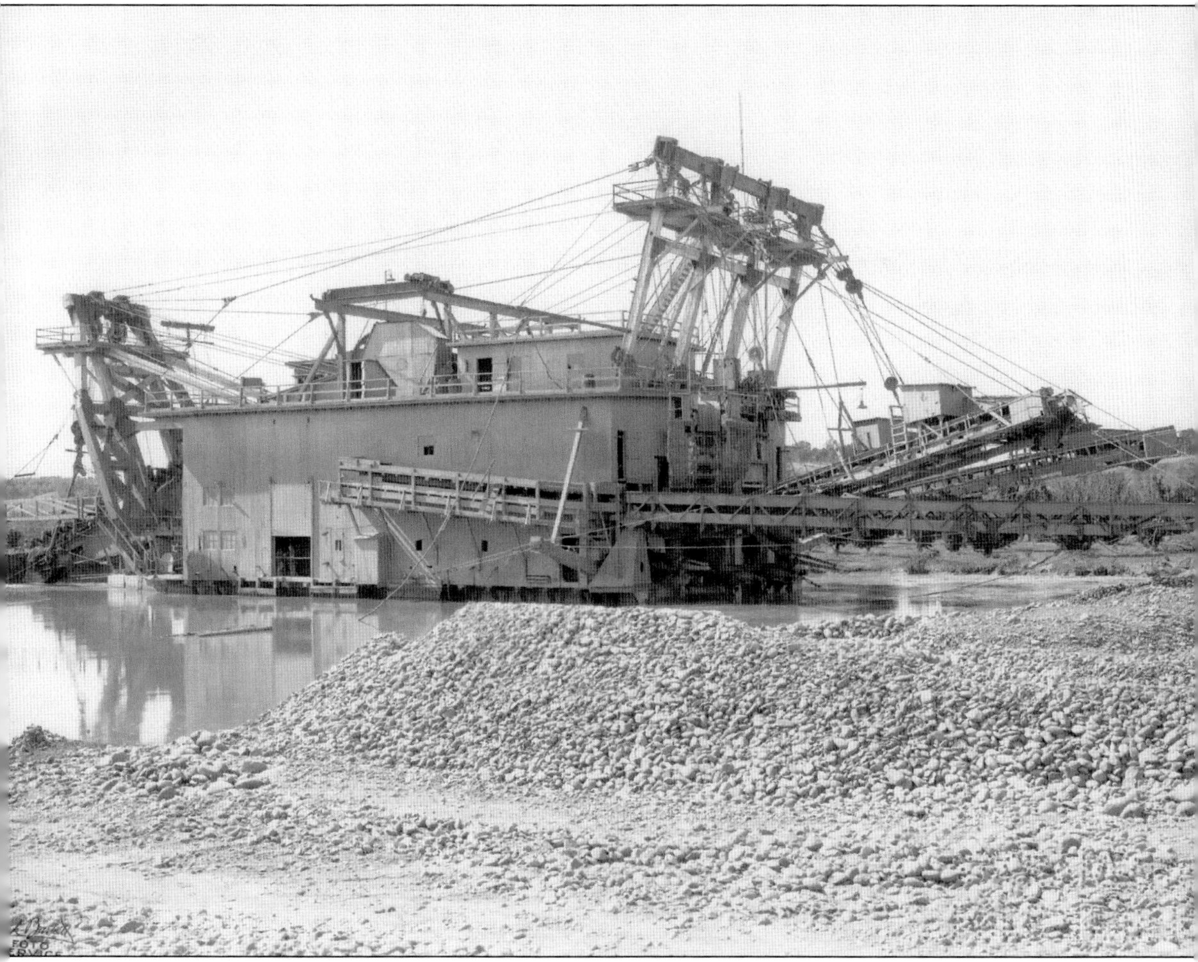

In the summer of 1903, the Folsom Development Company took advantage of an earlier option on Natomas property and built a town name Dredge south of the American River, where the machines were constructed and maintained. The growth of this new means of uncovering minerals changed the direction of the Natomas Vineyard Company; in 1906 its holdings and properties were merged with the Syndicate Dredging Company and the Colorado-Pacific Gold Dredging Company to form the Natomas Development Company. This was a move that brought in $600,000 but ended any beneficial use of the soil. Some of these monstrous machines developed in New Zealand were built on-site in a pond that, when flooded, floated the dredger as the attached bucket dug into earth and rock, then dropped them onto a large, revolving screen. As the gravel passed through the screen, it fell into a sluice containing mercury, which bonded with any gold present and made it easier to isolate and remove the precious metal. The dredger was then able to move forward, filling in behind with the rock tailings. (SPL.)

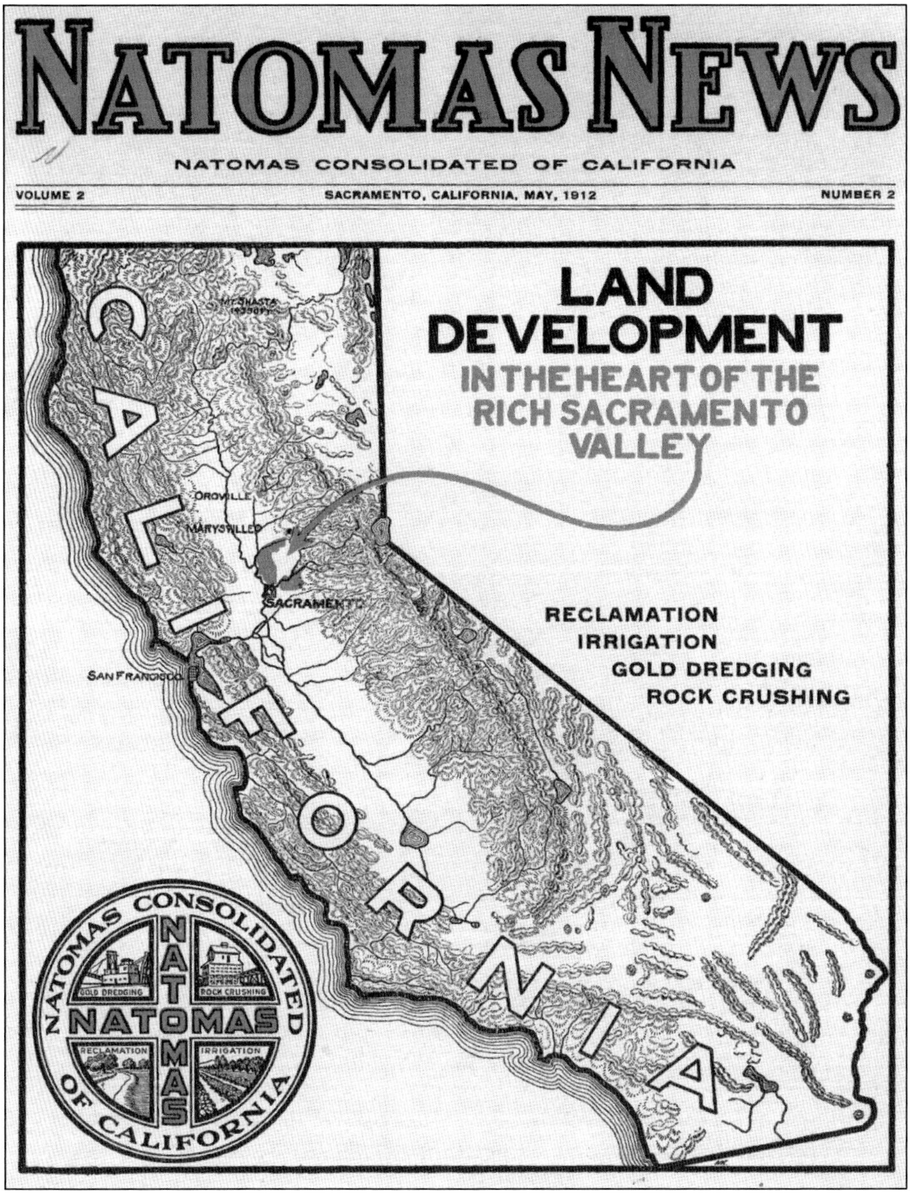

By the time the Civil War came to a close, the Natomas Company had entered the logging business, but funding troubles and flooding hindered plans and progress. Further exploitation of the company's mineral resources was limited, so leasing quarries containing granite, gravel, and cobble that lay on Natomas property kept some money coming in. With revenue drying up in the water business, Natomas left mining and minerals behind, as planting and agricultural development became the economic wheel. This kept Natomas in operation from 1872, when 200 acres were planted in grapevines, followed by 350 acres devoted to grapes and raisins. Within a dozen years, the company operated the largest winery in the state and owned orchards, acreage in hay and grain, and a fruit-drying and shipping business as a result of a reorganization that put Horace Putnam Livermore in charge of expansion. While the Natomas Vineyard Company focused on agriculture, new developments in mining found their way back to the area after R.G. Hanford introduced the newly developed continuous bucket line–configuration gold dredger. (SPL.)

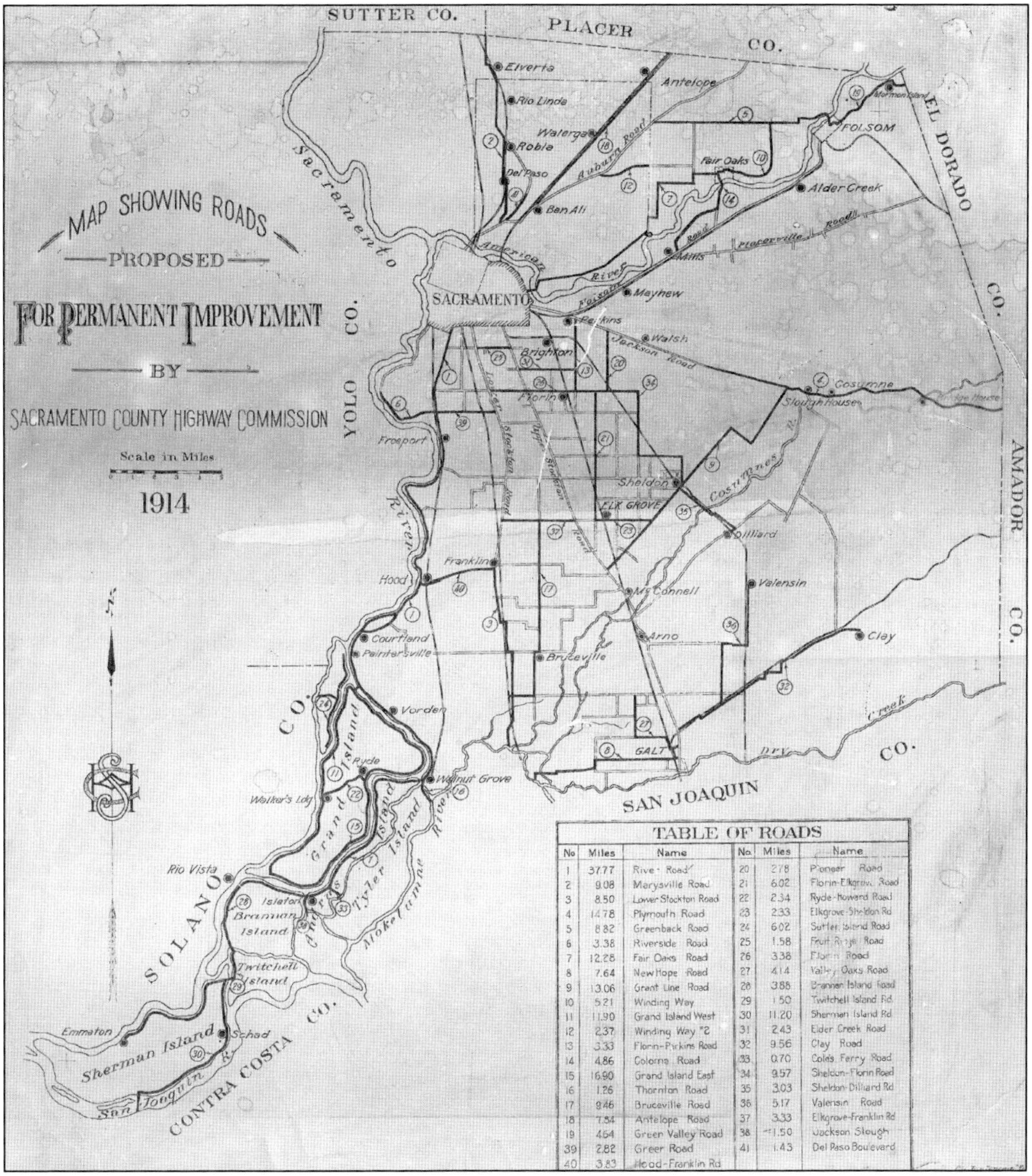

No	Miles	Name	No.	Miles	Name
1	37.77	River Road	20	2.78	Pioneer Road
2	9.08	Marysville Road	21	6.02	Florin-Elkgrove Road
3	8.50	Lower Stockton Road	22	2.34	Ryde-Howard Road
4	14.78	Plymouth Road	23	2.33	Elkgrove-Sheldon Rd
5	8.82	Greenback Road	24	6.02	Sutter Island Road
6	3.38	Riverside Road	25	1.58	Fruit Ridge Road
7	12.28	Fair Oaks Road	26	3.38	Florin Road
8	7.64	New Hope Road	27	4.14	Valley Oaks Road
9	13.06	Grant Line Road	28	3.88	Brannan Island Road
10	5.21	Winding Way	29	1.50	Twitchell Island Rd
11	11.90	Grand Island West	30	11.20	Sherman Island Rd
12	2.37	Winding Way #2	31	2.43	Elder Creek Road
13	3.33	Florin-Perkins Road	32	9.56	Clay Road
14	4.86	Coloma Road	33	0.70	Cole's Ferry Road
15	16.90	Grand Island East	34	9.57	Sheldon-Florin Road
16	1.26	Thornton Road	35	3.03	Sheldon-Dillard Rd
17	9.46	Bruceville Road	36	5.17	Valensin Road
18	7.84	Antelope Road	37	3.33	Elkgrove-Franklin Rd
19	4.64	Green Valley Road	38	1.50	Jackson Slough
39	2.82	Greer Road	41	1.43	Del Paso Boulevard
40	3.83	Hood-Franklin Rd			

The California Gold Rush brought thousands of immigrants to the Sacramento area within a few years, and by the time Theodore Judah mapped out the route for the Sacramento Valley Railroad in 1854, the main roads were established and remain so to this day. Though the first agrarian efforts in the area north of the Consumnes River were initiated by travelers new to California, the settlers thrived and grew large families to help build their own destiny through the land. Second-generation pioneers like John Studarus struck out on their own, buying acreage near the family property and going into retail business. John Joseph Smith was born near the Hangtown Crossing in 1868 on a ranch his father bought for $7. In 1889, the younger Smith left farm life and took employment as a guard at Folsom State Prison. Eventually appointed warden at Folsom Prison in late 1913, his knowledge of farming and livestock helped put the prison on a path to work that rehabilitated prisoners while making the facility as self-supporting as possible. (CSH.)

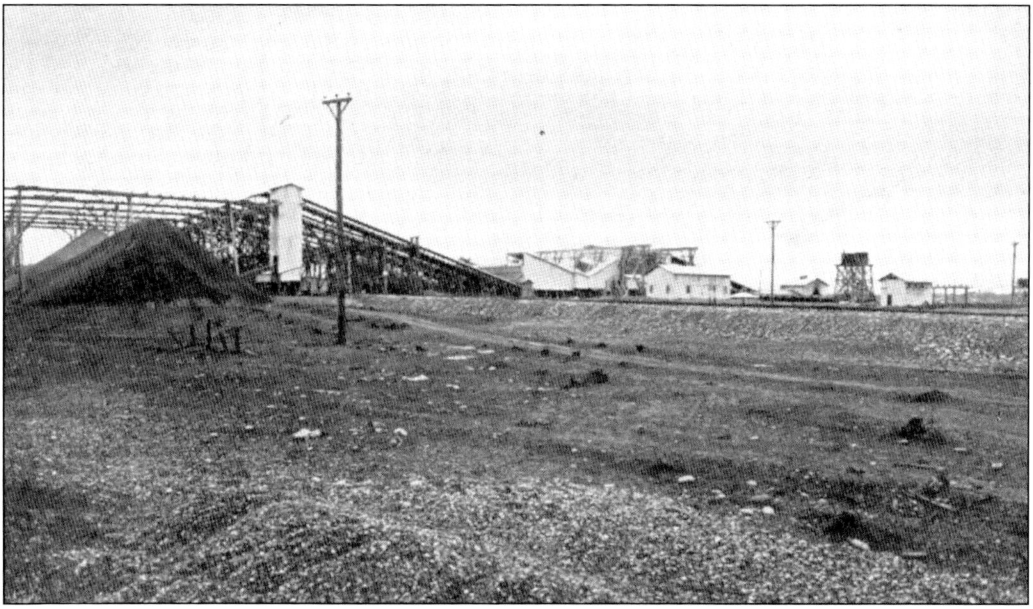

A Good Roads convention was held in Sacramento in 1893, and in March 1895, a state bureau of highways was established. These events led to the introduction of Senate Bill 513, which provided for the "construction of a State Highway or Wagon Road from Sacramento City to Folsom State Prison." A new rock-crushing machine at Folsom Prison and the Fair Oaks Rock-Crushing Plant (above) supplied the road surfacing for macadamizing the 22-mile highway from Sacramento to Folsom (below). This process involved scraping the existing roadway level, adding five inches of crushed rock flattened by a steamroller, then adding another smaller level and bedding it down with the roller. Finely crushed rock referred to as screenings was dusted on top of the elevated road, wet down, and rolled once again. The resulting surface was known as road metal. (Both, SPL.)

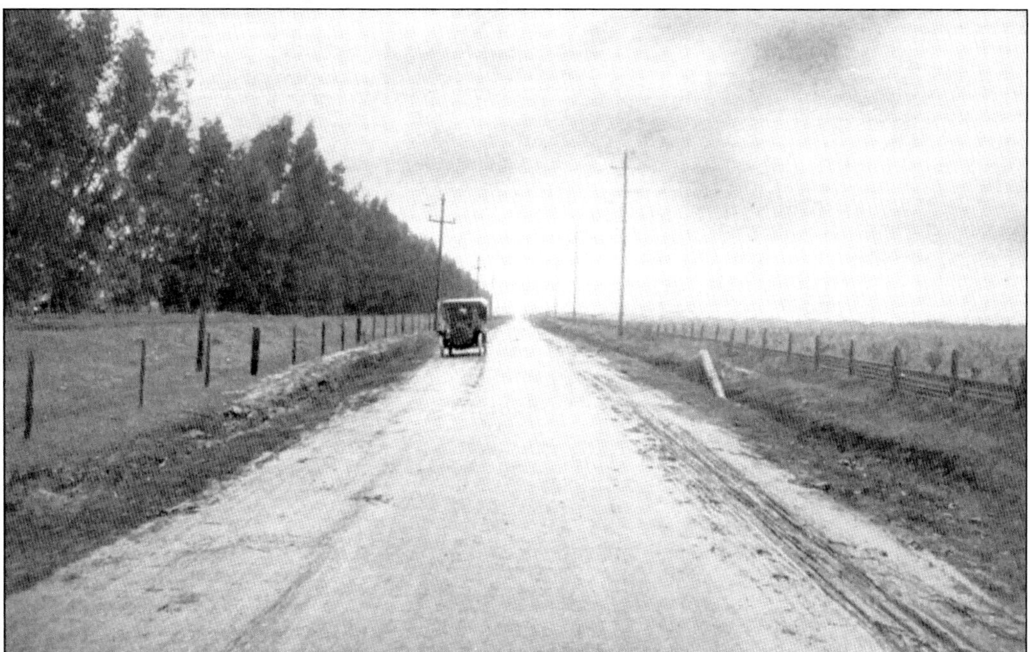

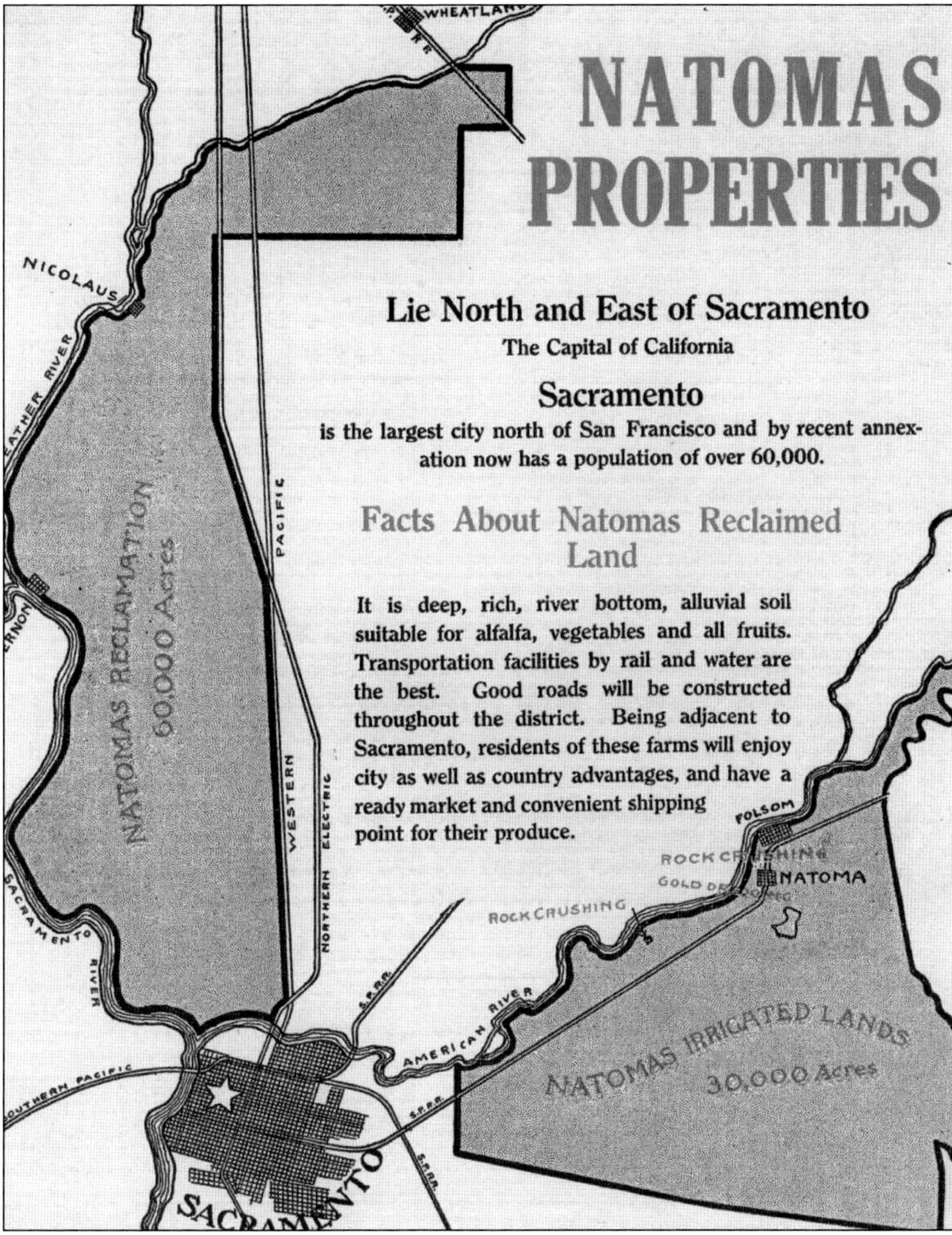

The Natomas Company offered 789 acres near Mills Station for five years at $1 a year, and on February 7, 1918, the federal government signed a contract with the Sacramento Chamber of Commerce with an option for the government to purchase the land at $100 an acre. The chamber arranged for the Southern Pacific Railroad to build a 2.5-mile spur to the site from the main track and sought an agreement with local service providers to bring electricity and means of communication to a proposed aviation school. The chamber was also expected to level the area, remove all obstructions, and guarantee wells capable of providing 100,000 gallons of water daily. A bond for $80,000 was required of the chamber of commerce to insure fulfillment of all conditions and terms of the lease. Good roads were a necessity since aircraft would be freighted to the airfield for assembly. (SPL.)

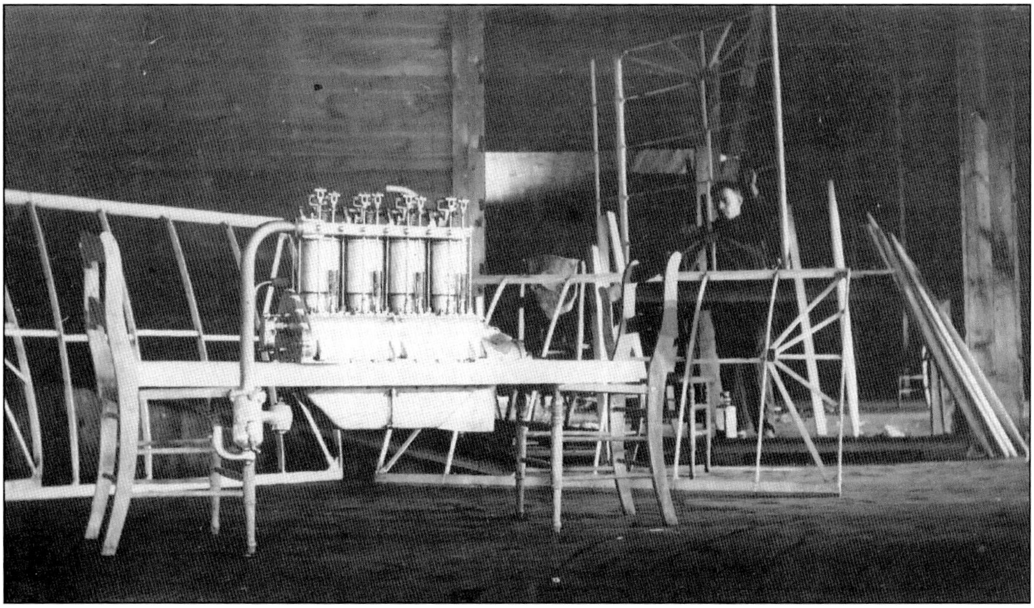

Born in 1894 in Paw Paw, Michigan, Carl Spencer Mather embraced aviation at an early age. He excelled in baseball and football in high school but channeled his natural curiosity and mechanical ability into the construction of airplanes and the study of flying. This photographic postcard captures Mather at work on a section of aircraft identified on the back as "Ruth Low's Plane." (CSH.)

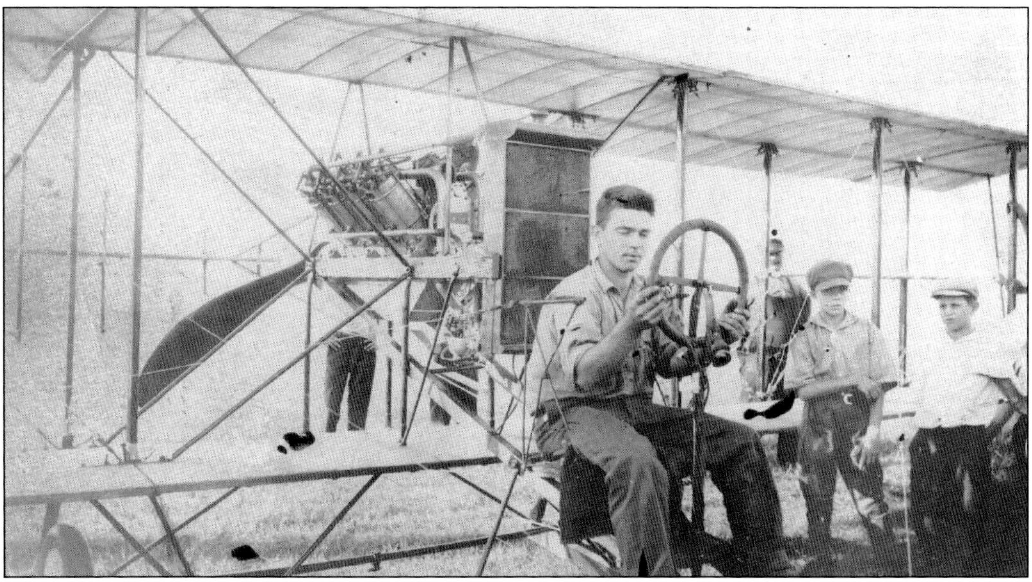

Mather, the idol of the neighborhood kids, sits behind the wheel of the crate he constructed and flew while still in high school. In 1915, he left Michigan to attend the Curtiss Aircraft Company flying school. Upon completion, he worked in the Curtiss plant before serving as chief flying instructor elsewhere. After two years of experience, Mather applied in July 1917 to the Aviation Section, Signal Officers Reserve Corps. (CSH.)

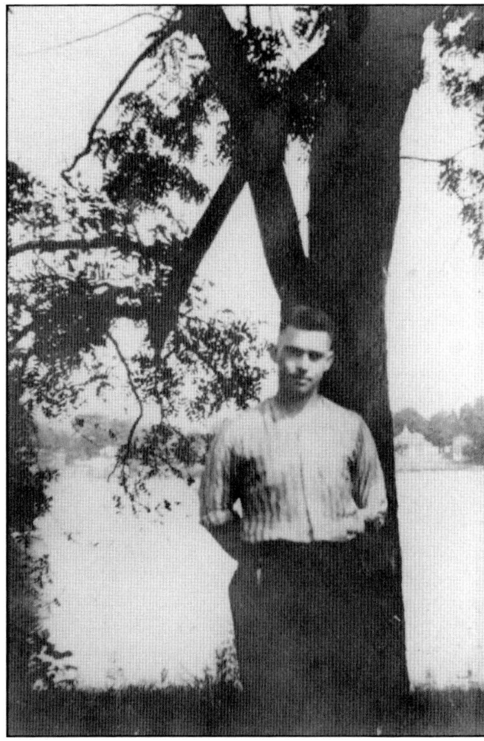

Carl Mather was a seasoned pilot by 1917, a skill now valuable to a country at war. Brig. Gen. George O. Squier, chief officer of the US Army Signal Corps, believed the nation could "put the Yankee punch into the war by building an army in the air," a "winged cavalry on gas-driven flying horses." The Aviation Act, signed by Pres. Woodrow Wilson on July 24, 1917, authorized a staggering $640 million appropriation to create an aerial extension of the US Army. On August 14, Mather signed on as a private in the Signal Enlisted Reserve Corps. When his current employer tried to hold Mather to his contract, Brigadier General Squier intervened on his behalf. On January 25, 1918, 2nd Lt. Carl Spencer Mather of Ellington Field, Texas, was appointed by President Wilson to the Signal Officers Reserve Corps. (Both, CSH.)

In future correspondence on this subject, refer to ______________

WAR DEPARTMENT
The Adjutant General's Office,
Washington.

January 25, 1918

Cadet Carl S. Mather,
Ellington Field, Texas.

Sir:

You are hereby informed that the President of the United States has appointed you, CARL SPENCER MATHER 2ND LIEUTENANT IN THE AVIATION SECTION, SIGNAL OFFICERS' RESERVE COPRS, to rank as such from the twenty-fifth day of January one thousand nine hundred eighteen.

Immediately on receipt hereof, return the oath herewith inclosed, properly filled in, subscribed and attested. This notice of appointment will be regarded as a commission for all purposes until a commission can be issued in due form.

By authority of the Secretary of War:

John F. Curry
Lt. Colonel, A.S., S.C.
Commanding, Signal Corps Aviation School
Ellington Field, Houston, Texas

3 Incls.

155(Com)

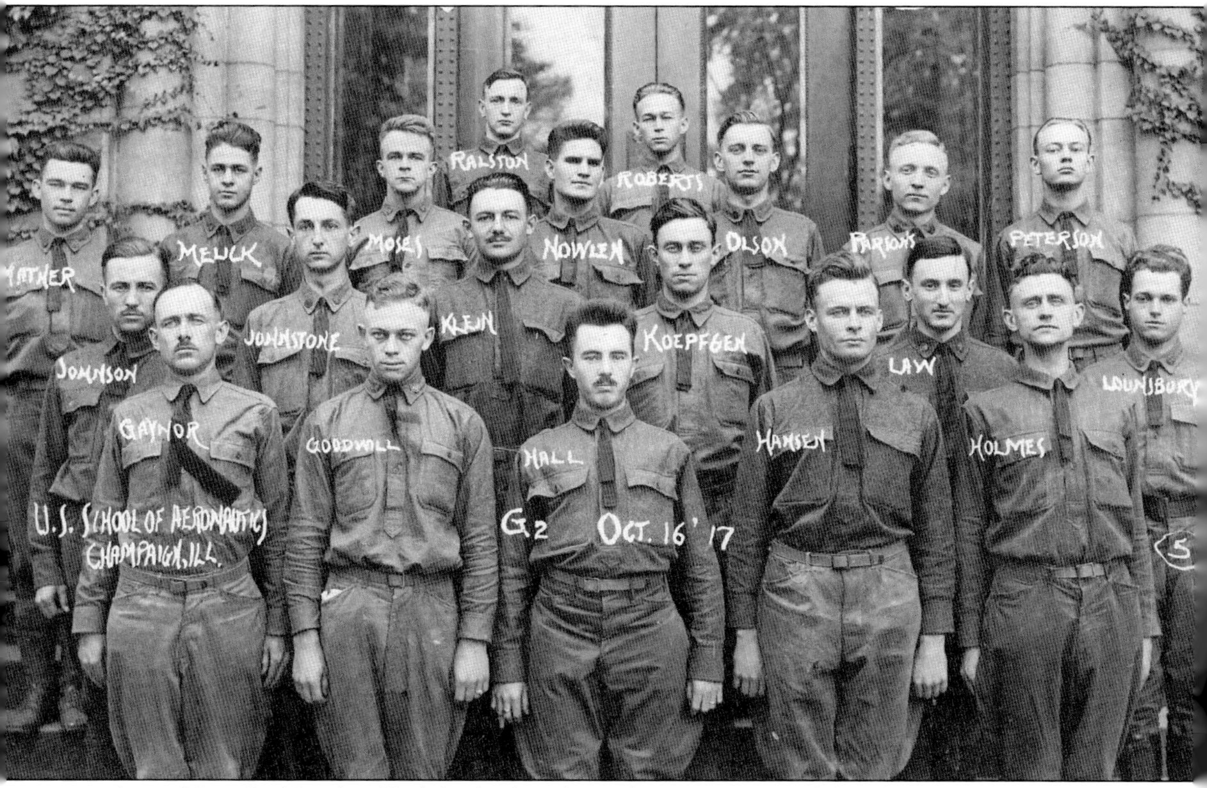

A confident Carl Mather (far left, third row) stands at attention with his class from the US School of Aeronautics at the University of Illinois on October 16, 1917, just a week before graduation. The 23-year-old Mather used this photograph as a postcard cover with the following message dated October 23: "Some bunch of would be Lieut, what? This is a official photo of this weeks graduating class, that is if we pass all the exams. With Love, Carl." Mather passed his final tests on January 20 at Ellington Field. Popular with his classmates, he was considered one of the most experienced graduates. Mather had gathered nicknames over the years, among them the "Curtiss Pusher," but his close calls and self-assured nature earned him the sobriquet "Sure" Mather. (CSH.)

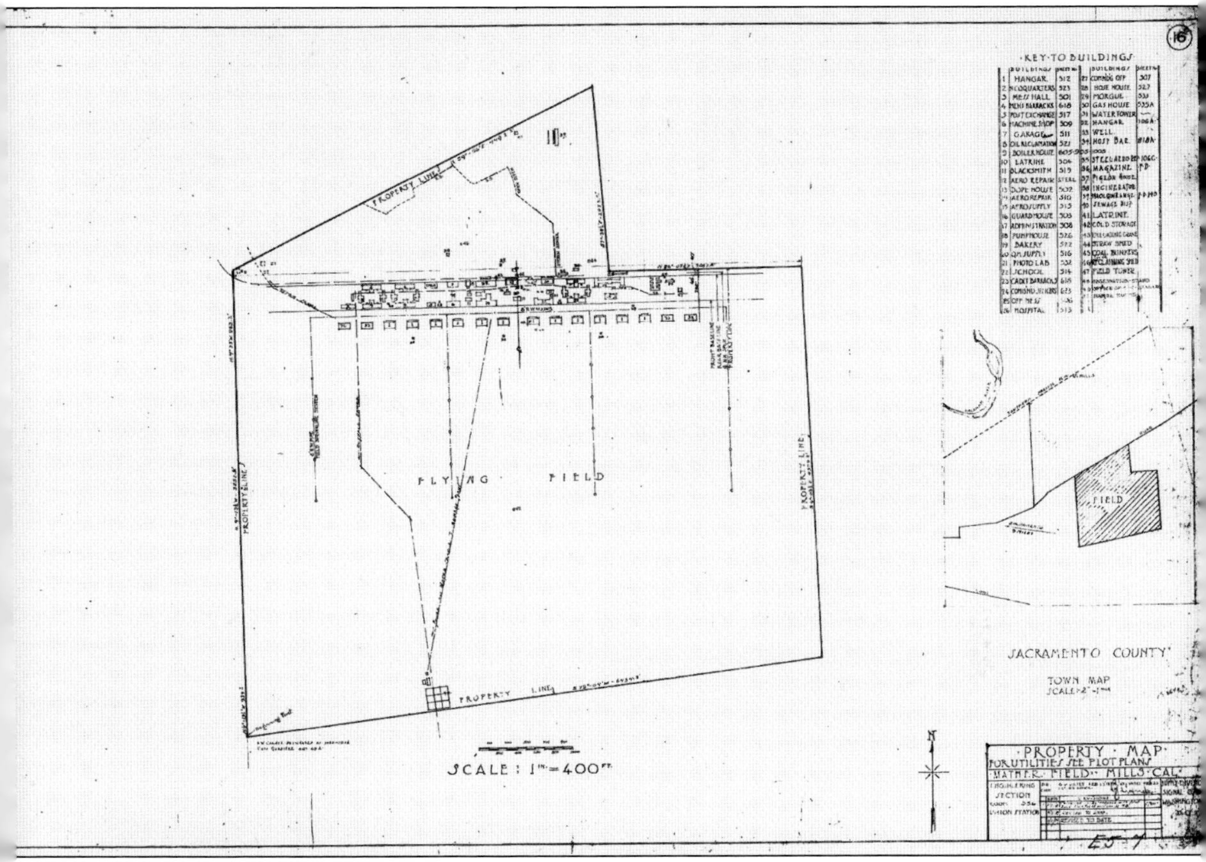

The construction of 52 buildings and 12 hangars blueprinted for the new school was estimated at $1 million. Federal approval of the Mills Station site in February opened the door for the low bid of $900,000. The *Sacramento Bee* announced on February 7, 1918, that the approval of the Mills Station area set into motion a three-month time frame for completion of the training field, but work on the site itself began a month later when Army 1st Lt. Sam P. Burnham arrived in March with 1,200 workers transported to the isolated area on a special 12-car train. Laborers and craftsmen supervised by Lieutenant Burnham commenced the projects, which all needed immediate attention. Crews framed and erected the hangars, barracks, classrooms, and other buildings necessary to maintain a self-sufficient base. Groups of workers graded the roads and streets within the airfield to accommodate access to the 700-acre site. Laborers toiled to level the land designated for the landing strips, uprooting acres of grapes dating back to when Joseph Routier established the first vineyard before the Civil War. (CSH.)

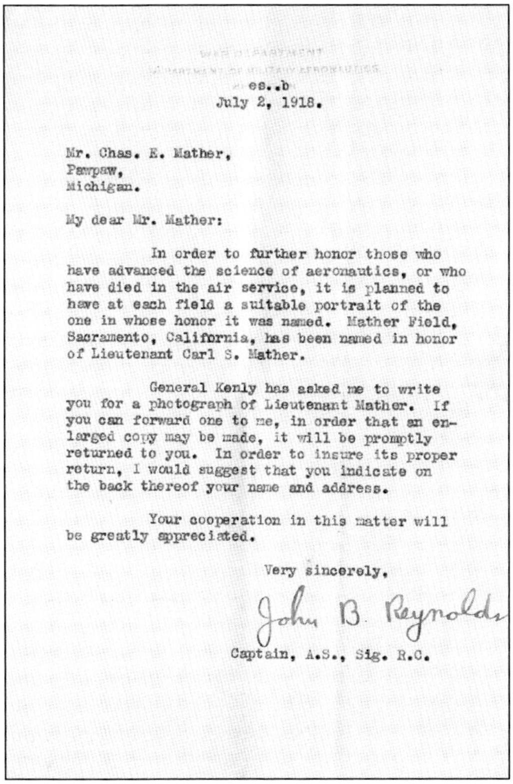

es..b
July 2, 1918.

Mr. Chas. E. Mather,
Pawpaw,
Michigan.

My dear Mr. Mather:

In order to further honor those who have advanced the science of aeronautics, or who have died in the air service, it is planned to have at each field a suitable portrait of the one in whose honor it was named. Mather Field, Sacramento, California, has been named in honor of Lieutenant Carl S. Mather.

General Kenly has asked me to write you for a photograph of Lieutenant Mather. If you can forward one to me, in order that an enlarged copy may be made, it will be promptly returned to you. In order to insure its proper return, I would suggest that you indicate on the back thereof your name and address.

Your cooperation in this matter will be greatly appreciated.

Very sincerely,

John B. Reynolds

Captain, A.S., Sig. R.C.

Carl "Sure" Mather was an exhibition and stunt pilot before joining the military, and he advertised "Nose dives, roller coaster, etc." on the postcard below. Hometown newspapers followed his exploits and reported that once, his crankshaft broke while he was 2,000 feet in the air, but he made a perfect landing. Five days after his appointment, Mather began what would become his last flight. A firsthand account written by Cpl. Scott P. Mathews states, "The men started out in formation of three. As Mather started to close in and take the lead the front two planes ran into a dense bank of fog from the gulf. They collided about 5,000 feet in the air." Mather and Lt. Edwin D. James were killed instantly. The newly built aviation field at Mills was named Mather at the request of newly arrived officers. (Both, CSH.)

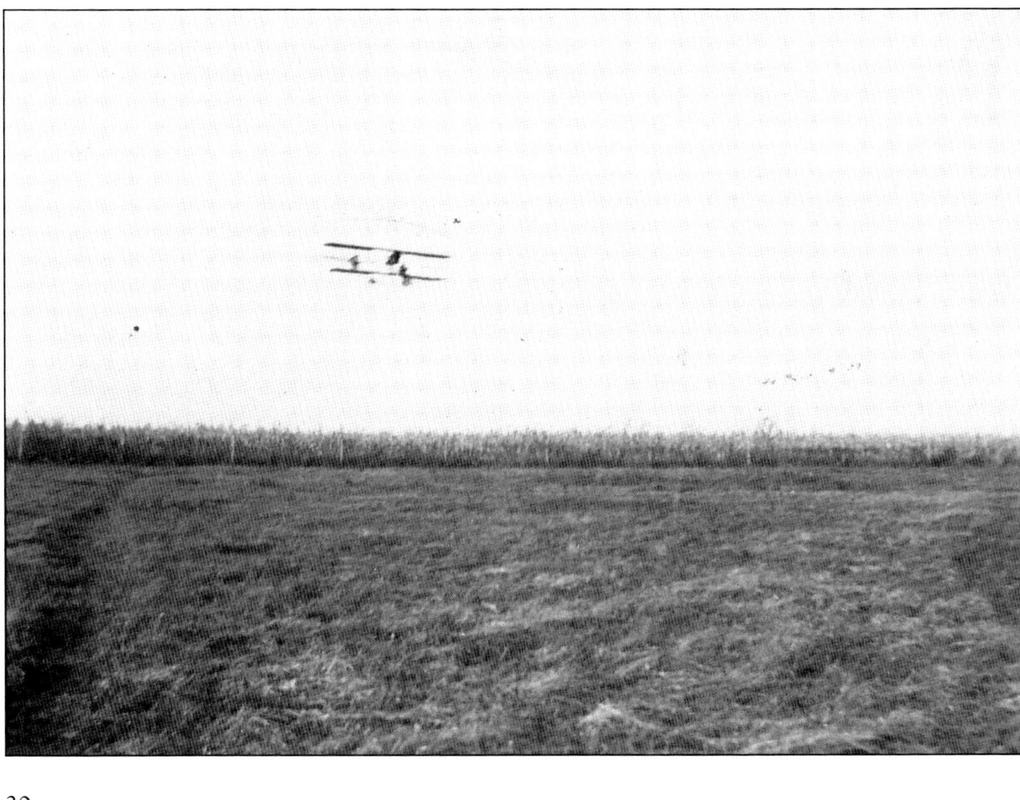

Two

Mather and the Great War

by James Scott

Nine months after Woodrow Wilson's April 1917 declaration of war against the Central Powers, the Department of War sent a cadre of officers to the Sacramento area to prospect sites for an aviation school. The group opted for a location some 12 miles southeast of the capital city known as Mills Station. In its initial form, the base—soon to take the moniker of Mather Field—covered over 700 acres and was comprised of over 50 buildings, enough to accommodate up to 1,000 personnel and bring 2,500 jobs to the area's economy.

The first cadets, a total of 44, arrived in mid-June from Berkeley's School of Military Aeronautics. During its seven months of wartime operation, Mather graduated 11 classes, with each required to do everything from clearing jammed machine guns (while in-flight) to dropping sandbag bombs on targets in a reservoir near Sloughhouse.

In search of diversion, Mather's tenants immediately took to building a baseball diamond, fielding marching and jazz bands, and forming a football team that was good enough to beat San Francisco's Presidio 45-0 at Buffalo Park in October 1918. The vineyards that surrounded the base also provided a ready source for jam.

Together, the City and County of Sacramento, along with the Southern Pacific Railroad (SP), built a spur to the field off the main SP line. The first daily train ran on March 26, although it would become a matter of status for any Sacramentan to say that he or she had transported an aviator in his or her automobile along the old Folsom Road.

For Sacramentans, the specter of Mather was enormous. How many residents had actually seen an airplane before, let alone an airport? The base's inaugural flight took place on the evening of June 12 in a JN-4 "Jenny," built at nearby North Sacramento's Liberty Iron Works. Weeks later, during Independence Day festivities, a squadron of Mather planes, armed with hundreds of small American flags, dropped their satiny ordnance over business and residential sections of Sacramento. Simply put, for both Sacramento and Mather, it was love at first sight.

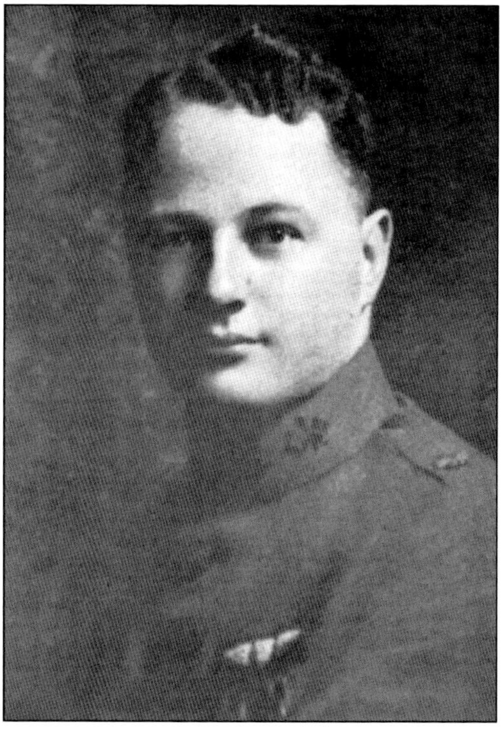

Pictured in 1918 is Lt. Col. Delos Emmons, Mather Field's first commanding officer. The 1905 West Point graduate took over in June 1918, declaring that "Mather Field must lead; other schools may follow!" Although transferred after the 1918 Armistice, Emmons later gained distinction in replacing Gen. Walter Short (head of the US Army's Hawaii Division), who was sacked after the Japanese Combined Fleet's attack on Pearl Harbor. (SPL.)

Standing before the University of California, Berkeley's Hearst Memorial Mining Building are cadets of the Berkeley Ground School. It, along with eight others nationwide, opened in May 1917 in response to the War Department's appeal for well-trained aviators. The first group of Berkeley cadets finished an eight-week regimen on June 8, arriving at Mather one week later. Courses addressed theory, radio operation, gunnery, flight mechanics, and tactics. (CSH.)

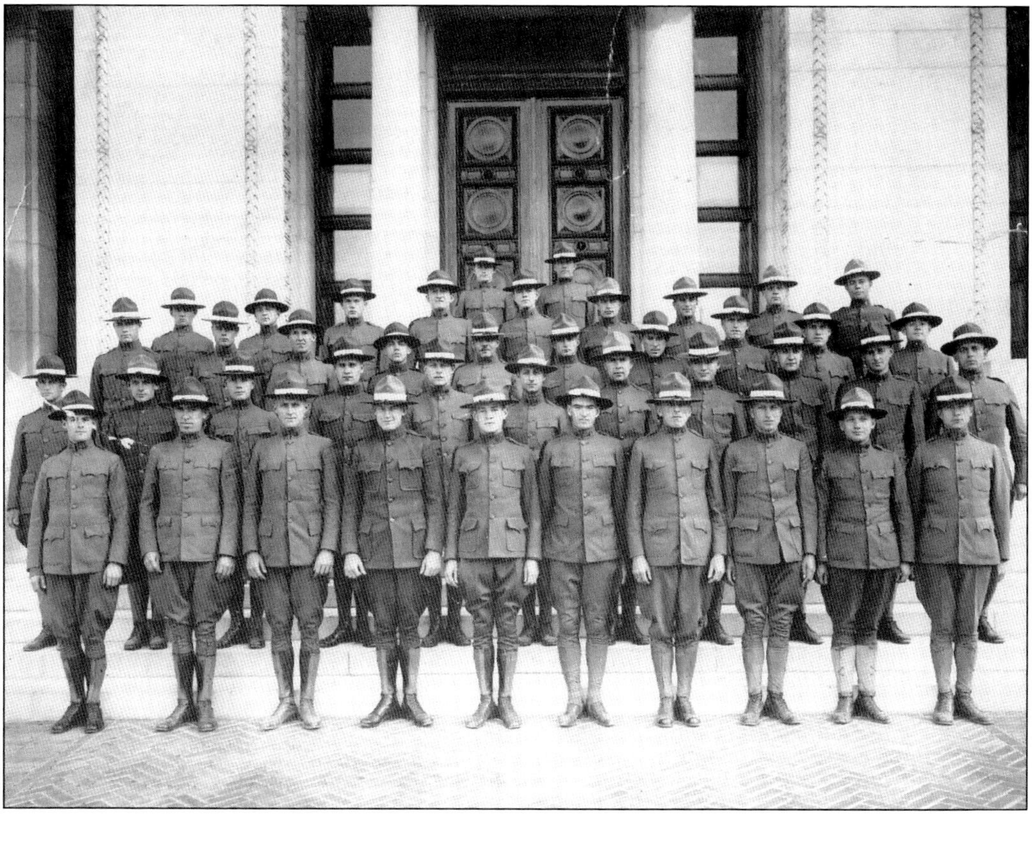

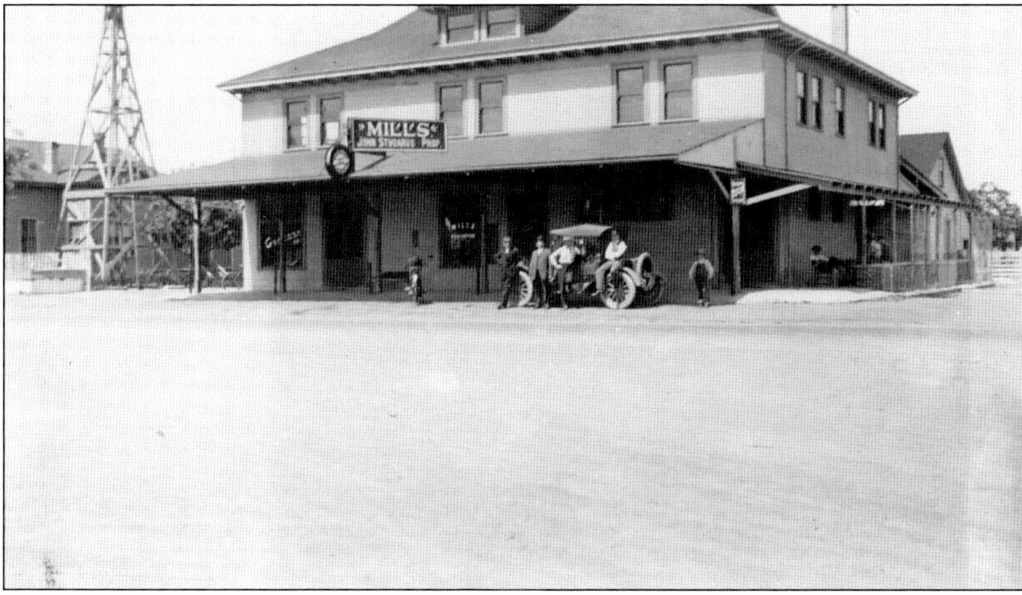

Shown in 1914 is John Studarus's Saloon, located at Mills Station. In an effort to insulate servicemen from vice, the War Department, in February 1918, placed a five-mile dry zone around all military installations, Mather included. In addition to Studarus's business, the Eagle's Nest Saloon at Jackson Road, the Arganda at Walsh's Station, Jack Hinter's Saloon at Routier Station, and the Moffatt Saloon at Mayhews Station were also closed. (Steve Abbott.)

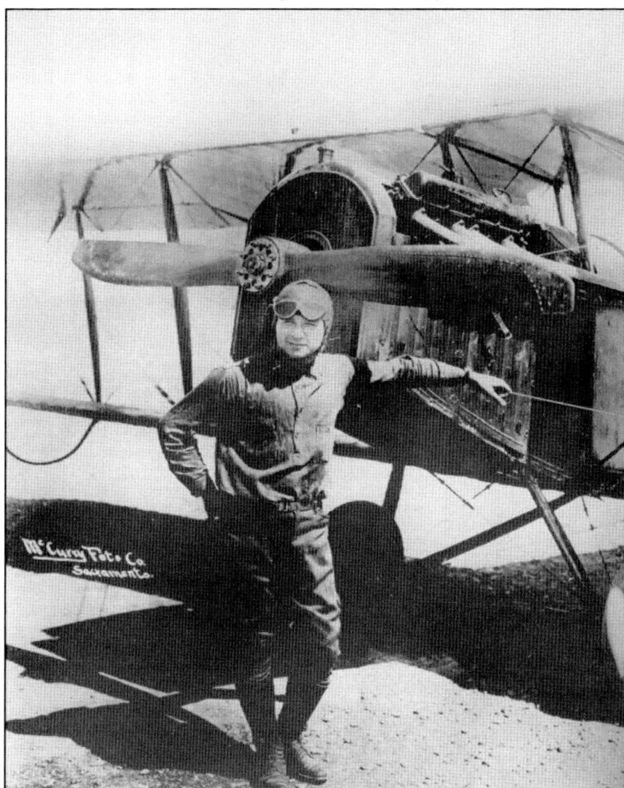

A Mather cadet poses, in 1918, before his JN-4 Jenny. The school employed the Gosport System of Instruction, an aggressive technique, whereby student and instructor, while aloft, communicated through rubbery Gosport tubing. The eight-week regimen included primary instruction (instructor flies) and secondary instruction (cadet flies), soloing, and long-range flying, all totaling 60 hours of flight time. Academic instruction was also required, taught by the aptly named "Kiwis"—instructors who did not fly. (CSH.)

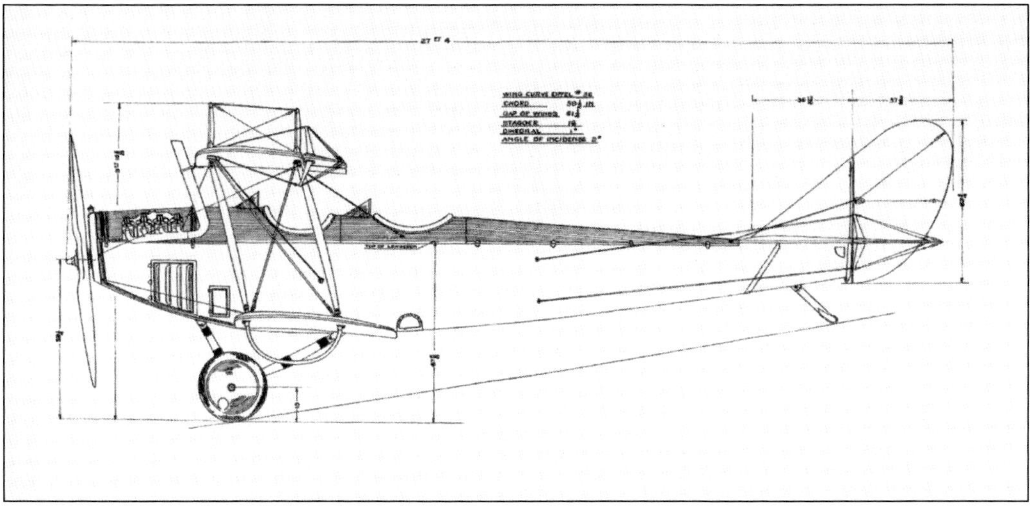

Curtiss Aeroplane Company fabrication plans show profile elevations of the JN-4, Mather's standard trainer. Known for durability and safety, the one-ton Jenny was also known for a lack of power, as maxing out at 65 miles-per-hour, the pilot was forced, upon takeoff, to lower the plane's nose until gathering enough airspeed (at least 65 mile per hour). Over its seven months of operation, Mather's JN-4s logged some 29,939 hours and two million miles of flight. (CSH.)

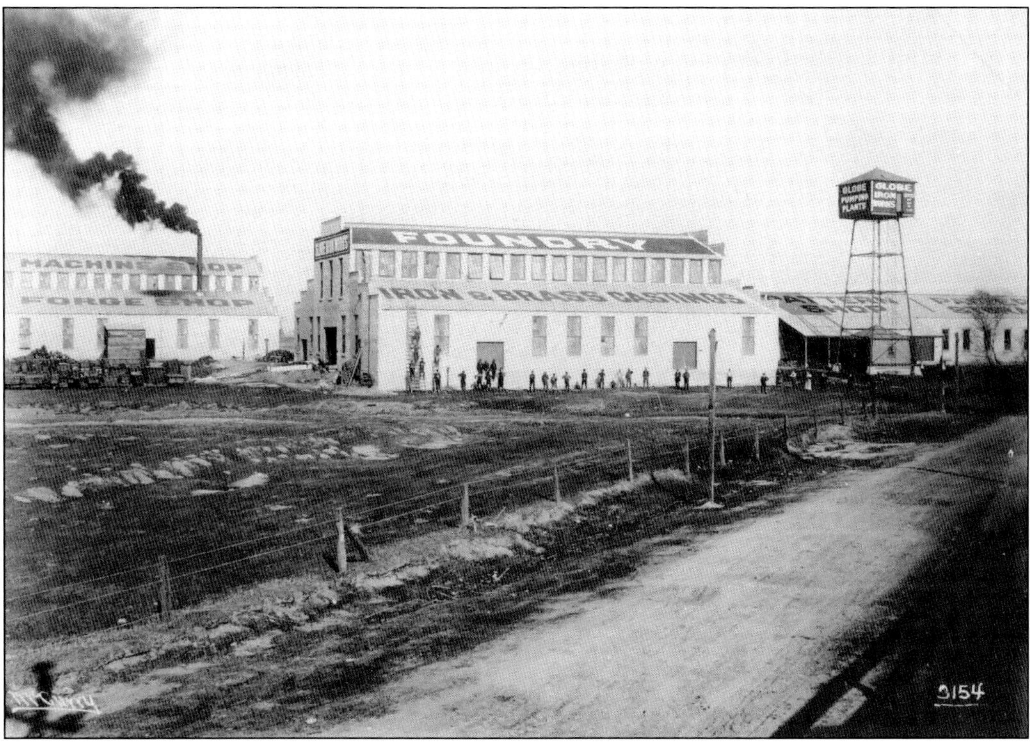

Shown in 1917 are twin fireproof buildings at Liberty Iron Works. In October 1917, the company won an $18 million contract to produce JN-4s. Accordingly, a 10-man engineering and production crew was transferred to Sacramento from Curtiss's Buffalo, New York, plant. Liberty's proximity to the Sierra-Nevada Mountains' bounty of spruce—a vital material in the JN-4's construction—was thought to have sealed the contract. In the foreground is Del Paso Boulevard. (CSH.)

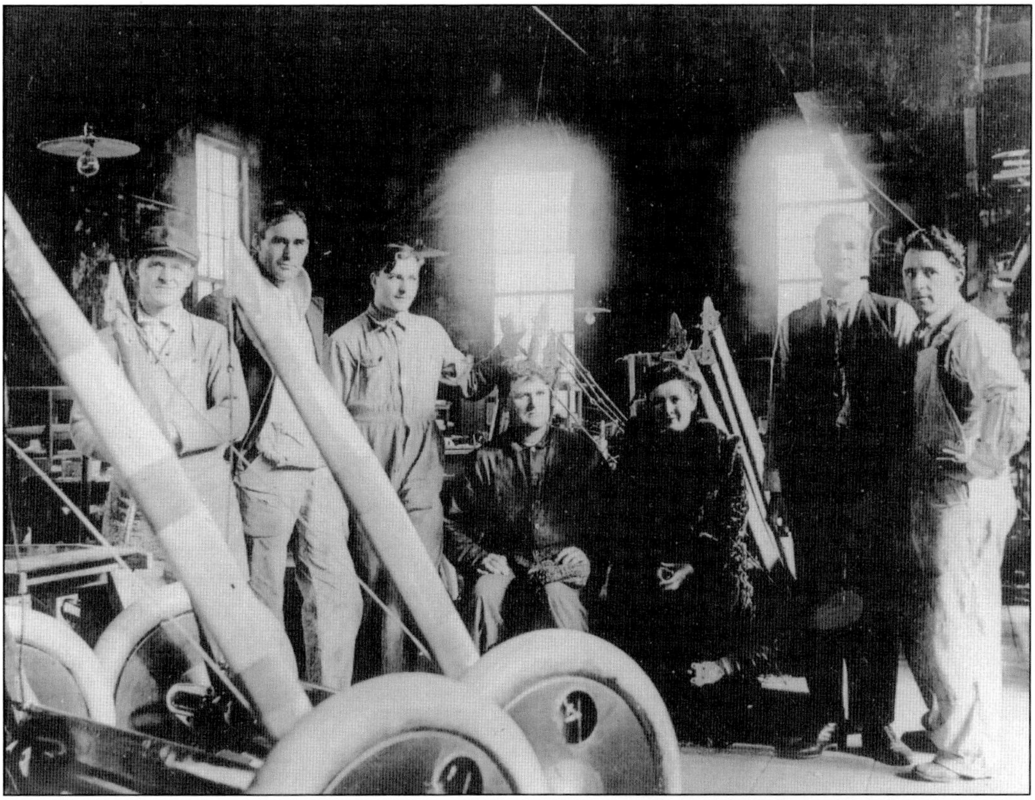

Liberty Iron Works employees pose for this 1918 portrait. Their campus occupied some eight acres of North Sacramento, with a 300-foot frontage on the American River. Liberty quickly fell under the ambitious thumb of the War Department, which expected the production of five planes a day and 150 a month—numbers which the Army viewed to be instrumental in achieving the greater national goal of a 75,000-man, 22,625-plane Air Corps. (CSH.)

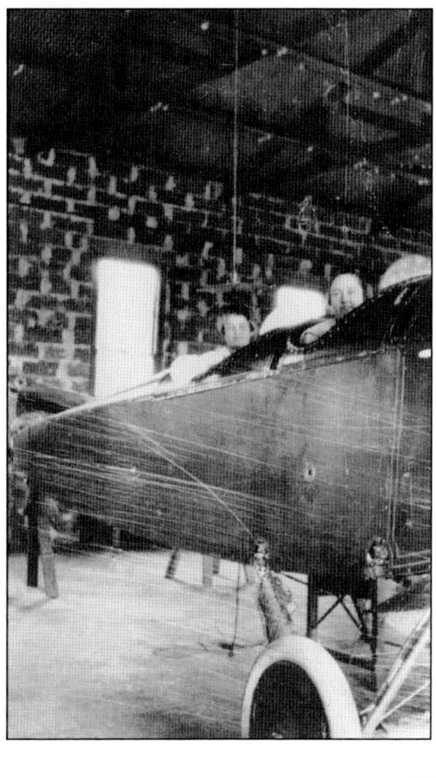

Pictured at Liberty in 1918, two female workers happily sit within the fuselage of a wingless Jenny. With nearly 800 Sacramento County men swept from employment rolls and sent to either Camp Lewis (Washington State) or Camp Kearny (San Diego County), female labor proved essential to the war effort. According to the 1920 census, there were as many women as men employed in California's munitions industry for 1918 and 1919. (CSH.)

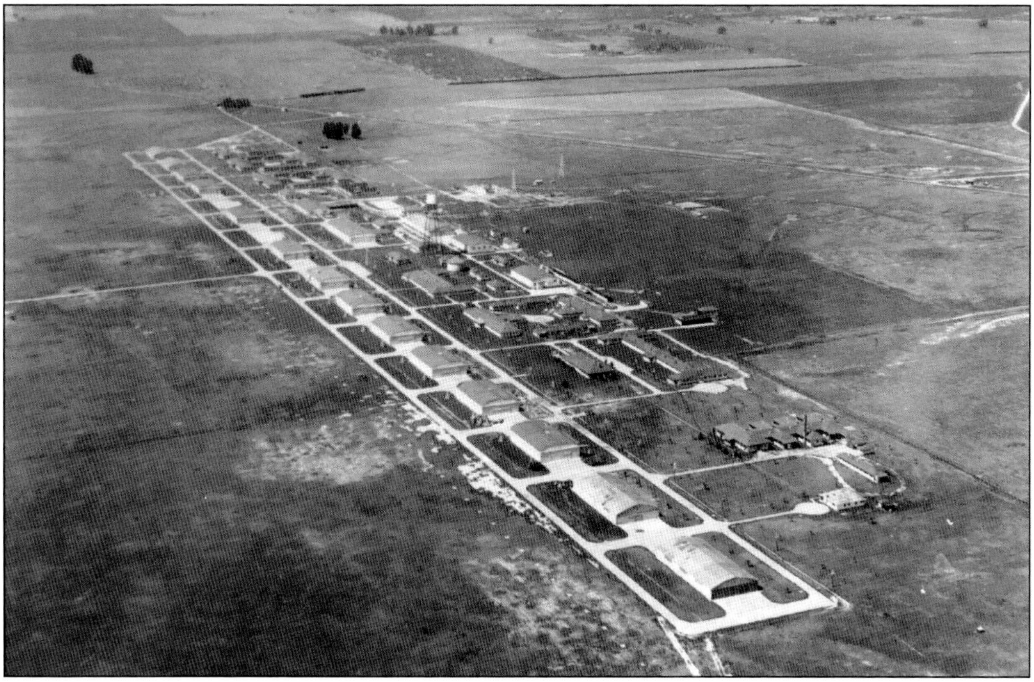

Looking west, this 1918 aerial photograph captures a youngish Mather. Near the top, and running diagonally, is the base's northern property line. Above that, as evidenced by railcars, is the 2.5-mile-long, $46,000 Southern Pacific spur. When the War Department came calling, area landowners—tending orchards, vineyards, and cattle—ceded their "land at the lowest possible figures, in some cases suffering great personal losses," according to the *Sacramento Bee*. (CSH.)

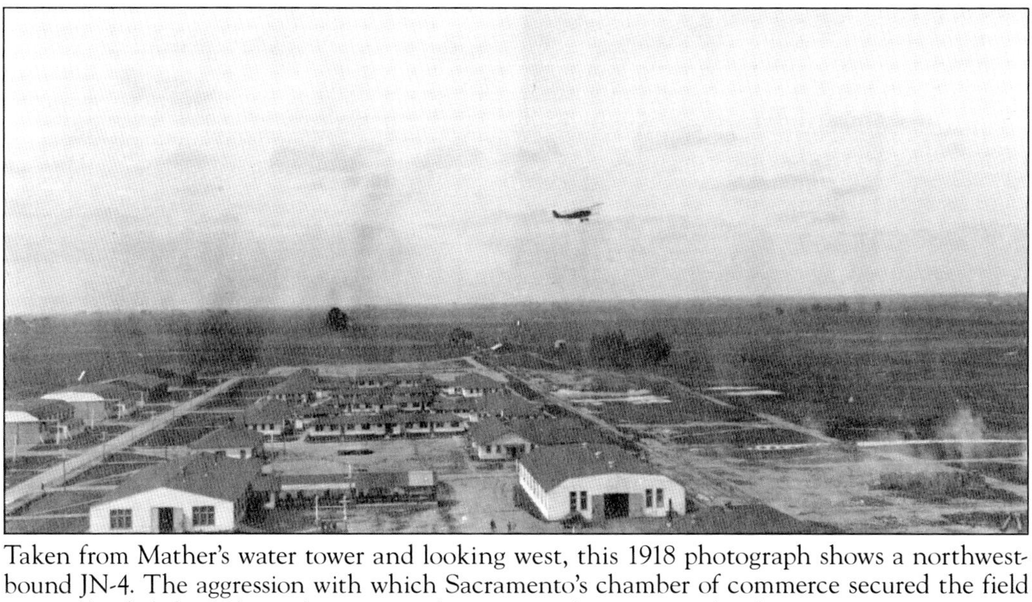

Taken from Mather's water tower and looking west, this 1918 photograph shows a northwest-bound JN-4. The aggression with which Sacramento's chamber of commerce secured the field was applauded throughout the city's media, many indicating it to be the organization's greatest accomplishment. Sacramento's favorable weather proved pivotal, with the Signal Corps checking meteorological conditions back to 1848. Dust wafts about in the lower left-hand corner of the frame. (CSH.)

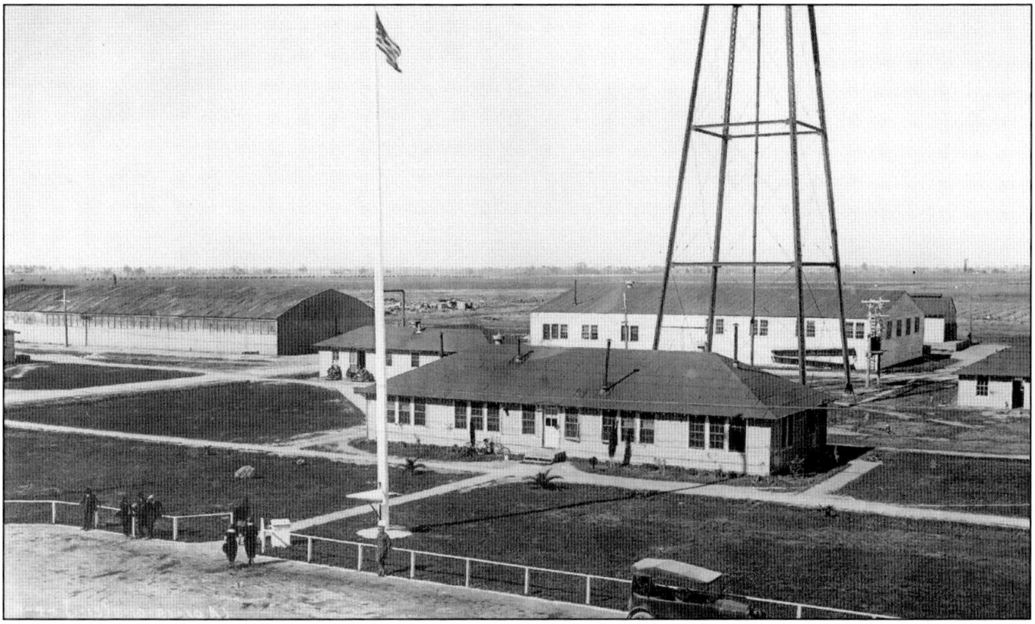

Pictured in 1918 is Mather's Headquarters Building, backed by the water tower and Aero Supply Building. The American River flows along the distant line of trees. In the foreground are several civilians, a sign of the public's enduring love for the base. It was especially common for tourists to park to the northwest edge of Mather to watch flights. The remaining perimeter was enclosed by opaque fencing in June 1918. (CSH.)

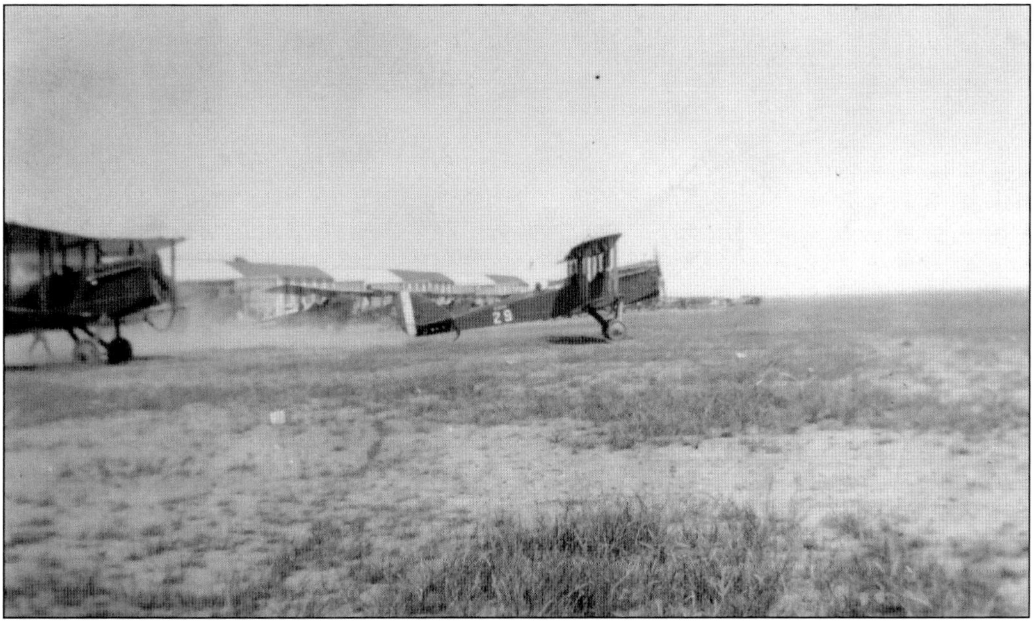

Departing Mather's flight line in 1918 is a group of De Havilland Airco day bombers. The lead plane kicks up a plume of dust, a frequent gremlin during Mather's summer months. Dust not only impacted visibility, but swirling grit could affect engine operation. To counteract this, in July, two massive motor-driven water sprinklers were installed, whereas water was onerously delivered by animal-drawn wagon prior to this. Bermuda and rye grass were planted in September. (SPL.)

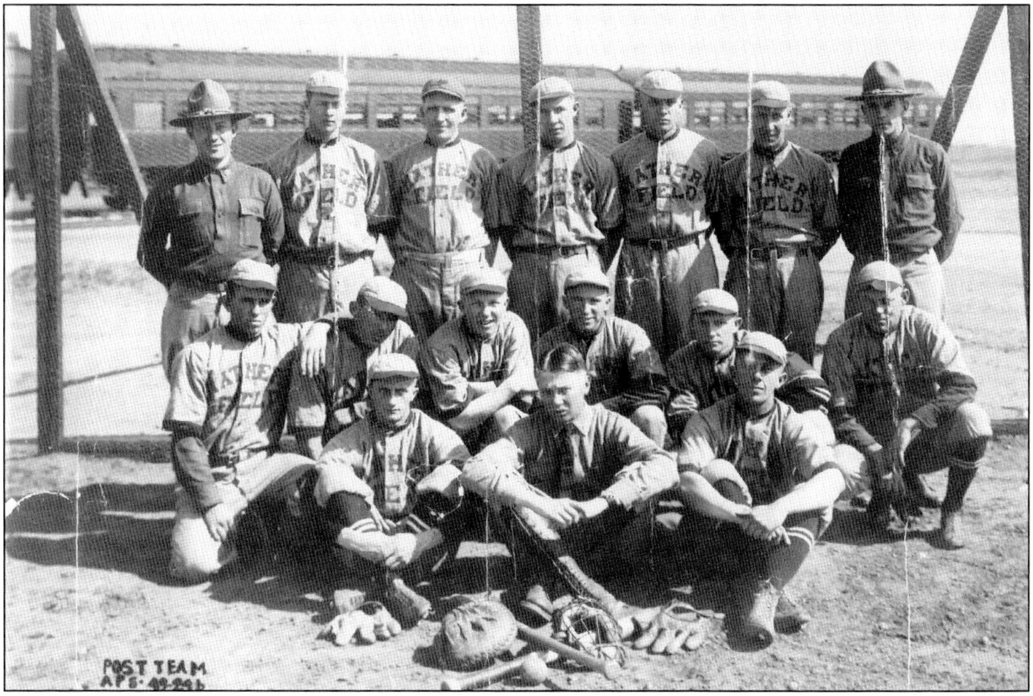

Pictured in September 1918 is Mather's baseball team, posing before a backstop and coach cars along the base's Southern Pacific spur. Uniforms and equipment were purchased with a $500 donation from the Sacramento Masons. Perhaps one of the team's most humbling tilts came a month earlier at the hands of the Represa Giants, a squad comprised of inmates from Folsom State Prison, who blanked the Aces 8-0. (SPL.)

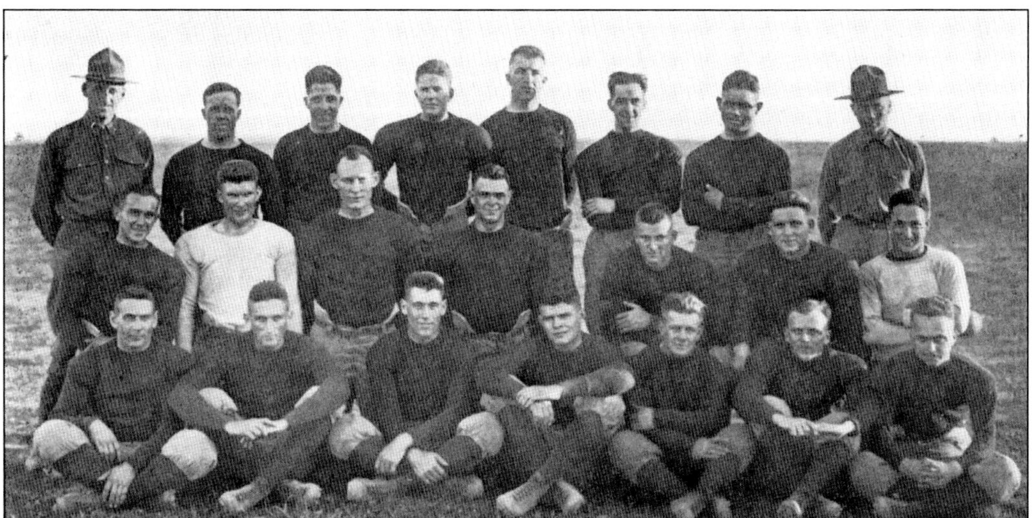

Mather Field's football team poses in 1918. Despite patchy scheduling due to the havoc-wreaking influenza epidemic, the team bested the Presidio, Berkeley, St. Mary's College, and Stanford University. Mather's coach and star player was Lt. James De Hart (third row, second from left), an All-American from the University of Pittsburgh and future Pittsburgh Pirate. Team manager Lt. John Buffington (first row, sixth from left) made Mather's inaugural flight. (SPL.)

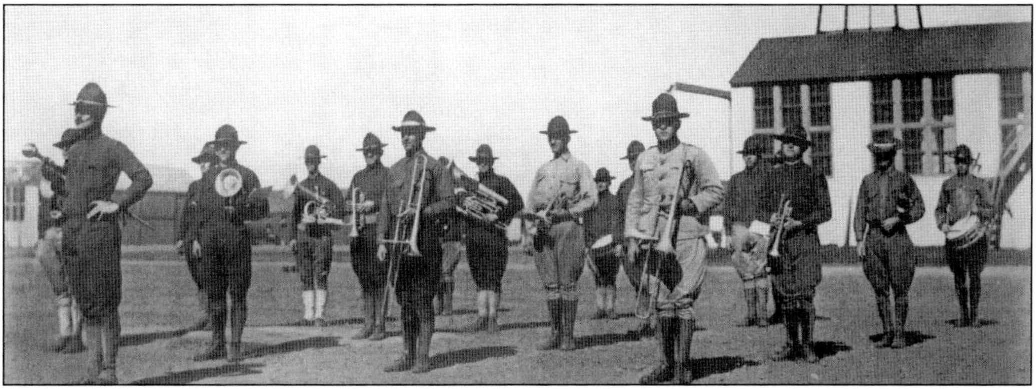

The 20-member Mather Band marches in formation in 1918. Led by Lt. N.E. Jones and Private Ward of Squadron C, it offered daily concerts outside the base's Headquarters Building. It was also used during drills and parade hours to provide cadence and instill pep. Mather personnel found additional musical outlets through visits from several area organizations, including Sacramento's YMCA and even Berkeley's Californians choral group. (CSH.)

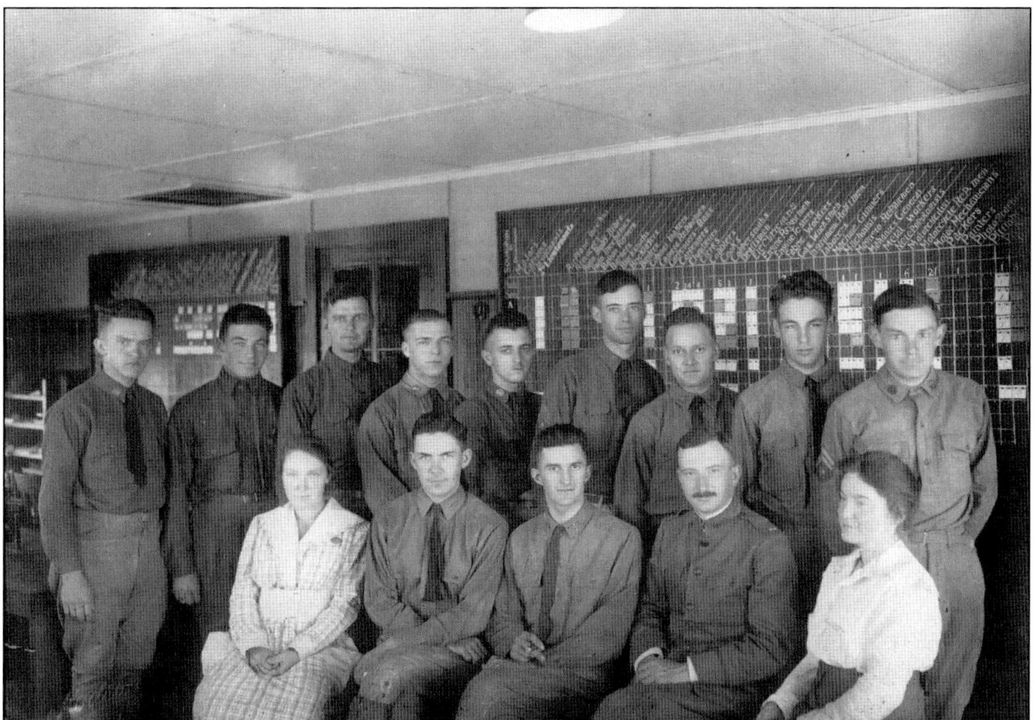

Pictured in 1918 is Mather's personnel department. Excepting cadets, its charge was to determine the overall ability of each recruit and assign accordingly. Determined through examination, recruit skill sets were then distilled into qualification cards. To the right is the trade test board, showing each man's number and degree of proficiency. To the left, the special duty board shows the number of men assigned to each department. (CSH.)

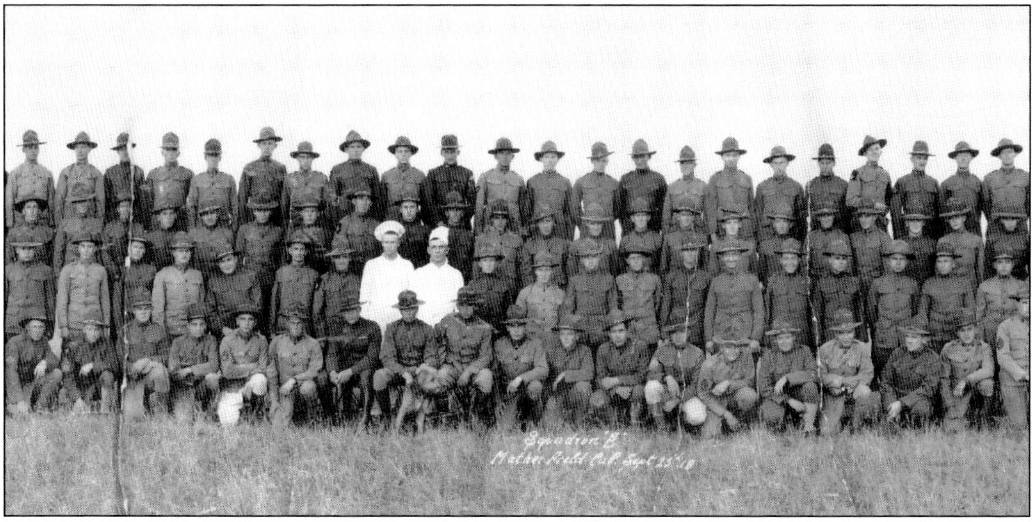

Members of Squadron E pose in September 1918. The unit was typical of Mather's four other squadrons, comprised of both cadets and support personnel, and keen on impromptu vaudeville acts and league athletics. The typical primary flying school (Mather was one of 15 nationwide) handled 300 cadets at any given time, and was well aligned with supreme commander John Pershing's goal of 60 battle-ready squadrons by June 1918. (CSH.)

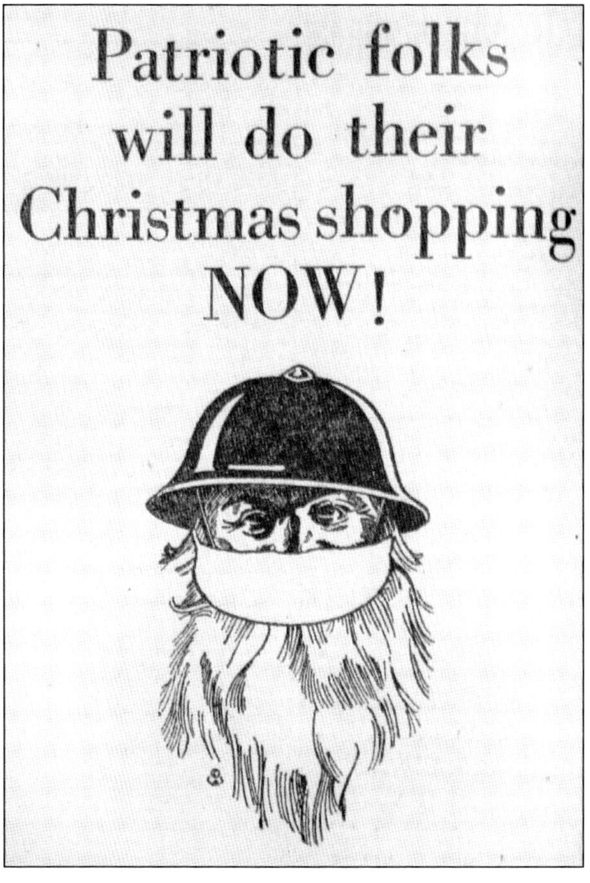

With the influenza death of four aviators and the infection of 90 more, Mather was quarantined in mid-November 1918. Sacramento health officials admonished citizens to wear masks, an act hardly lost on local department store giant Weinstock, Lubin & Company. Imploring consumers to do their capitalist duty, this November 1918 advertisement features a helmeted and masked Santa Claus. By November, over 10,000 Californians had been felled by the epidemic. (SPL.)

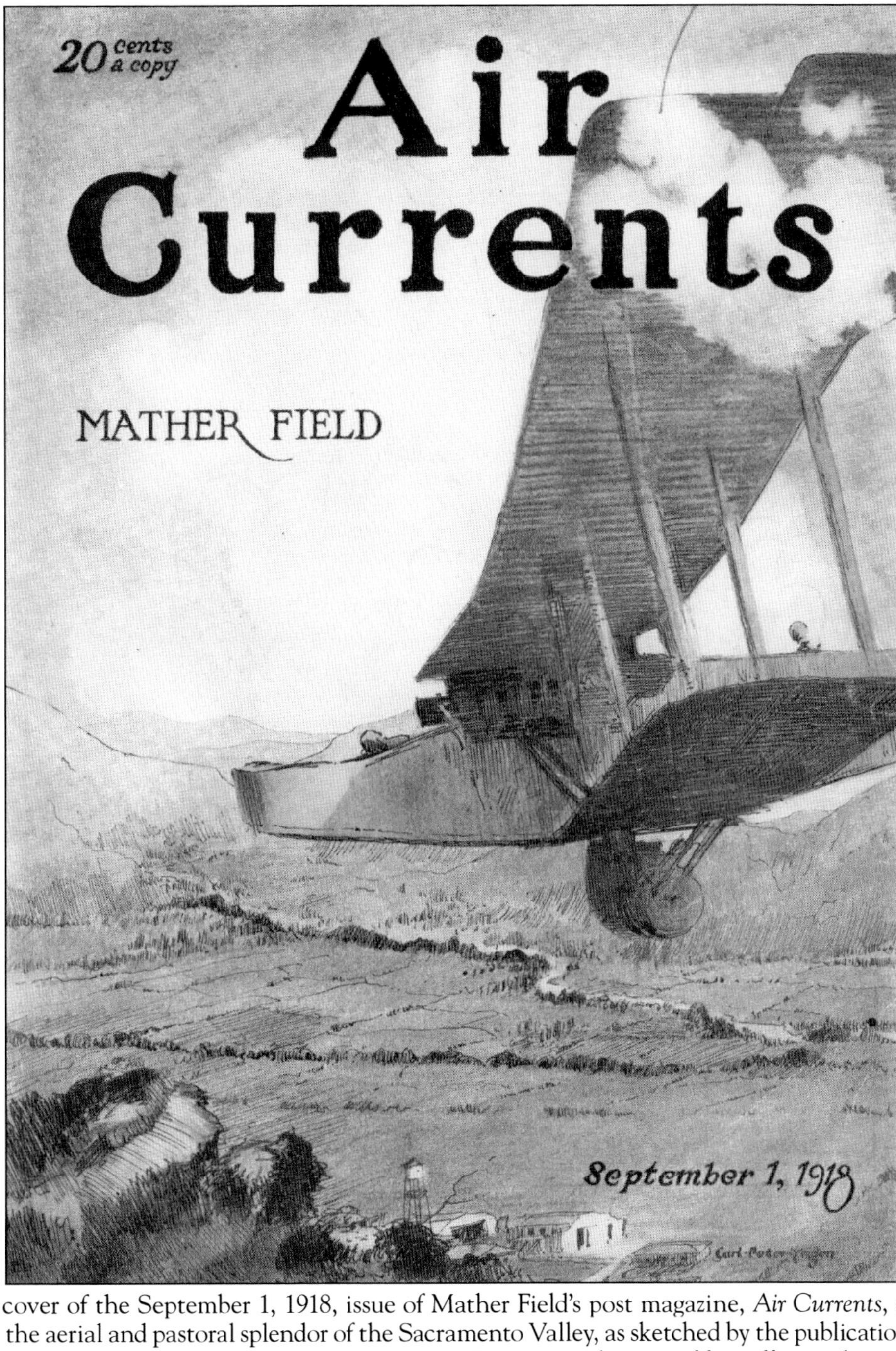

The cover of the September 1, 1918, issue of Mather Field's post magazine, *Air Currents*, shows both the aerial and pastoral splendor of the Sacramento Valley, as sketched by the publication's art editor, Lt. Carl Peter Teigen, a Minnesota-native. Teigen was also one of five officers who oversaw the operation of the magazine, a self-described "nonpolitical, nonsectarian, non-agitating and none-of-your-business publication." Teigen's British-built Handley-Page 400 heavy bomber soars its way over a creatively placed Mather Field and nearby American River. Eventually supplemented by a free weekly newsletter, *Fly Paper*, the magazine was printed by J.N. Larkin and Son Publishing at 2211 K Street in Sacramento. (SPL.)

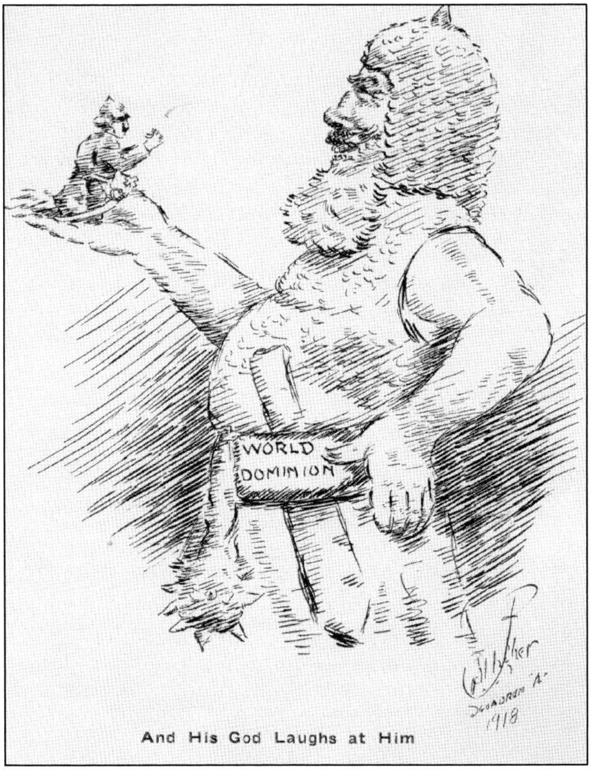

September 1918's *Air Currents* ran P. Callaghan's impression of a tiny Kaiser Wilhelm II and his Teutonic overlord, foretelling a rich lineage of world-class Mather artists. So intense was Mather's enmity for Imperial Germany that personnel played "Swat the Kaiser" whereby, with leather strap in hand, one soldier chased another around a circle of 25, attempting to hit the pursued before he could get back to his original spot. (SPL.)

Pictured here on September 25, 1918, is Mather's first graduating class. What started off in June as a group of 44 was down to 26 by the time this photograph was taken. In the image's center, a cadet accepts his diploma. Each aviator was then commissioned as a second lieutenant and given the coveted honor of wearing the Reserve Military Aviator's winged-propeller badge. (SPL.)

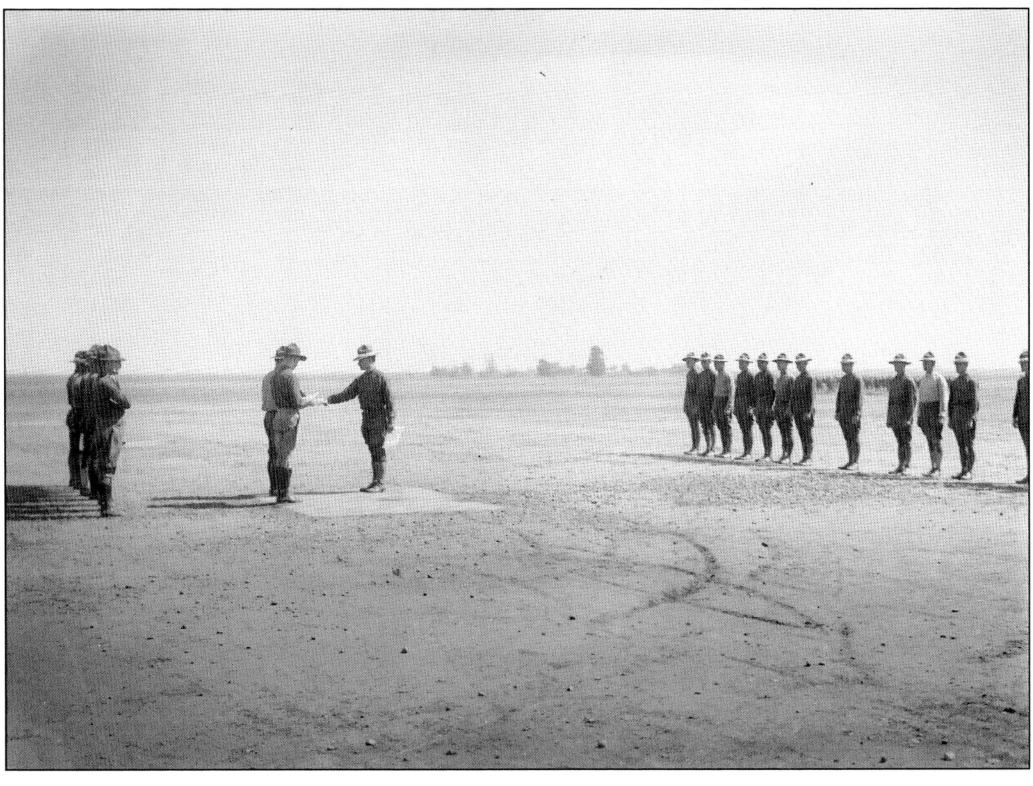

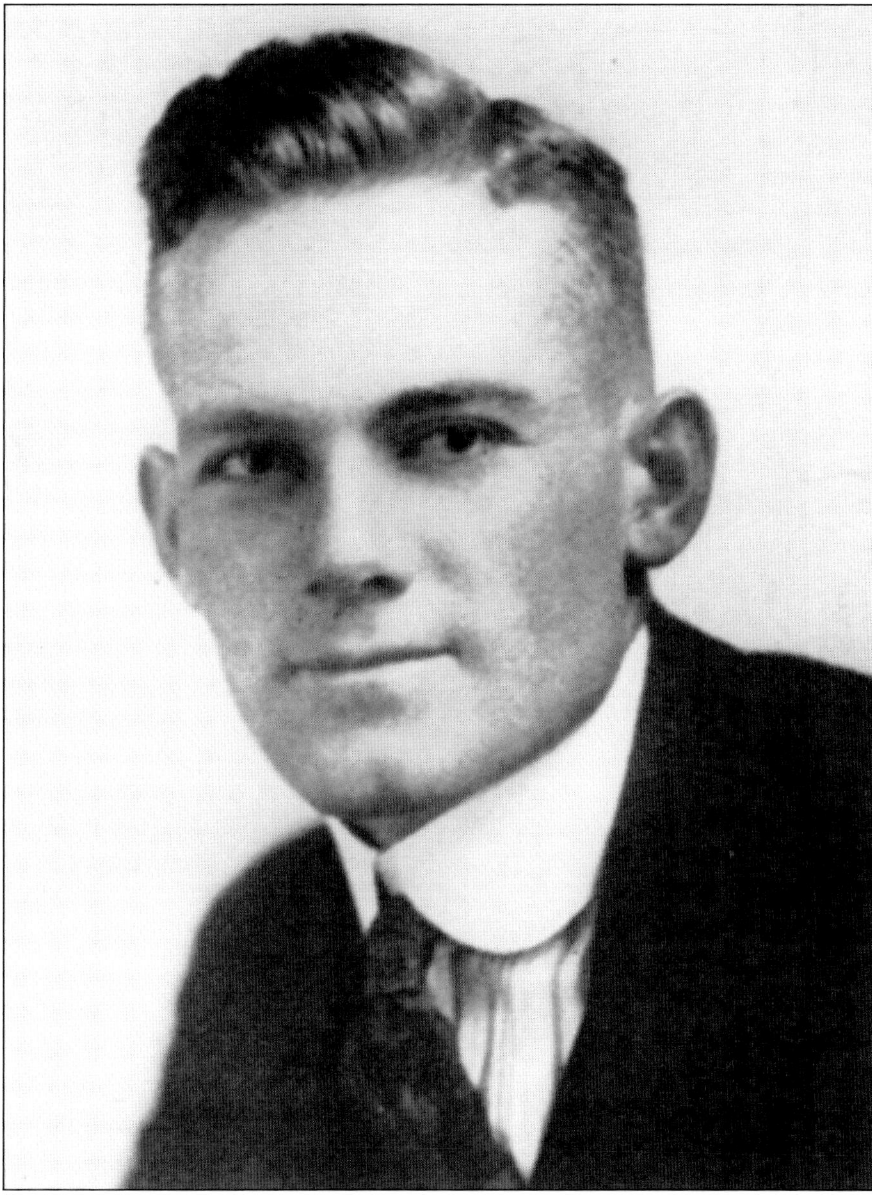

Mather's first fatality was the 283rd Aero Squadron's James Ward Jr., a cook who, in June 1918, drowned in the American River during a base outing. One of Mather's first training deaths was that of Lt. Gladstone Wilson (pictured), a University of California, Berkeley graduate and son of former Socialist mayor of Berkeley and onetime gubernatorial candidate J. Stitt Wilson. In September 1918, the 25-year-old Gladstone Wilson was killed when his JN-4 trainer collided with that of cadet James E. Wilson, who also perished. The deceased were not related. Over 1,000 cadets attended Gladstone Wilson's funeral in Berkeley. Three days after the collision, his father eulogized that "a week ago he told us that, as he looked down on California from the airplane, the most gratifying expression of his heart was the recollection of any little work he had done for the progress of humanity such as his work for the cause of temperance." Upon graduation from Berkeley, Gladstone Wilson had toured the state as an orator, promoting temperance and the prohibition of saloons. (CSL.)

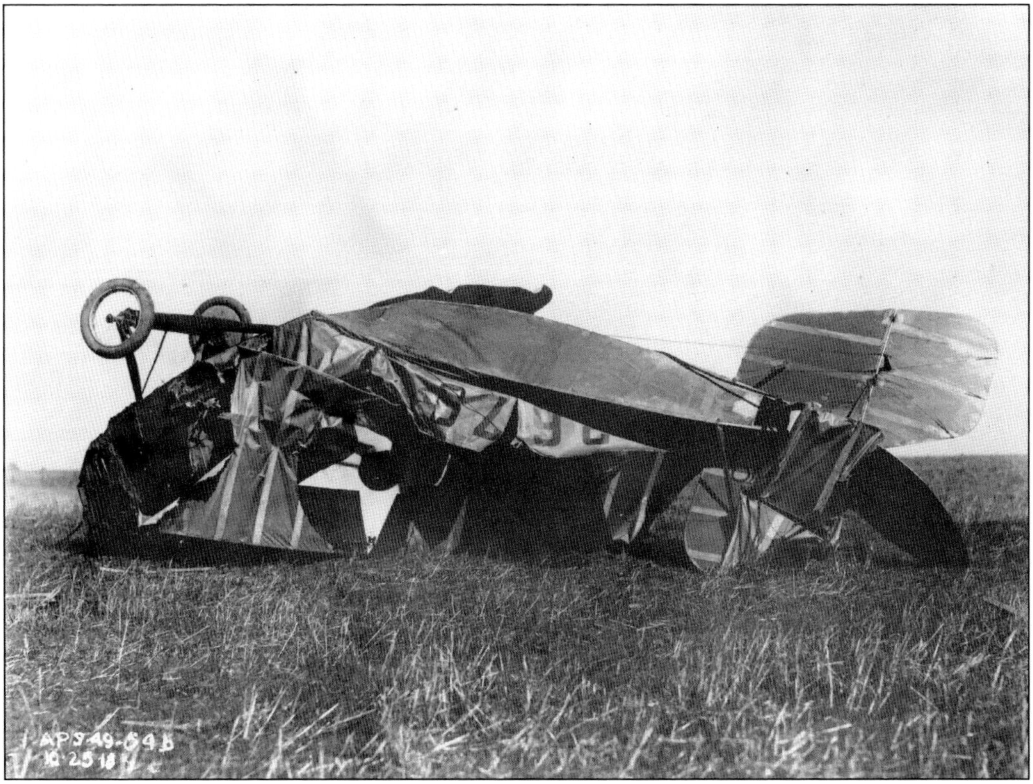

Pictured near Mather in October 1918 is a wrecked JN-4. In its first seven months of operation, the school lost five aviators, including the Wilsons, cadet Marion Burns, Lt. Arthur Thigpen, and Lt. Edward Wall. Nationwide, flight schools saw near parity between instructor and cadet fatalities while also averaging one death for every 65 cadets who went on to receive their wings. (CSH.)

LIBRARY WINDOWS

OF late the air is full of flying things:
Home-making linnets, busy with romance,
New-risen butterflies that flit and glance,
And downy elm seeds trying out their wings;
Quite frequently is heard the whirr which brings
The airplane near, and searching the expanse
From side to side, we note the swift advance
Of man-made bird which through the ether sings:
The task of these has been to practice war
From the adjacent camp of Mather Field;
But now, most happily, war measures yield
To arts of peace, and monster planes fly o'er
The land, depositing their human freight
And friendly letters; seeds of love for hate.

April the Fourteenth

In 1920, Retta Parrott, a librarian for the Sacramento City Free Library, wrote a collection of 26 sonnets, entitled *Library Windows*. They were meant to capture the "Heart of California's" seasonal changes as viewed through the windows of a newish Central Library. This sonnet, entitled "Winged Seeds," celebrates the advent of spring and the transition of an airfield, city, and world from war-making to peaceful renewal. (SPL.)

Three

Interwar Mather
by Tom Tolley

Deactivated in the summer of 1922, Mather Field led a feast-or-famine existence for most of the next two decades, never completely forgotten by the federal government and lobbied-for heavily by the Sacramento Chamber of Commerce. Forest Patrol aircraft utilized Mather's facilities and field for years, and a weekend air circus in 1925 brought throngs of spectators and aviators from around the world. The airmail service came via Mather, and one of the greatest celebrities of the 1920s, Charles Lindbergh, piloted the *Spirit of St. Louis* onto the unpaved runway in 1927. The US government sponsored the nation's largest aerial maneuvers in April 1930, sending men and machines to a spruced-up Mather Field for 10 days of intense flying, testing, and training. Representative personnel from most of America's government airfields and the majority of their aircraft were brought to Northern California for the event. Airmen with nearly 20 years of experience rubbed flight jackets with rookie pilots, as they would again at Mather Field during the next few years. By the end of the decade, the original buildings along the flight line were dilapidated beyond repair and torn down, leaving the field as quiet as it had been before World War I and awaiting activity and a renewed call to arms.

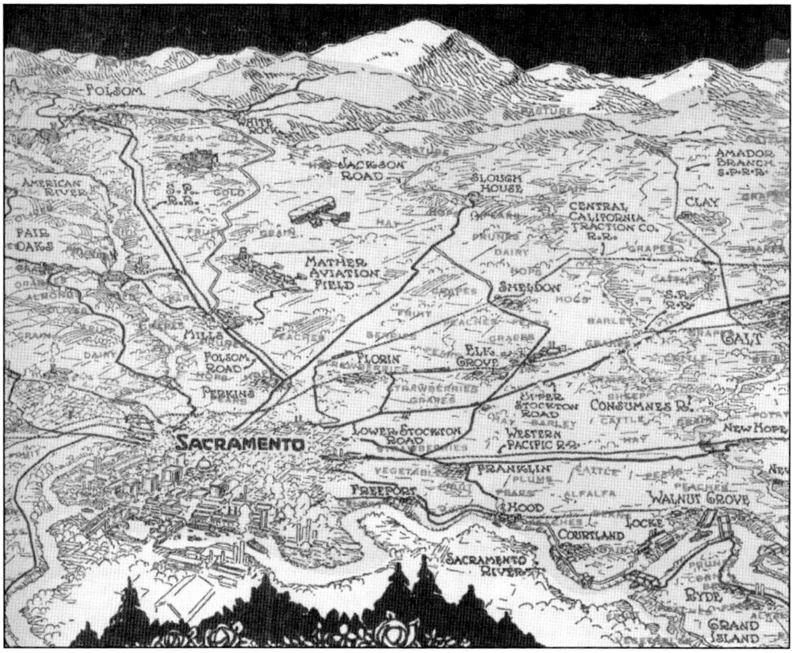

The Sacramento Chamber of Commerce was united in its belief that Mather Air Field could continue to benefit the Sacramento Valley and sought new venues to populate the area after the base was deactivated. This section of a foldout map included in a brochure features an airplane flying toward Folsom, with local towns, townships, and crops prominent. (SPL.)

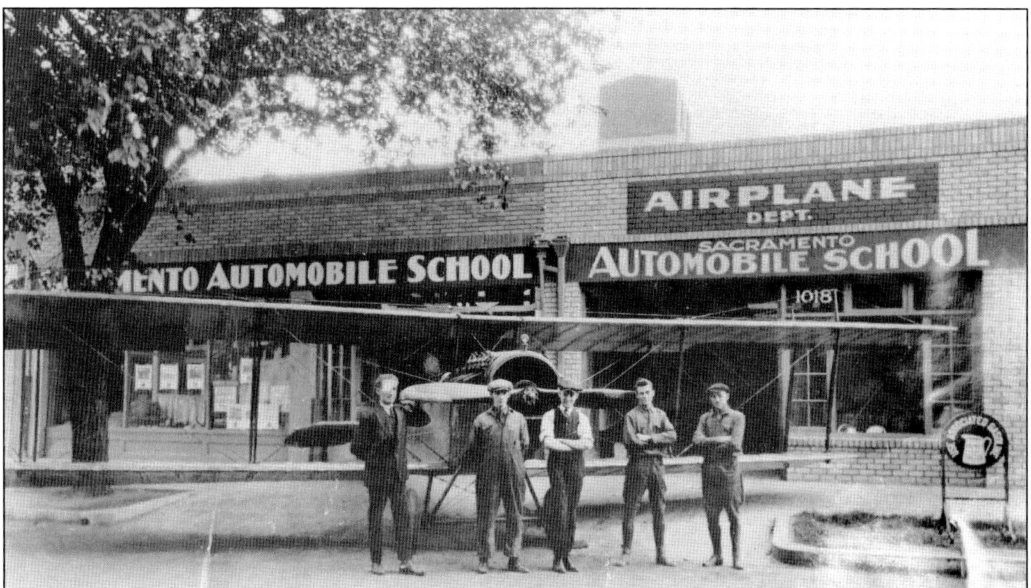

Sacramento went plane-crazy in a time when livery stables were being transformed into garages, and the enterprising owners of the Sacramento Automobile and Engineering School at 1018–1022 Fourteenth Street in Sacramento took the next step and expanded their business into aviation. The five men in front of the business are not identified, and how the airplane settled where it is remains a mystery. (CSH.)

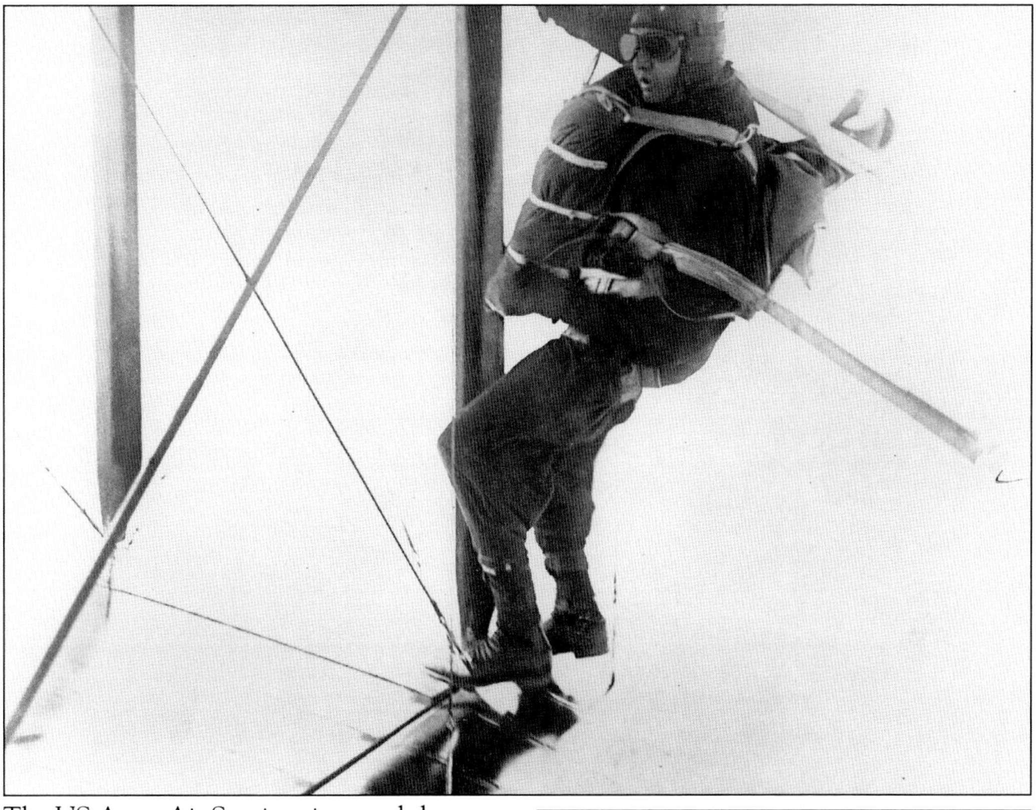

The US Army Air Service pioneered the development and use of free-fall parachutes, but the supply did not always meet the demand in the early days. There were over 270 fatalities from air crashes between 1920 and 1925, and the requirement for carrying parachutes on all flights and instructing all personnel in their use joined improvements in ship design, construction, equipment, and communication to improve flying safety. Charles "Lucky Lindy" Lindbergh earned his nickname between 1925 and 1926 when he made four emergency jumps using a parachute from planes that had either collided, been disabled in flight, or run out of fuel, earning him charter membership in the Caterpillar Club of daredevil aviators. In writing about the value of a parachute in flying, he commented, "If you need it and haven't got it, you'll never need it again!" A note on the back of the photograph above reads, "1920 . . . a moment before the jump, 8,000 feet up." (Both, CSH.)

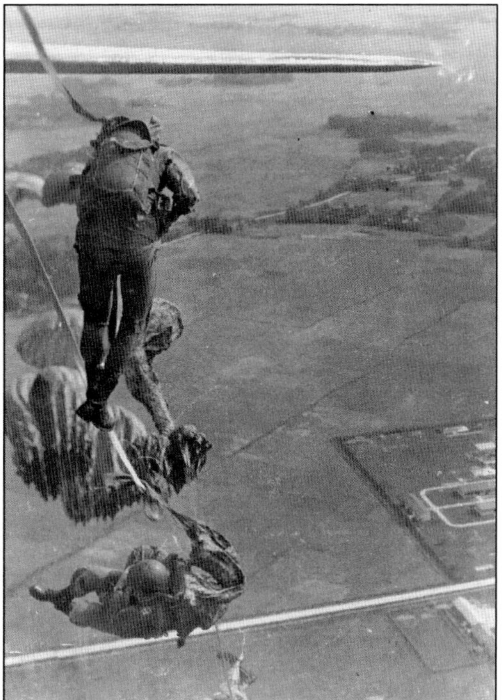

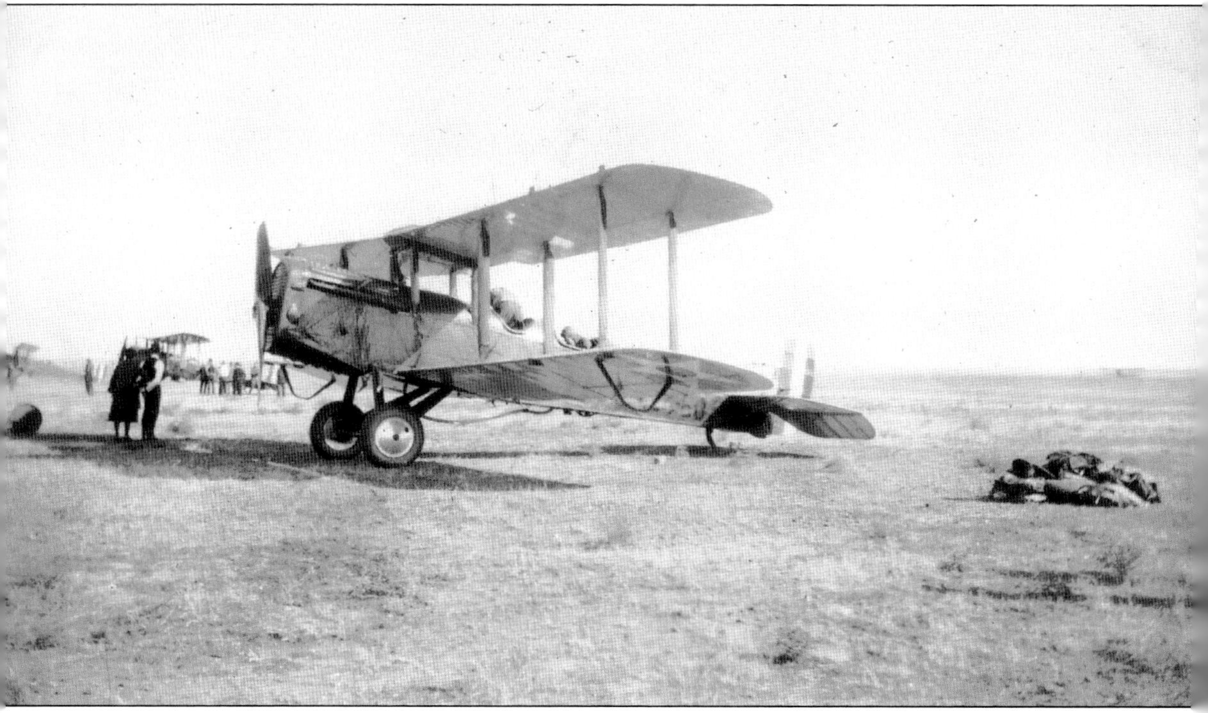

When federal funding for maintenance and improvement of Mather Field failed to materialize in 1922, the Sacramento Chamber of Commerce began an aggressive campaign to house the Army 9th Corps air service at Mather. Air service at the time flew from the East Coast to San Francisco, and the capital city's mail was brought by rail. Things took a positive spin in 1925 when Mather hosted a successful international air circus in May, followed by contracts secured for the Forest Service patrol and government airmail, both beginning July 1. Within a year, the mail service was contracted out to private concerns, and the first airmail service under private contract began in 1929 with Boeing supplying the aircraft. In this photograph, a Boeing C-7 on Contract Air Mail Route 18 idles on the natural landing field at Mather on April 26, 1929. Private contracts for airmail service were cancelled in 1934 by Pres. Franklin W. Roosevelt in an effort to stimulate federal involvement in aviation and defense. (SPL.)

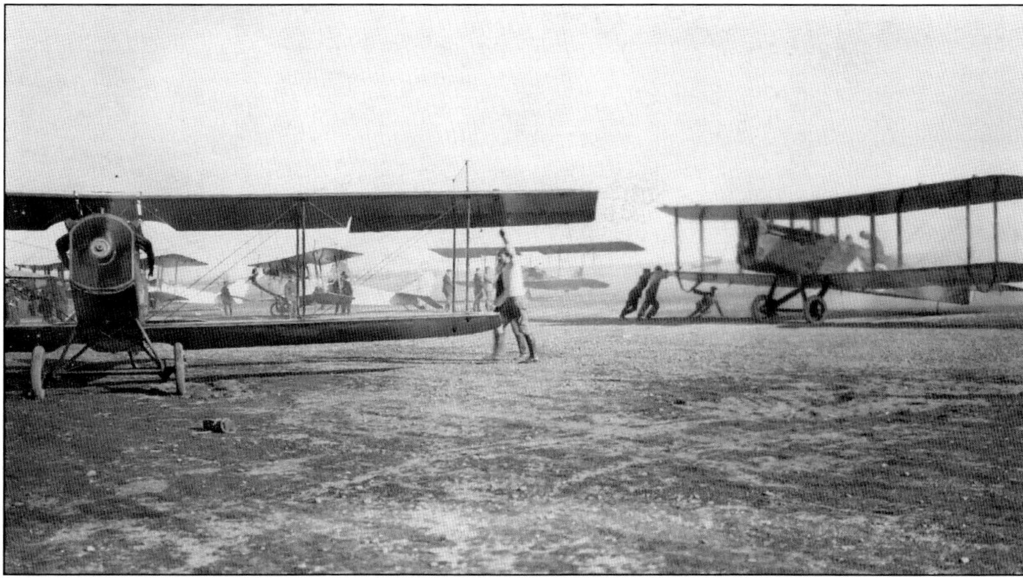

Propellers whirl as airmen and ground crews ready aircraft for flight during an exercise at Mather Field. A pilot in a sweater and flying cap signals to someone, while officers and civilians stand in the background. The straps used to turn the craft on the right were also used by wing walkers and daredevils during flying exhibitions. (CSH.)

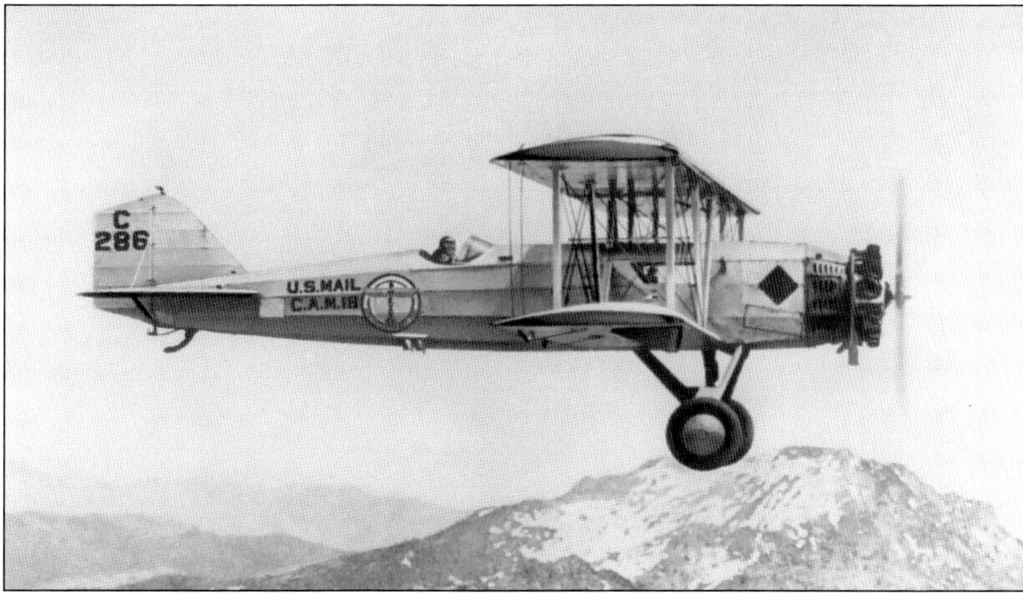

A Boeing Model 40 biplane powered by a 425-horsepower Wasp engine capable of flying 125 miles-per-hour cruises above the Sierra Nevada Range. The two-passenger Air Transport 40A could carry a cargo of 1,400 pounds. The original aircraft built for the post office had a composite wood-and-tube fuselage. The designation C.A.M. 18 indicates the airplane was following Contract Air Route 18. (CSH.)

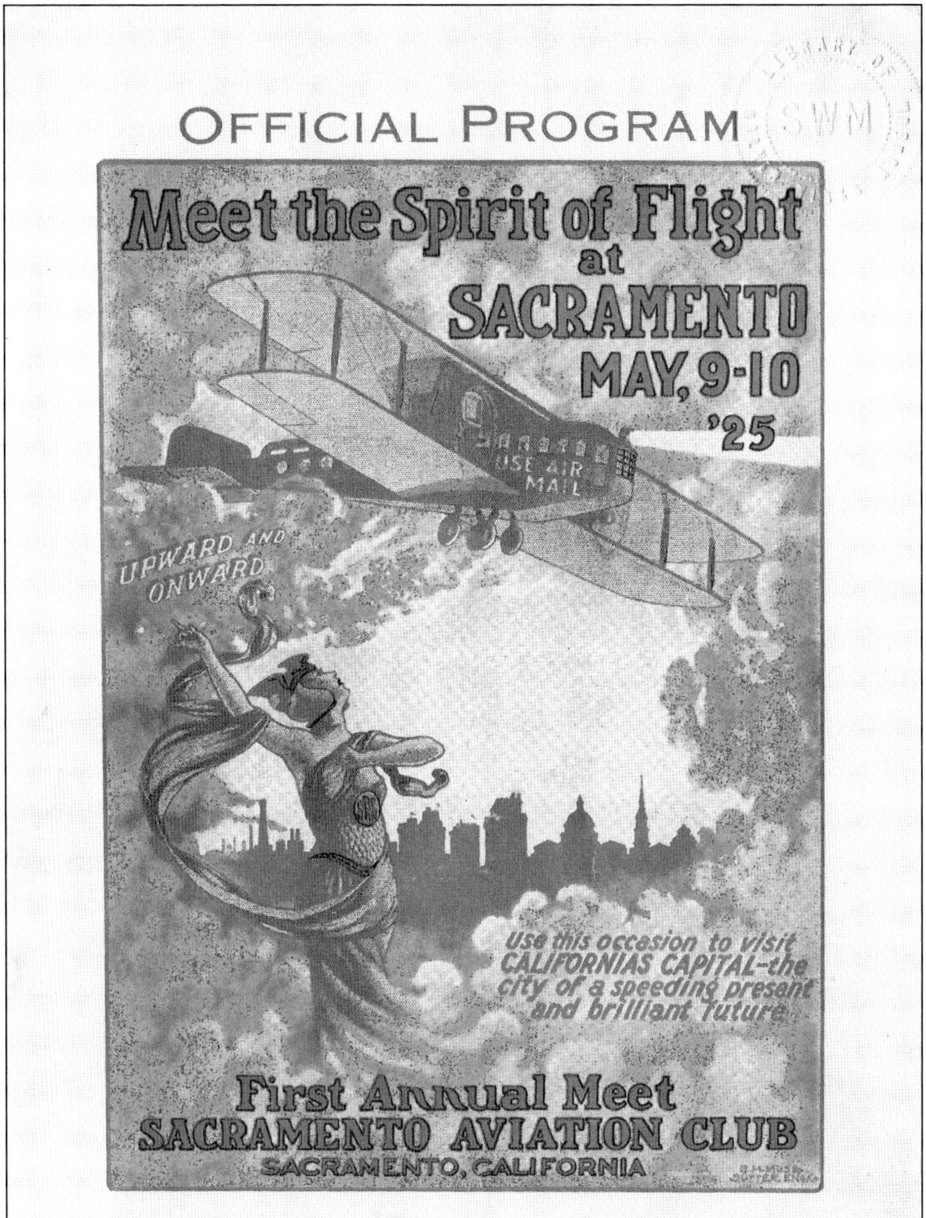

The spirit of flight entered the Sacramento Valley in May 1925 in the form of an aerial meet held at Mather Field and sponsored by the Sacramento Aviation Club. Over 90 airplanes, the largest concentration of engine-driven aircraft assembled in California up to that time, took to the air in flyby reviews and tests of speed. The scheduled events and unexpected occurrences thrilled people who had no exposure to airplanes beyond magazines, movies, and newspapers. Both days featured a "battle in the clouds" late in the afternoon, with airships attacking each other with machine guns blazing while an airplane went down as the pilot "hit the silk." SSgt. Fred Kelly suffered a fractured skull and a broken leg during a jump from 2,000 feet on opening day, the only serious accident during the weekend. Both days ended with smoke and phosphorus bombs dropped on a mythical city. (CSH.)

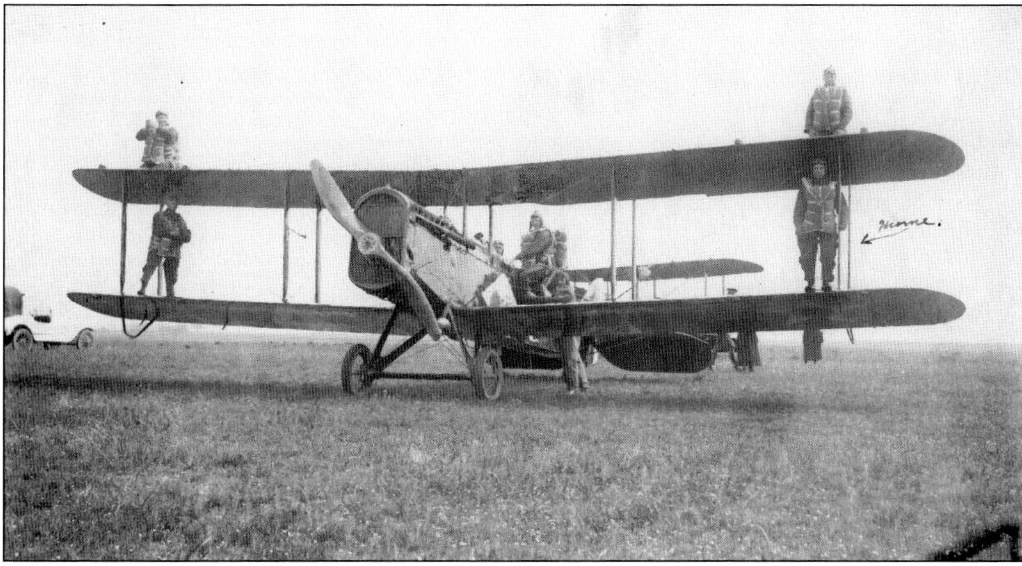

Festivities on both days of Mather Field's 1925 air circus included fancy flying by Lt. Henry Andrews and acrobatic stunts performed by his partner Jimmy(?) Angel, who sat, hung, and posed on the wings with hands raised while Andrews put the plane through its paces six full turns above the crowd. These two photographs capture four unidentified daredevils wearing parachutes as they stand prior to flight and hunker down on the wings at take off, hanging tightly to the straps or struts that hold them in place against the wind currents. The refinement of the parachute made such stunts somewhat safer, as evidenced by a small but growing fraternity of flyers who belonged to the Caterpillar Club of airmen who survived forced exits from crippled aircraft. (Both, CSH.)

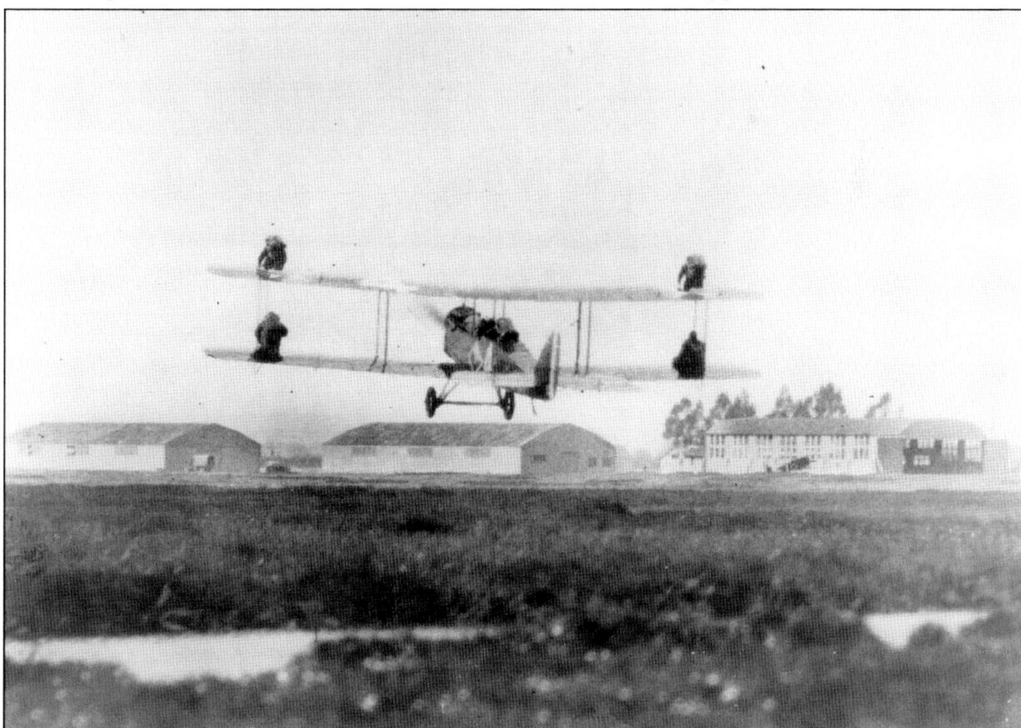

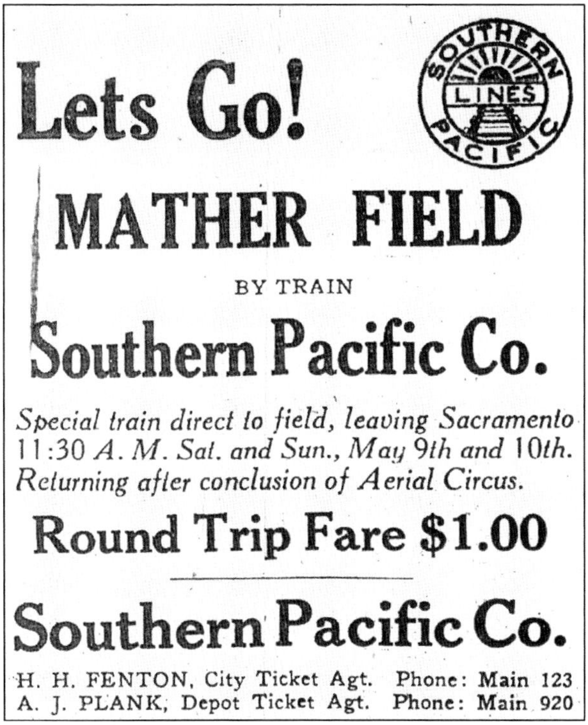

An arrangement with the Southern Pacific Railroad for the required spur to Mather Field cost the chamber $21,000 in 1918. The line proved its worth during the air circus in 1925, when the chamber teamed with local press and Southern Pacific to run a special train to the events both days for a round-trip fare of $1. Visitors arriving early had a chance to inspect the aircraft or take advantage of free rides offered by experienced pilots. Prize races, formation flying, and feats of daring kept audiences from Sacramento and San Francisco on the edge of their bleachers while locals and passersby, drawn by the unusual noise and activity, craned their necks from beyond the gates. (Both, SPL.)

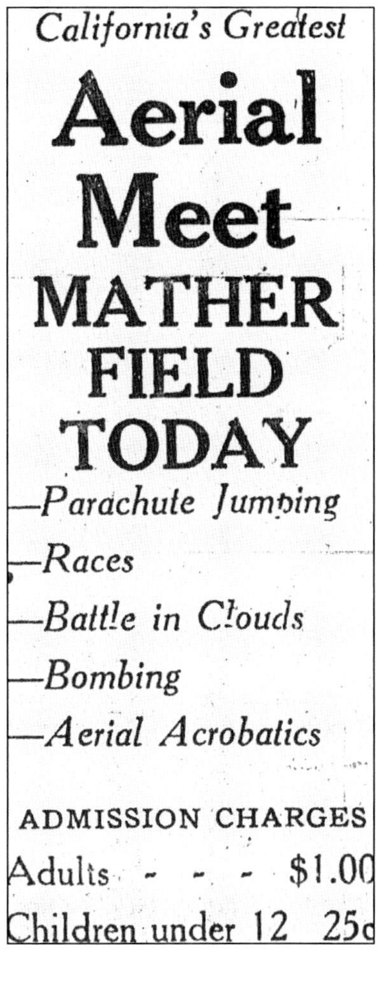

Aerial meet queen Fay Lamphere presided over the 25-mile civilian aerial race held opening day, but the $125 trophy hardly matched the $1,000 prize offered by the Sacramento Chamber of Commerce for the winner of the 50-mile race between competing De Havilland aircraft. Finishing second was local man Lt. Willis Taylor, son of Sacramento and Signal Corps meteorologist Nathaniel R. Taylor, who had accompanied a committee inspecting Mills Station in early 1918 and spent nearly 50 years with the US Signal Corps. Both days featured dead-stick landings, where contestants stalled their engines at 2,500 feet and attempted to land closest to a mark on the field. The top six contestants competed again on Sunday for a sterling-silver trophy. (Both, CSH.)

PROGRAM—Saturday

9:30 A.M. Gates opened to public. Public may inspect ships, view grounds, and take rides in planes.
12:30 P.M. Cross-country handicap race. Start at Richmond, end at Sacramento. (Ric. C. C.)
1:30 P.M. Competitive Formation Flying. All reserve squadrons eligible. A $125.00 trophy to be awarded to the winner.
2:00 P.M. Queen of the Aerial Meet arrives.
2:10 P.M. Andrews-Angel Acrobatic Stunts. (a) Ship to fly past crowd six times with Aviator Angel hanging or sitting in different positions on ship. (b) Aviator Angel sitting on top of center section while ship does two Immelman turns. (c) Aviator Angel standing with arms outspread on top of center section while ship does a Loop-the-Loop. (d) Parachute jumping.
2:50 P.M. Civilian's Race over a course of twenty-five miles. A beautiful trophy to winner. Value of trophy, $125.00.
3:25 P.M. Dead Stick Landings. Contestants kill their engine at 2500 feet altitude and land ship for a mark. The best six will compete in finals on Sunday.
4:15 P.M. Battle in the Clouds. Ships to attack each other. Machine gun firing. One ship will be shot down in mid-air with pilot jumping out with parachute.
4:45 P.M. Air Mail arrives and leaves a pouch of mail at field.
4:50 P.M. Airplanes will drop spectacular smoke and phosphorus bombs around the Mythical City.

Sacramento Chamber of Commerce
Trophy
Presented as
FIRST AWARD
in the
Main Event
Sacramento Aerial Meet
Mather Field
May 9th and 10th, 1925

Sold by

H. Wachhorst Co.

Jewelers and Silversmiths
Since 1850

801 K Street **Sacramento**

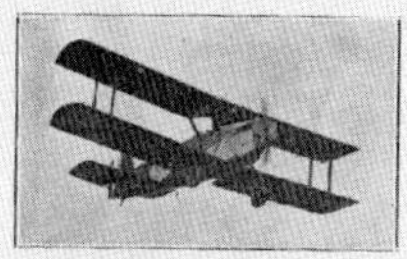

ONE OF THE AIRPLANES THAT FLEW AROUND THE WORLD

Page Five

PROGRAM—Sunday

10:00 A.M. Gates opened to public. Public may inspect ships, view grounds, and take rides in planes.

1:30 P.M. Formation Flying, demonstrating all types of formations.

1:50 P.M. Navy Ships Demonstration. A demonstration consisting of a T. S. Pursuit Plane, Vought Plane, and a Navy Torpedo Plane, being the three latest types of aerial craft.

2:10 P.M. Andrews-Angel Acrobatic Stunts. (a) Ship to fly past crowd six times with Aviator Angel hanging or sitting in different positions on ship. (b) Aviator Angel sitting on top of center section while ship does two Immelman turns. (c) Aviator Angel standing with arms outspread on top of center section while ship does a Loop-the-Loop. (d) Parachute jumping.

2:50 P.M. De Haviland Race. A fifty-mile race. Feature race of the meet. The $1,000 Chamber of Commerce trophy to be given to the winner as his possession until the next annual race. Suitable permanent trophies will also be awarded.

3:20 P.M. Dead Stick landings. Finals. A $200 sterling silver trophy to be given as first prize and a $75 trophy as second prize. (Hotel men and Sacramento Aviation Club.)

4:00 P.M. Battle in the Clouds. Ships to attack each other. Machine gun gun firing. One ship will be shot down in mid-air with pilot jumping out with parachute.

4:30 P.M. Aerial mail arrives.

4:40 P.M. Presentation of Cups.

5:00 P.M. Bombing of Mythical City. Planes will fly over a small city and drop bombs, etc. Village will be set afire.

Page Nine

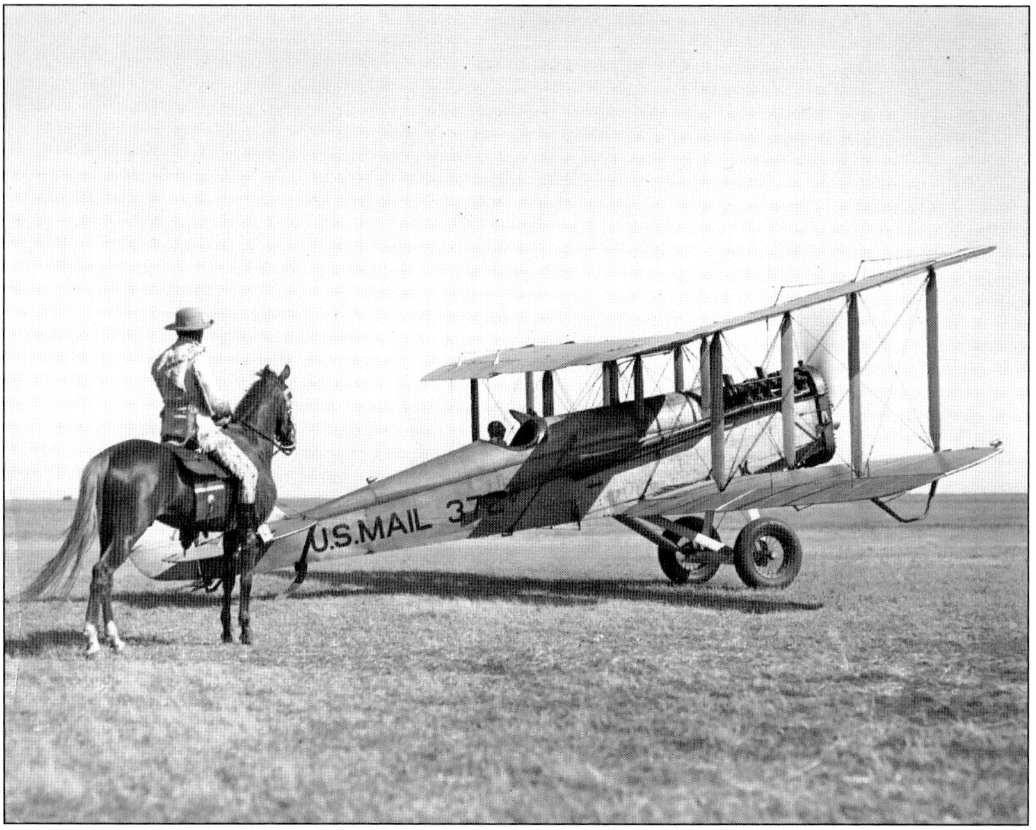

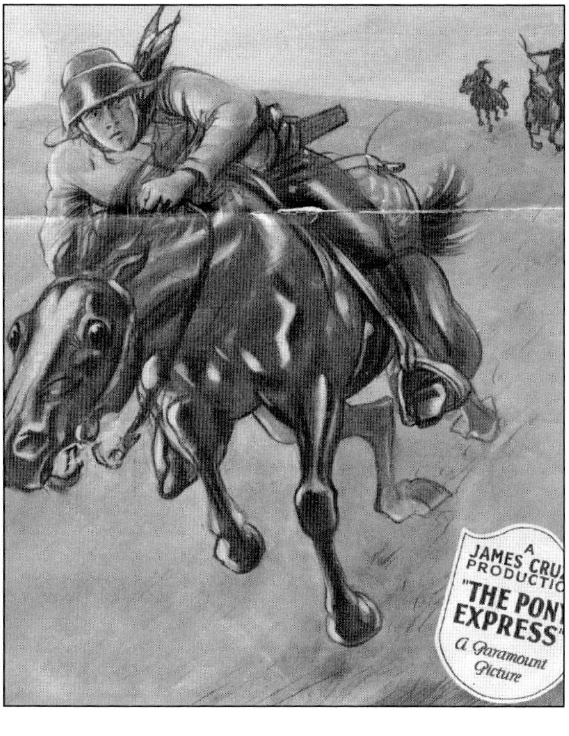

A stunt rider for the Paramount Pictures blockbuster *The Pony Express* sits astride his mount as a De Havilland DH-4, used in the newly inaugurated airmail service between Sacramento and San Francisco, prepares to go aloft with the mail sack transferred at Mather from pony to plane. Four thousand spectators had gathered at Mather Field on May 10 for the air circus and witnessed the arrival of the first transcontinental airmail plane in Sacramento County. James Cruze filmed *The Pony Express* on location along the Sacramento River utilizing available old riverboats to double for 1860 craft. The real Pony Express followed two routes during the first few months of its existence (April to June 1860); the southern route followed White Rock Road to Mormon Tavern, then on to Henry Deterding's 15-Mile House to 5-Mile House and Sacramento. (Both, SPL.)

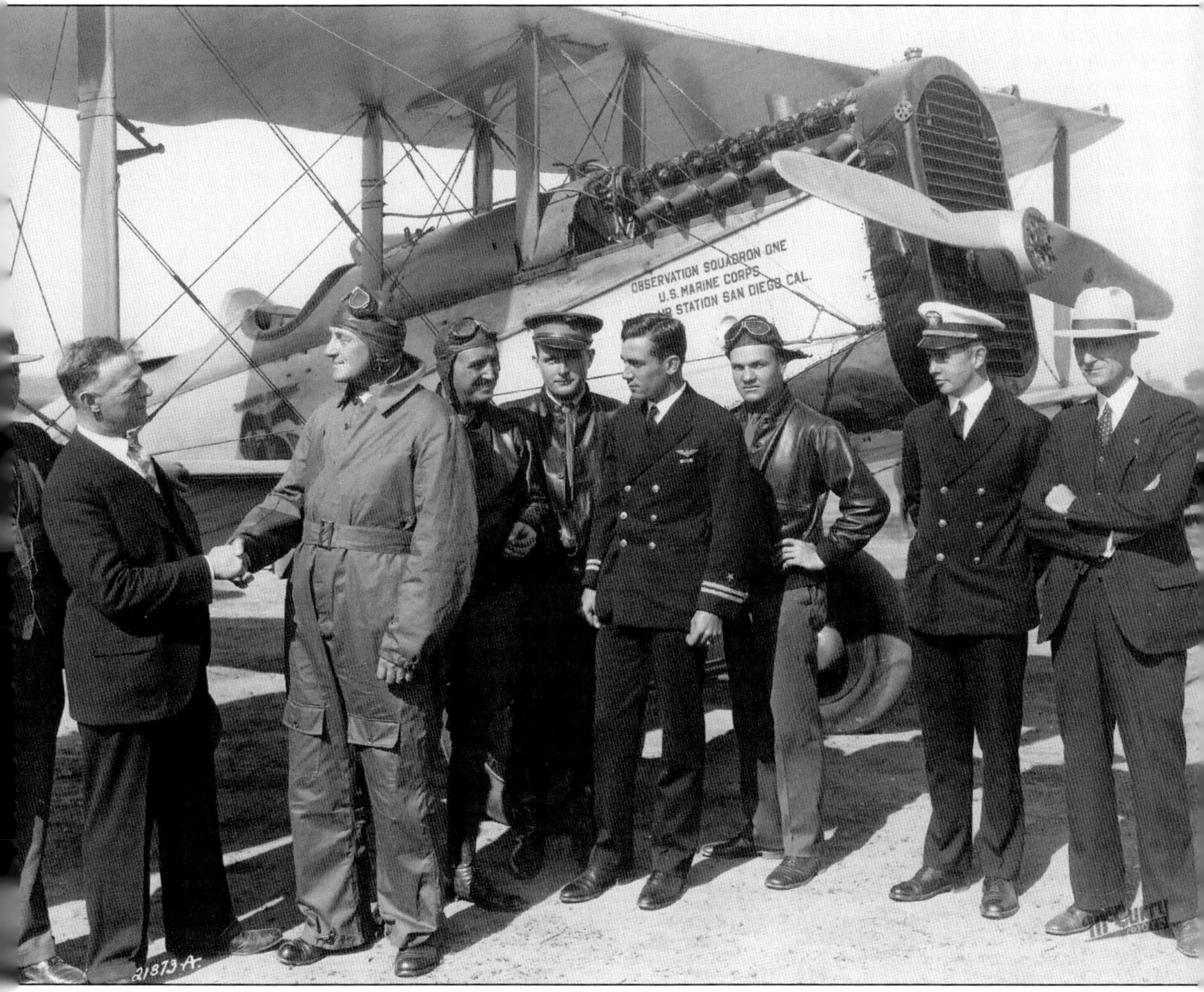

California state senator Roy J. Nielsen (second from left) shakes hands with Maj. Ross E. Rowell, commanding officer of Observation Squadron One, US Marine Corps, during a visit to Mather Field on Navy Day in 1926. Receiving the new designation in July 1922, the squadron evolved from the Northern Bombing Group operating in France in 1918. Intense practice in aerial bombing off the North Island base in San Diego proved invaluable when Rowell and his squadron executed a dive-bombing attack against insurgents in Nicaragua during July 1927, earning the future lieutenant general the Distinguished Flying Cross and Distinguished Service Medal. Navy Day was originally celebrated in 1922 on October 27, the birthday of former assistant secretary of the Navy Theodore Roosevelt, via a proclamation by Pres. Warren G. Harding. The tradition was discontinued in 1949. Nielsen and Rowell stand in front of a De Havilland 4-B airplane. (CSH.)

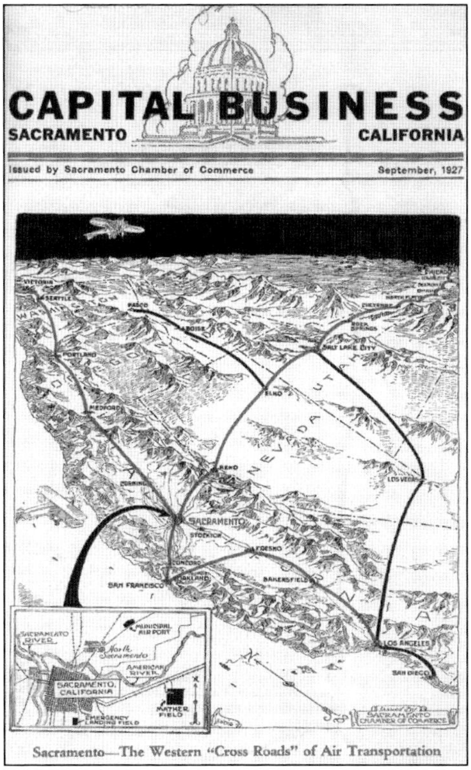

The future of aviation seemed limitless to the American public, but the federal government had limited the growth of air power, and many of the bases established in 1918 were closed or received little use. The arrival of Charles Lindbergh at Mather Field in September provided an opportunity for the Sacramento Chamber of Commerce to reaffirm its belief in Sacramento as the "Western 'Cross Roads' of Air Transportation."(SPL.)

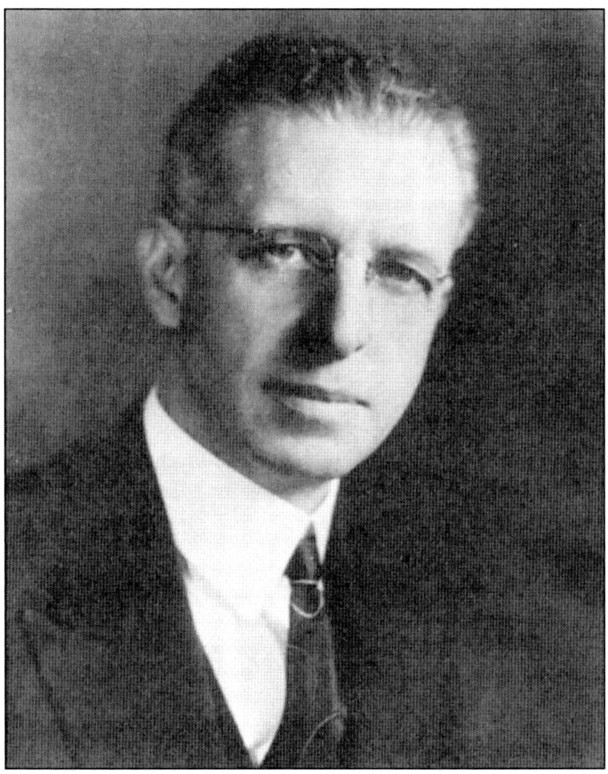

Arthur Serviss Dudley was the guiding force behind the Sacramento Chamber of Commerce from 1927 to 1950, though in 1923, he became involved in the struggle to keep Mather Airfield active through contracts with the Forest Service. He paid full attention to lobbying for reactivation of Mather Field, and the efforts were successful in large part through special events and visits by aviators and airships from across the country. (SPL.)

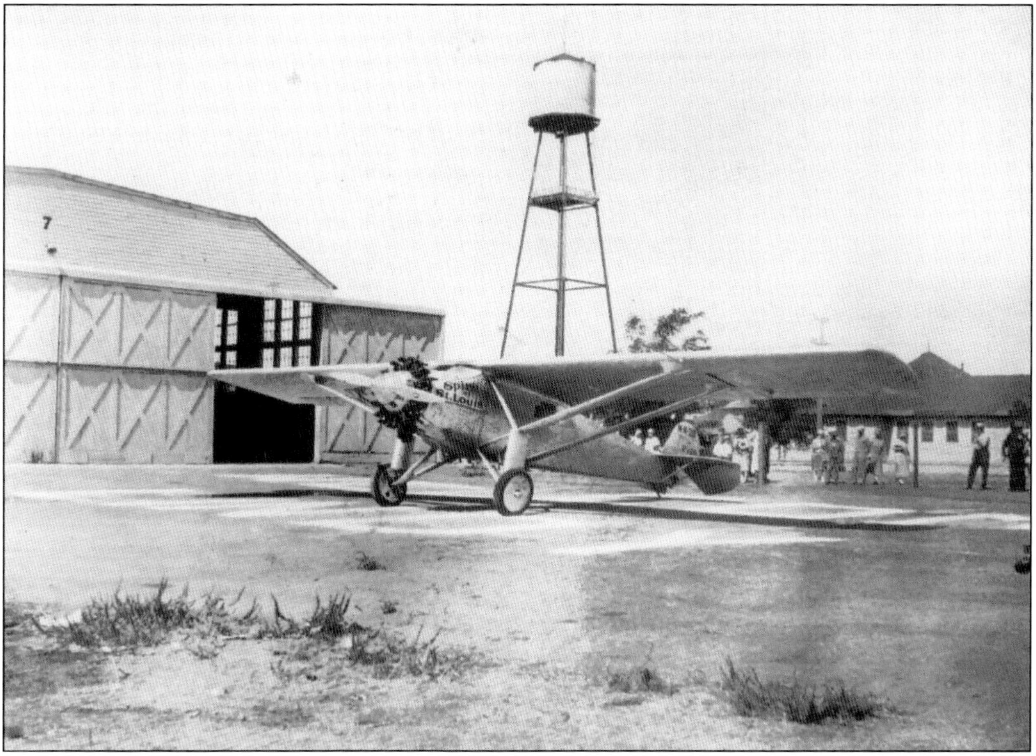

At 21 years old, Charles A. Lindbergh took his first solo flight in a war-surplus Curtiss Jenny. No license was required and no flight plans had to be filed, so the young aviation enthusiast filled the airship with gasoline and took off. Lindbergh's solo flight from New York to Paris in May 1927 made the "Lone Eagle" an instant and lifelong celebrity. On September 17, he visited Mather Field amidst thousands of exultant fans before being whisked away by a motorcade past cheering crowds to Moreing Field at Riverside and Y Streets. A banquet in his honor was held at the Hotel Senator, with tickets running $5. The photograph above shows Lindbergh's famous *Spirit of St. Louis* at Mather Field. The sheet music at right conveys the fascination the public had with the shy aviator, whom many felt embodied the American spirit. (Above, SPL; right, Tom Tolley.)

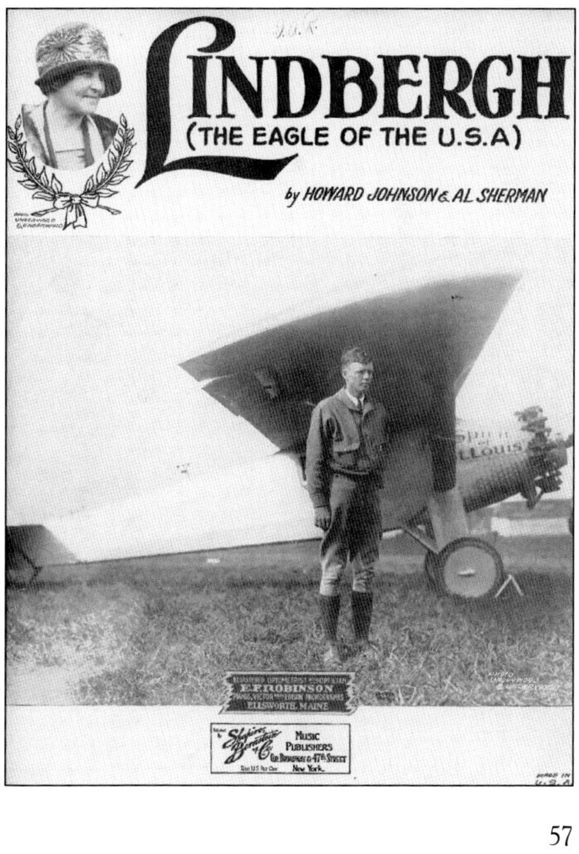

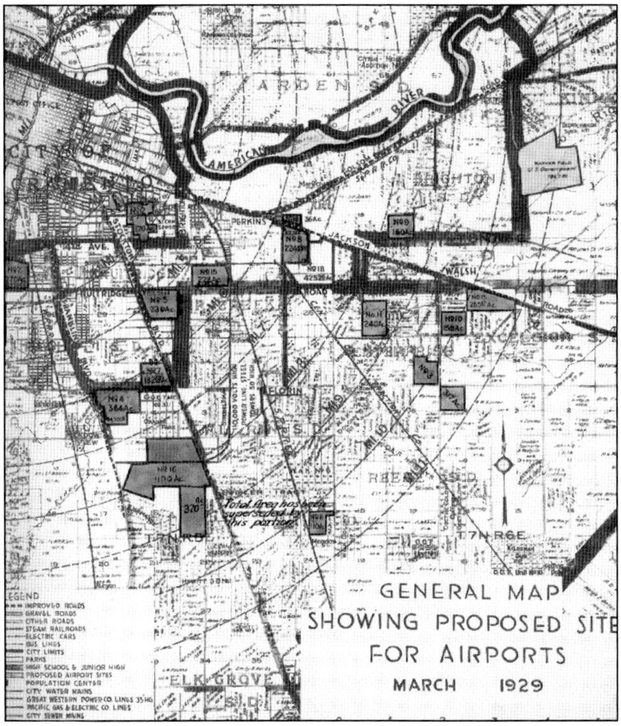

The search for a site to lay out a municipal airfield for Sacramento began in earnest by the late 1920s. A location by Del Paso Park was never completely developed and eventually proved to be too far from town for practical consideration. A report published in 1929 detailed the advantages of sites chosen, provided blueprints and data on several spots, and included a detailed map (left). Acreage on Freeport Boulevard beyond the city limits, where Sacramento Executive Airport now stands, was chosen, and by mid-April 1930, a dedication was held at the new airfield. A special commemorative postal seal marked the opening of the new airport along with the Army Air Corps maneuvers held at Mather Field the same month. (Left, SPL; below, CSH.)

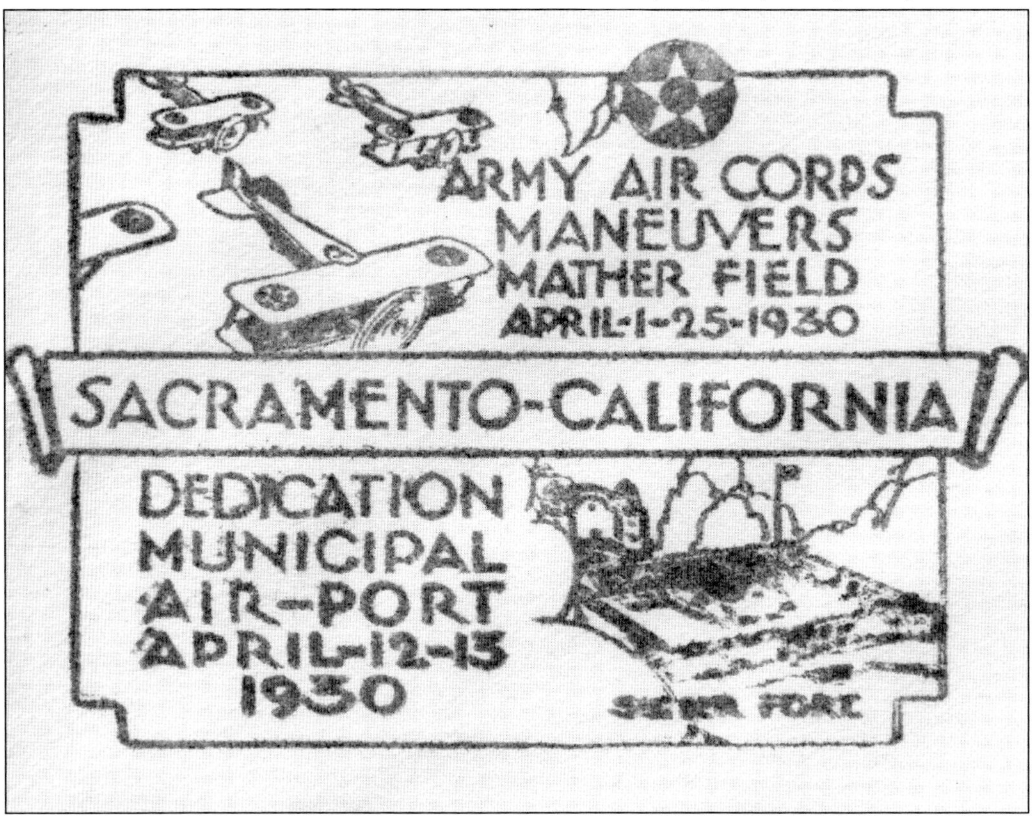

Mather Field's front gate lies open as the first of a procession of vehicles enters for an event during the interim period between wars, when the installation struggled for survival. The California Highway Patrol Academy was founded in 1930 and originally used Mather facilities for classes until moving in under the grandstands at the state fairgrounds until 1938. (CSH.)

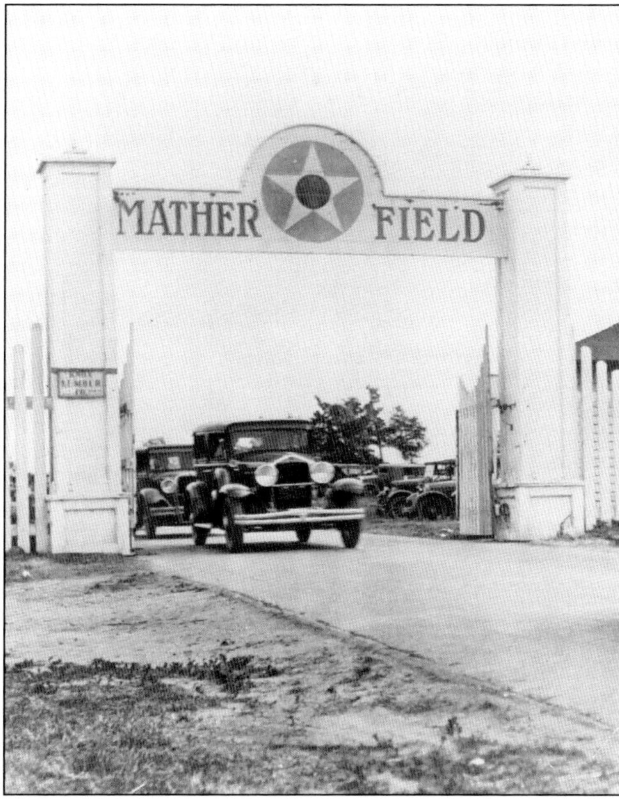

High-booted chauffeurs and enlisted men lean against tightly packed touring cars and De Havilland aircraft during an event at Mather Field, possibly the aerial circus, which was held the second weekend of May 1925. Mather would become a testing ground for new military transportation of all kinds in exercises held during the 1930s. (CSH.)

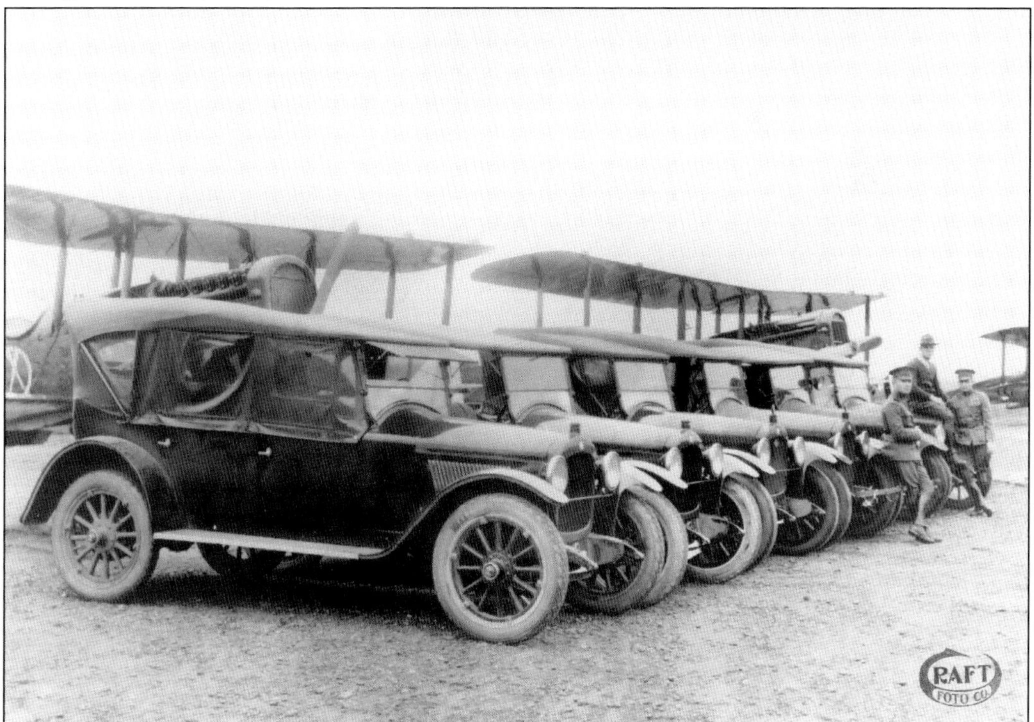

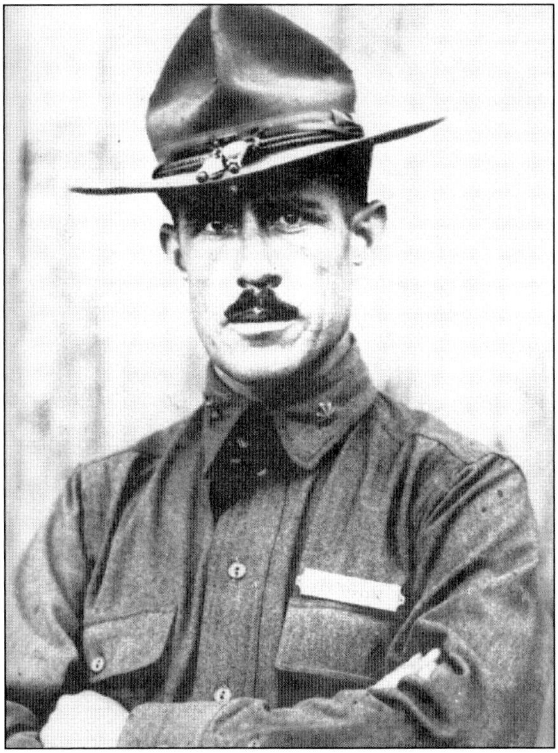

Col. Clarence L. Tinker, who commanded the 20th Pursuit Group at Mather Field from 1930 to 1932, was noted for his affability and fairness, despite a steely gaze. The first Native American major general in the United States, he took command of American forces in Hawaii during January 1942. Tinker and the B-25 Mitchell bombers he was leading to attack Japanese vessels off Wake Island disappeared without a trace on June 7, 1942. (CSH.)

A group of aviators and ground crewmen poses in front of aircraft on Mather Field during the maneuvers and games in 1930. For three weeks, about 40 percent of American airplanes, pilots, and support staff were dispatched to the isolated location to engage in mock battles, put on demonstrations for the public, and test new equipment. (CSH.)

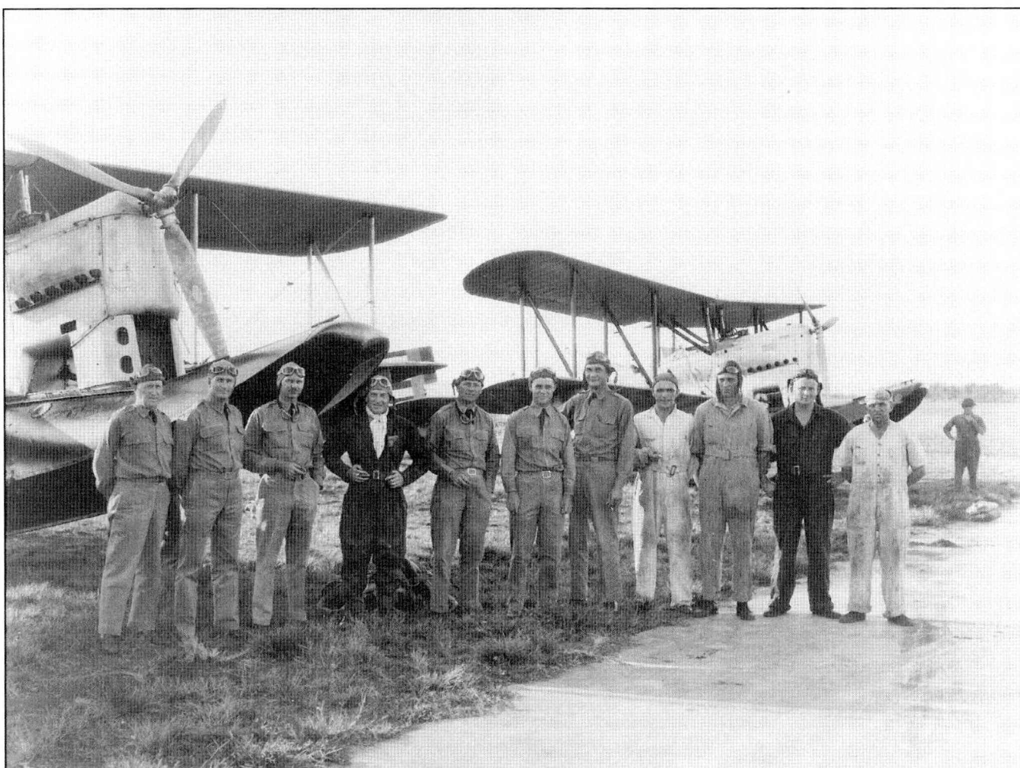

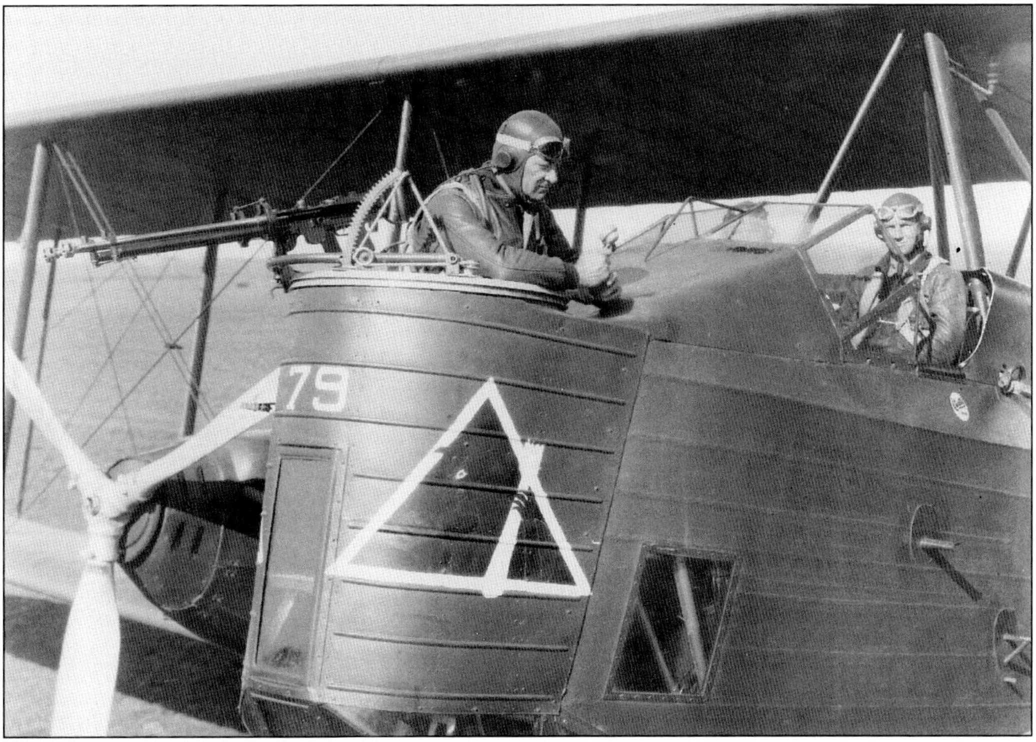

Brig. Gen. William E. Gillmore holds the radiophone used to communicate wireless instructions to the 1st Pursuit Squadron and 150 aircraft during maneuvers in 1930. Gillmore, assistant chief of the Air Corps from 1926 to 1930, led simulated air attacks over San Francisco, where winged armies thrilled citizens. The early nose-cone art below General Gillmore depicts a horned devil with a large nose holding a bomb in his left hand. (CSH.)

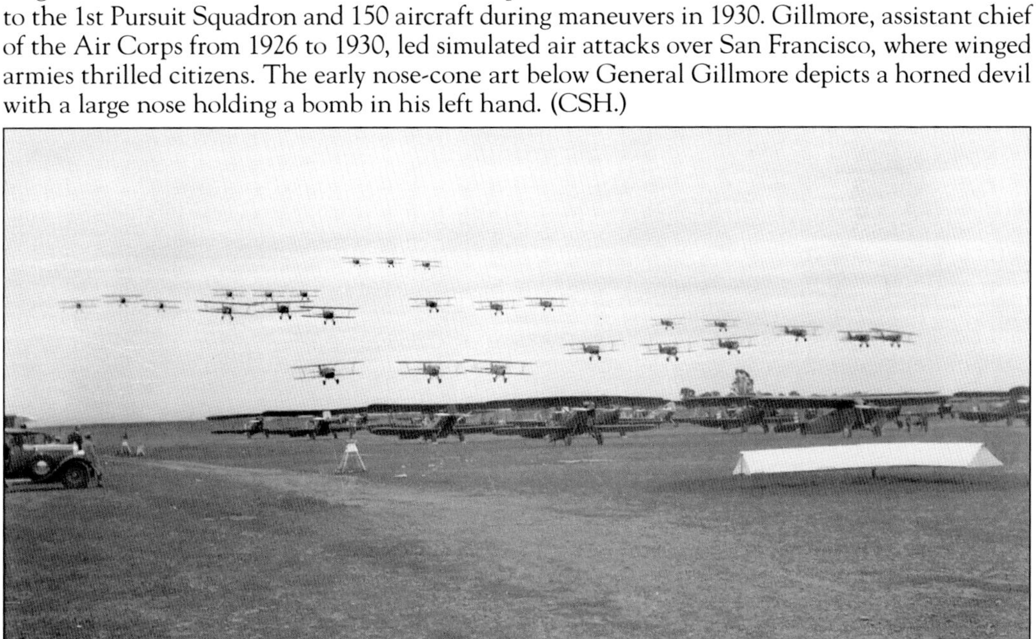

Twenty-six A-3 pursuit planes in groups of three fly above bombers and ground crews at Mather Field. Army Air Corps maneuvers took place over three weeks early in 1930 and lasted from dawn until dusk. Observers lean against automobiles and ambulances visible to the left as they wait for a long day to end. (CSH.)

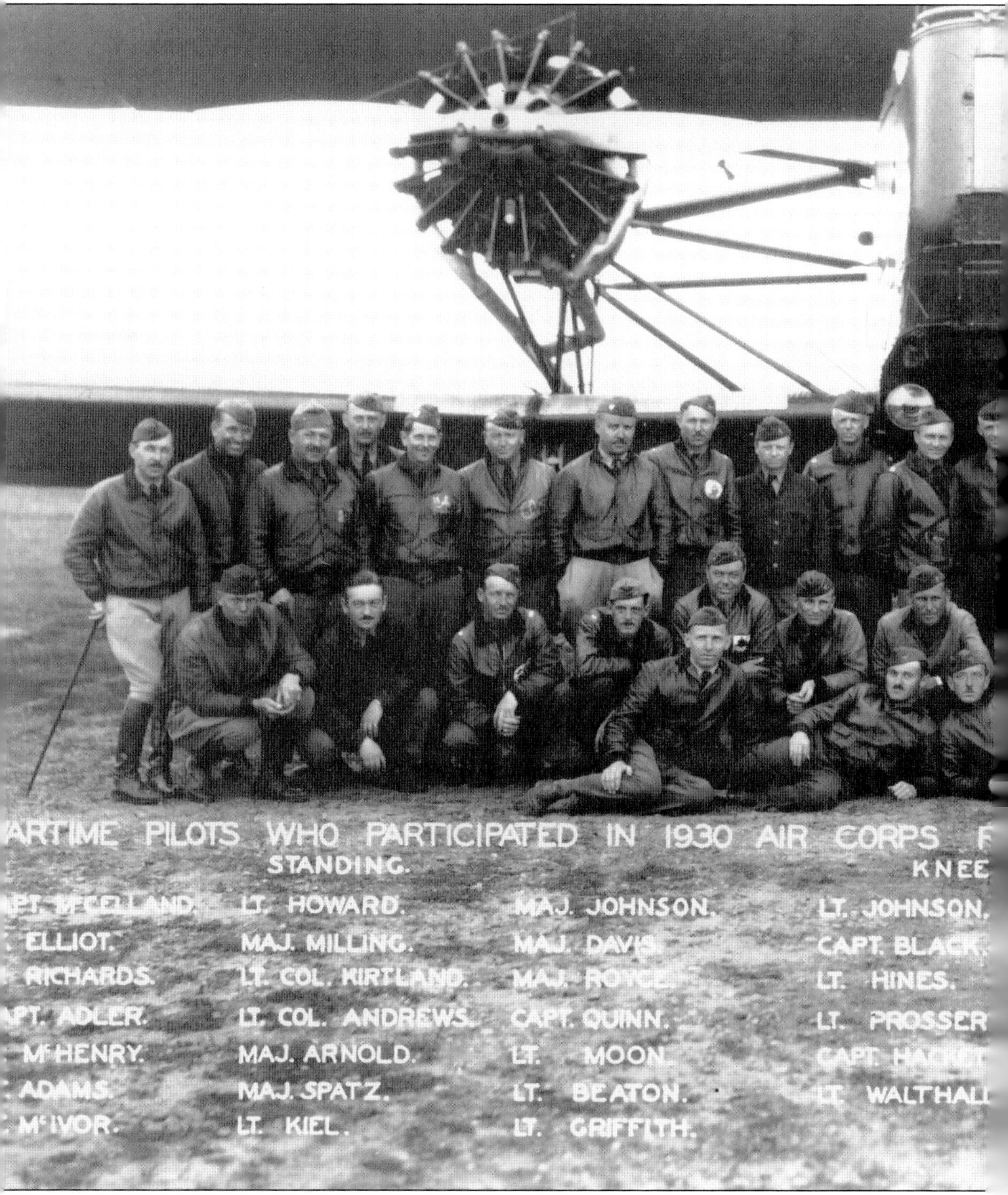
ARTIME PILOTS WHO PARTICIPATED IN 1930 AIR CORPS
STANDING.
KNEE
LT. HOWARD.
MAJ. JOHNSON.
LT. JOHNSON.
ELLIOT.
MAJ. MILLING.
MAJ. DAVIS.
CAPT. BLACK.
RICHARDS.
LT. COL. KIRTLAND.
MAJ. ROYCE.
LT. HINES.
PT. ADLER.
LT. COL. ANDREWS.
CAPT. QUINN.
LT. PROSSER
M^c HENRY.
MAJ. ARNOLD.
LT. MOON.
ADAMS.
MAJ. SPATZ.
LT. BEATON.
LT. WALTHALL
M^c IVOR.
LT. KIEL.
LT. GRIFFITH.

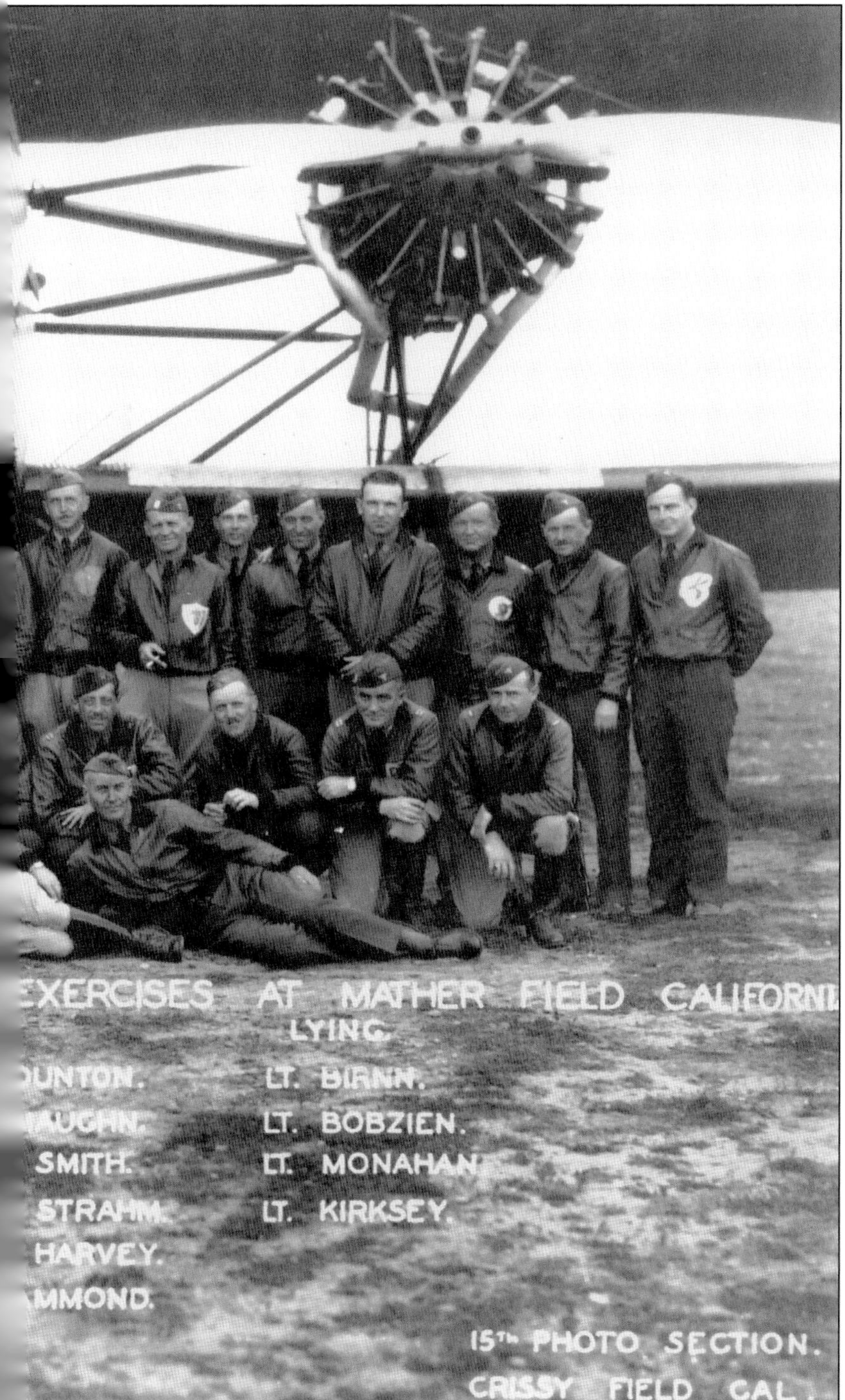

A veritable Mount Olympus of American military aviation was photographed during the spring of 1930's Army Air Corps maneuvers, held at Mather. Of particular note, the three aviators standing directly beneath the nose of the plane are, from left to right, Lt. Col. Frank Andrews (future commander of all US troops in the European theater of operations and namesake of Andrews Air Force base), Maj. Henry "Hap" Arnold (later commanding general of the US Army Air Forces during World War II), and Maj. Carl "Tooey" Spaatz (future chief of staff of the US Air Force). The aviators pose before a Keystone B-6A Panther bomber. (CSH.)

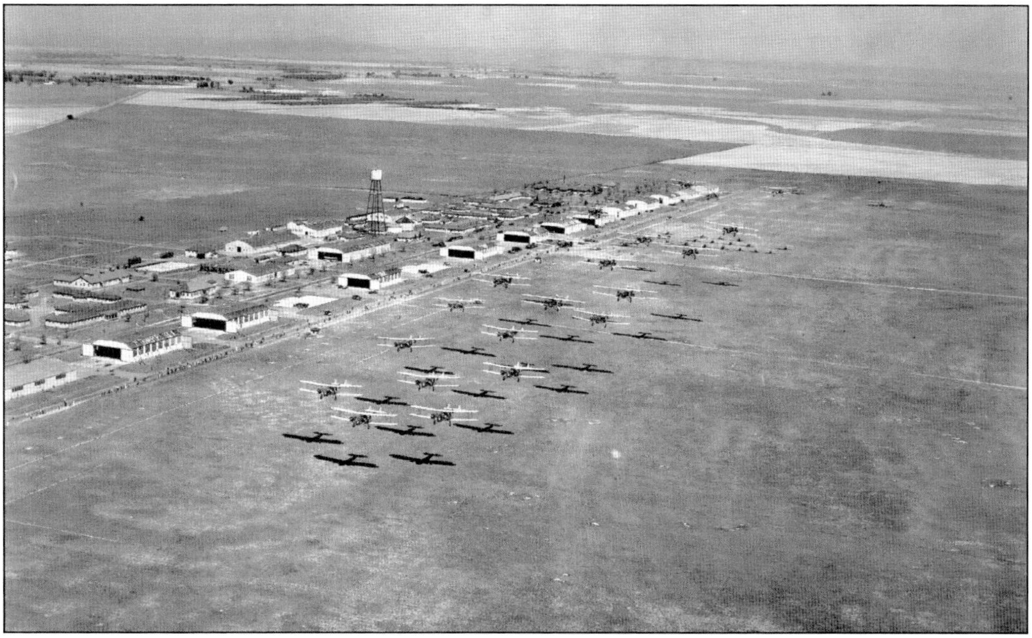

A formation of Curtiss B-2 Condor bombers followed by A-3 attack airplanes takes off from Mather Air Field on April 4, 1930, during the open house celebrating American air power. The photographic unit of the Air Corps stationed at Crissy Field in San Francisco's Presidio printed many quality shots taken during the run of the maneuvers, producing dramatic images of warbirds over scenic vistas—a melding of land and machine. (CSH.)

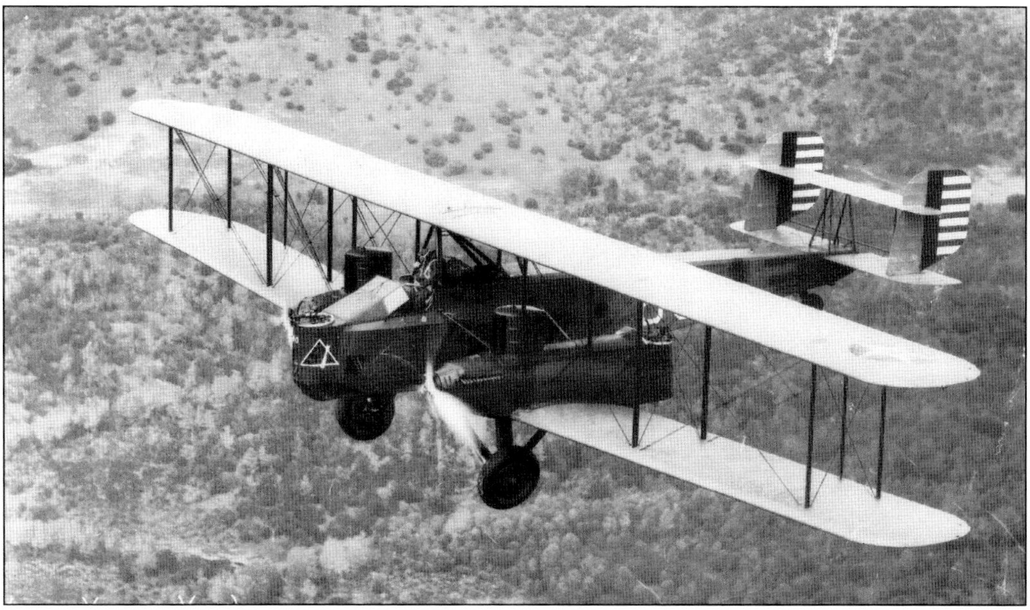

The pilot of this Curtiss B-2 Condor flying on autopilot stands in the cockpit while his copilot lies on top of the fuselage during a round-trip flight to San Francisco. The pilot handled the controls only for takeoff and landing. Tests of radio communications and high-altitude flying were key parts of the 1930 exercises flown over much of Northern California during the month of April. (CSH.)

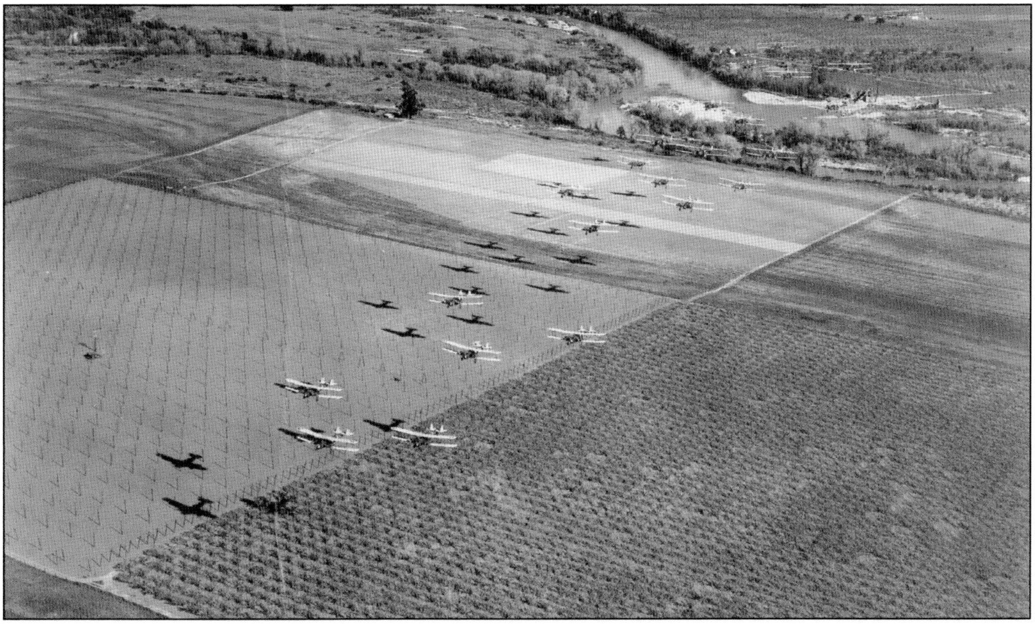

A group of Keystone LB-7 Panther bombers and Curtiss B-2 Condors crosses the American River in groups of three during the open house maneuvers held at Mather Field in April 1930, which showcased the Army Air Corps and tested new aircraft and technology. The soaring airplanes pass over fields planted with crops and vines, reminiscent of what the Mather side looked like a little over a dozen years earlier. (CSH.)

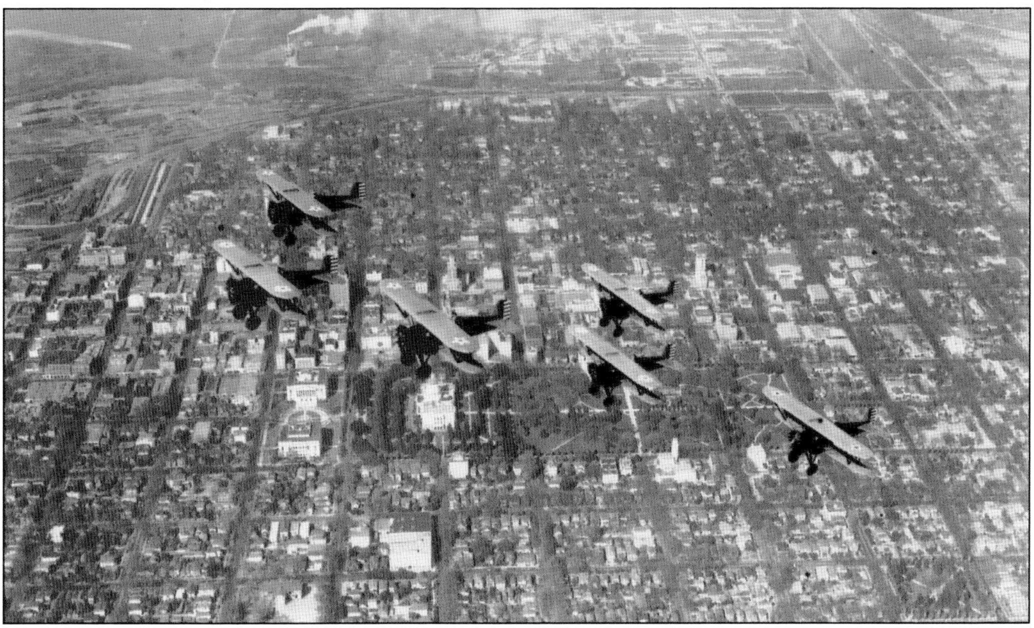

The Army Air Corps Maneuvers at Mather Field in April 1930 captured the attention of most of Northern California as airplanes and pilots waged mock war above San Francisco, flew radio-communication and high-altitude tests over the Sierra Nevada Mountains, including Mount Whitney, and practiced formation flying. In this photograph, a group of A-3 pursuit aircraft flies high above Sacramento, with the capitol and grounds and the new state library visible. (CSH.)

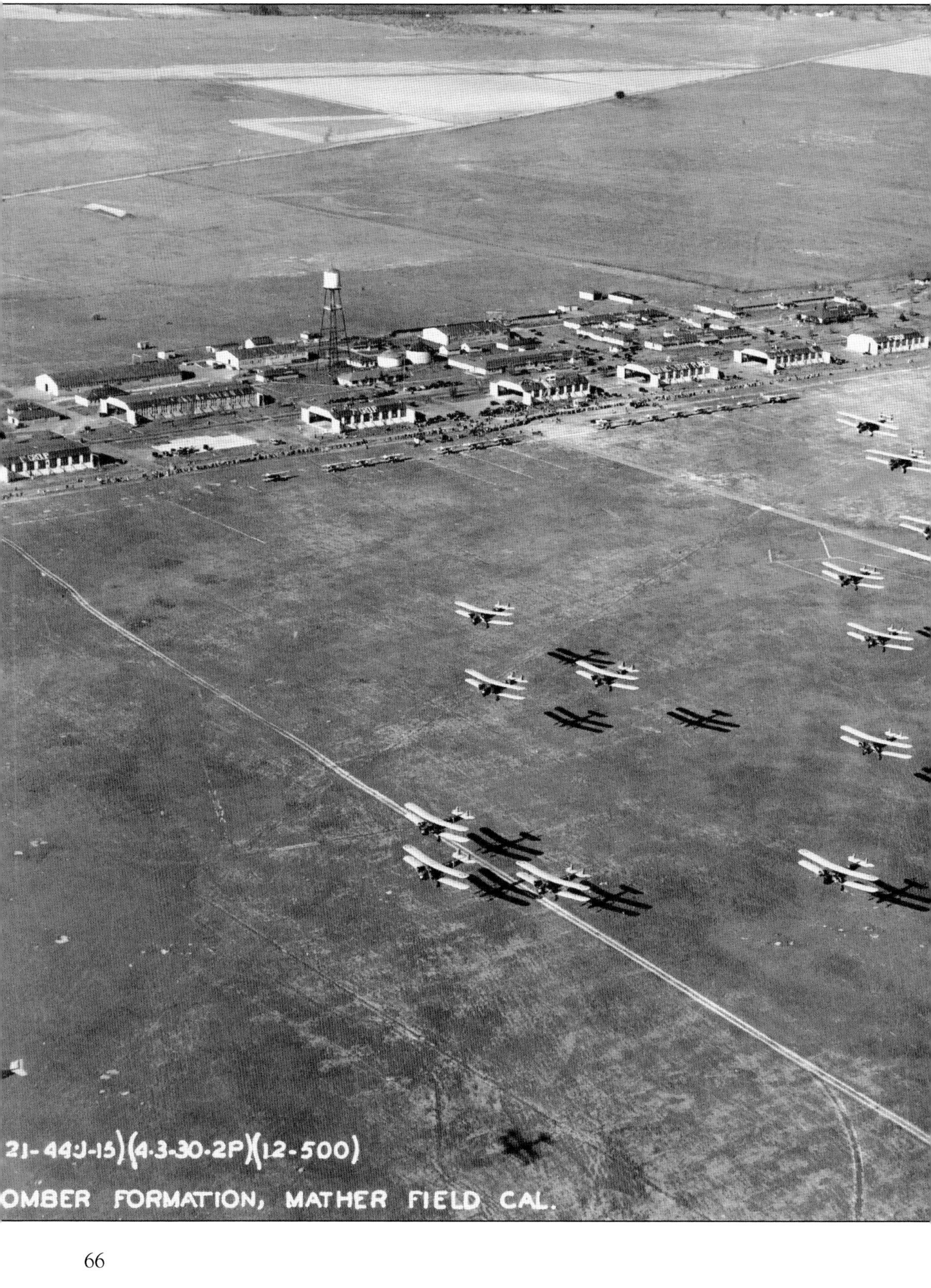
21-44J-15)(4-3-30-2P)(12-500)
OMBER FORMATION, MATHER FIELD CAL.

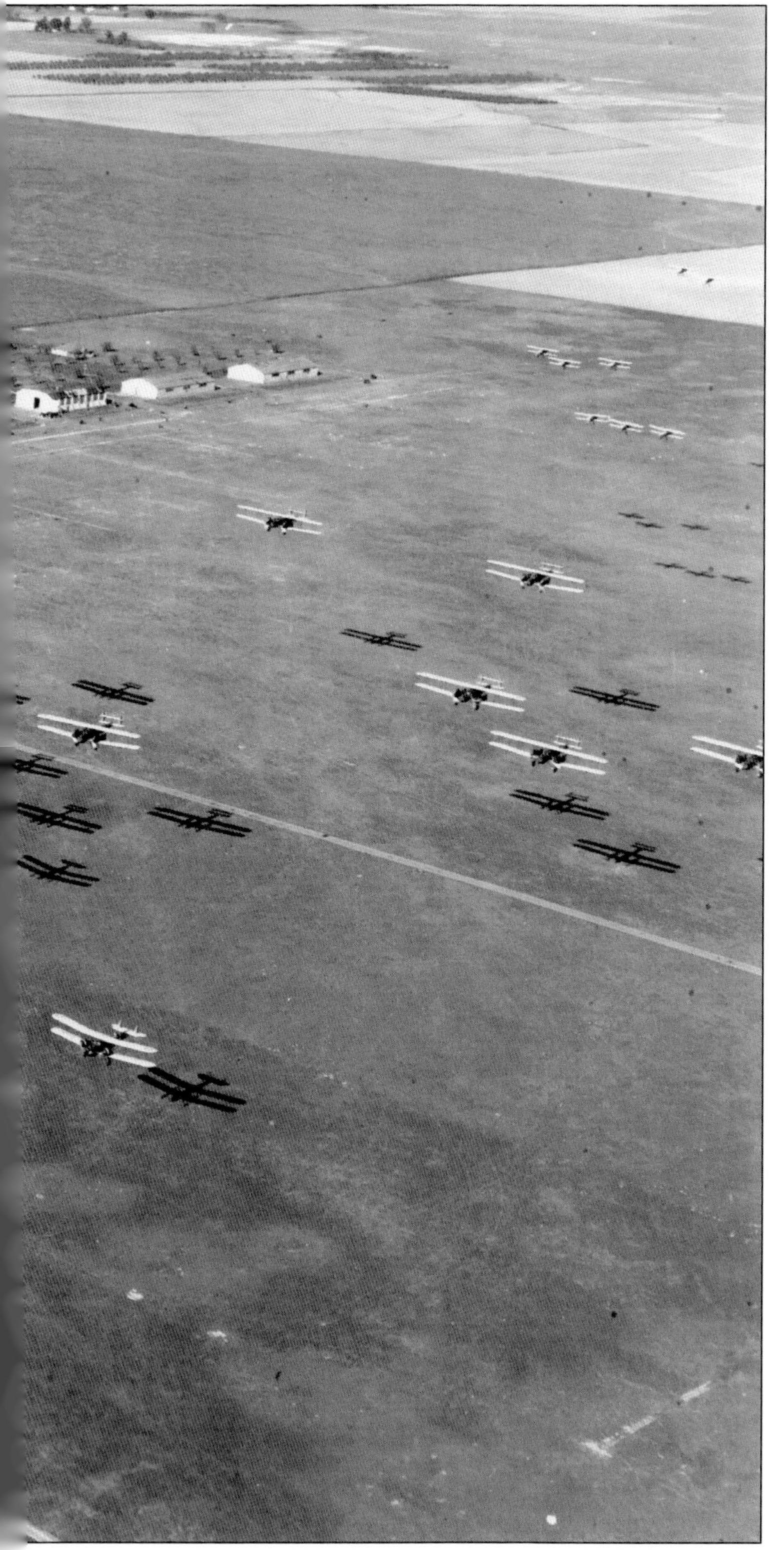

Wings glistening in the sun and planes' shadows below and away, a formation of bombers flies above Mather Field during aerial maneuvers in April 1930. Many of the more than 50 buildings constructed by teams of laborers, many of them transients gathered from Sacramento's notorious West End, are visible, along with more than a dozen aircraft parked along this flight line. Formerly fertile farmland lay flat and fallow to the north of Mather, along the southern edge of the American River. Some of the large hangars have hand-painted signs, visible from the air and identifying the flight groups involved. Spectators stand along the flight line and sit or stand atop the massive hangars. (CSH.)

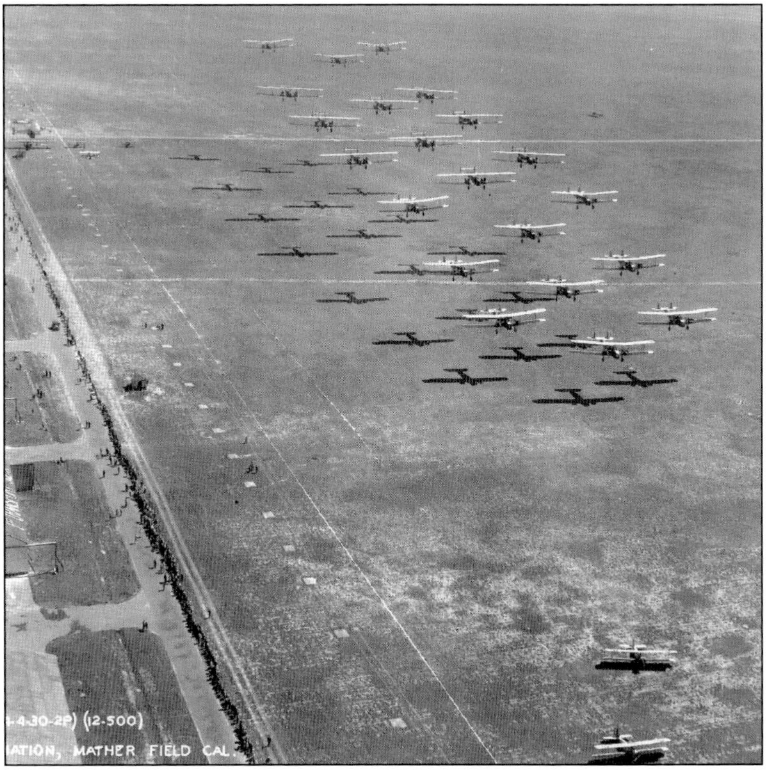

When word reached the Sacramento Chamber of Commerce late in 1929 that the Army Air Corps was planning the largest aerial exercises up to that time, the group jumped into action. Bringing as many men and machines as possible together for maneuvers was the goal of the government, and the clear skies and mild weather above Mather Field proved ideal for the event. (CSH.)

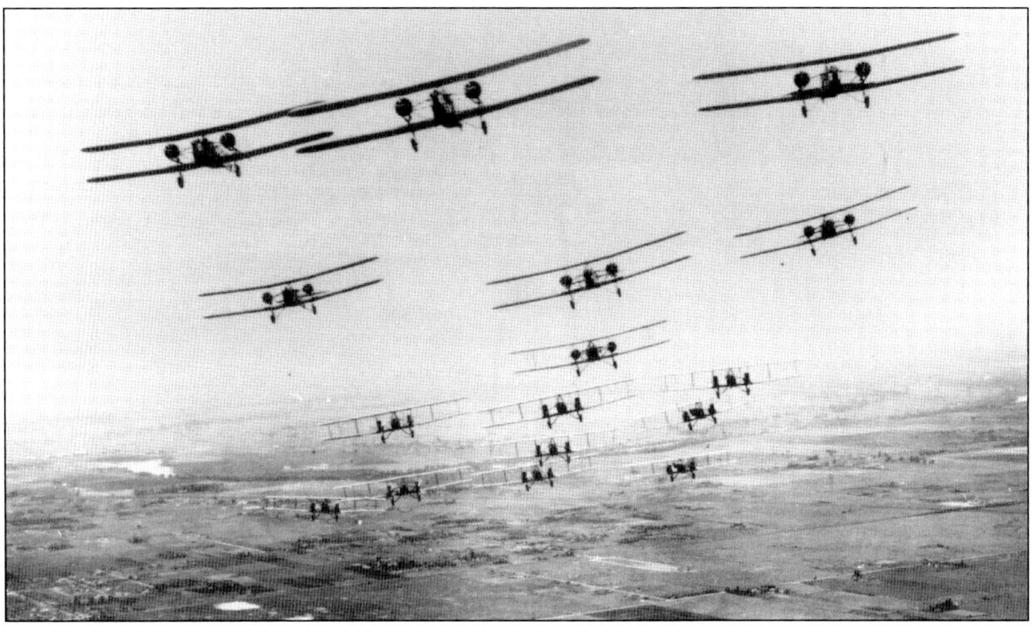

LB-7 Keystone Panthers lead Curtiss B-2 Condors during the US Army Air Corps aerial maneuvers hosted by Mather Field in 1930. The 16 aircraft fly in unison, with the wings of two lead planes nearly touching. Brig. Gen. William E. Gillmore commanded the exercises, and for the first time in military history, directed aviators via radio communication, although written orders for flights were also carried in the event of problems with wireless transmission. (CSH.)

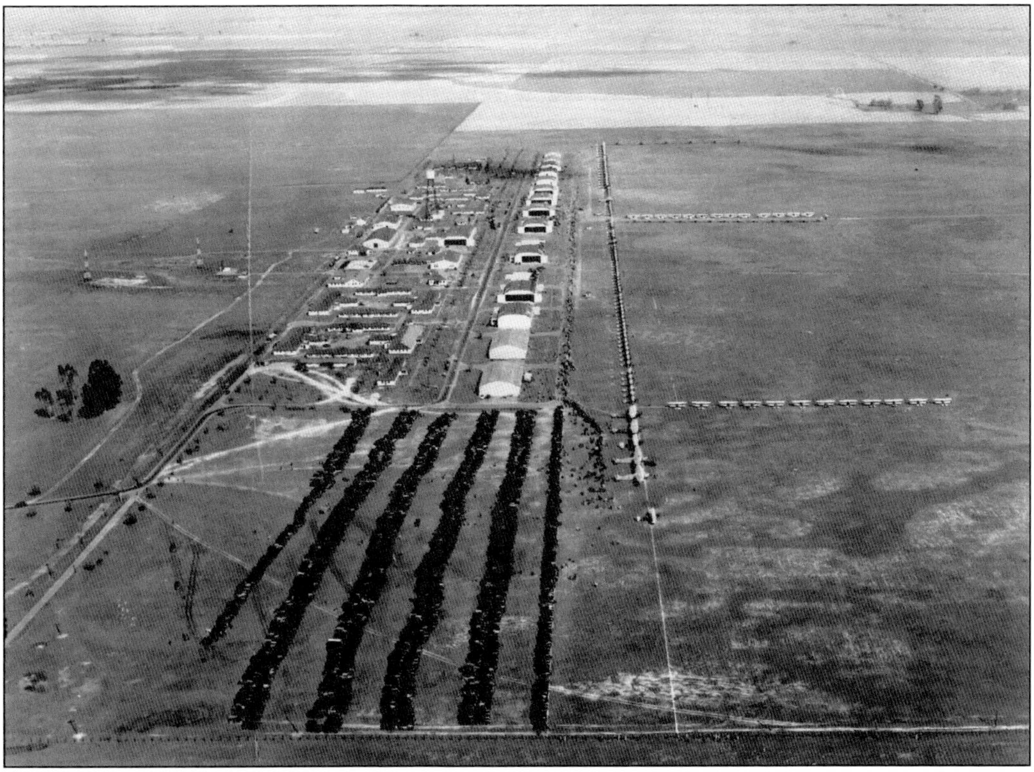

American airpower was on full display as Mather Field sponsored an open house on April 3, 1930. Over one-third of the nation's aircraft, pilots, and personnel drawn from every major airbase in the country attended. Six thick rows of automobiles parallel the line of hangars, while scores of attack, pursuit, and heavy transport planes form a perfect row along the flight line, with two rows of bombers perpendicular. (CSH.)

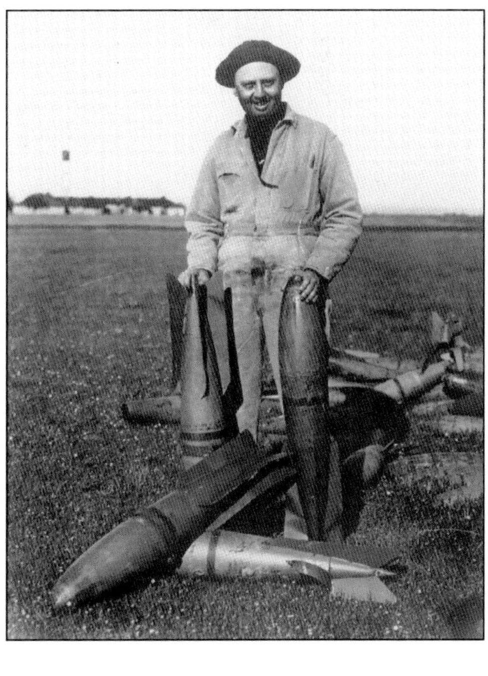

An ordnance worker manages a grin as he poses with a pair of mid-sized bombs at Mather Field during the aerial maneuvers and games held during April 1930. In 1931, a displacing gear was developed to avoid accidents common when a bomb lodged in landing gear or struck a propeller when dropped. Dive-bombing was used successfully by the Marine Corps in 1927 at a height of 300 feet, and Mather's bombing range received sporadic but heavy use over the next decade. Part of Mather Field had come from the Natomas Company, eager to unload land near White Rock Road that test digging had proved valueless for dredging. In 1937, Natomas released 3,200 more acres for use as a bombing range. During the maneuvers centered at Mather Field in 1935, Martin bombers dropped loads over designated areas in the Stanislaus Forest. (CSH.)

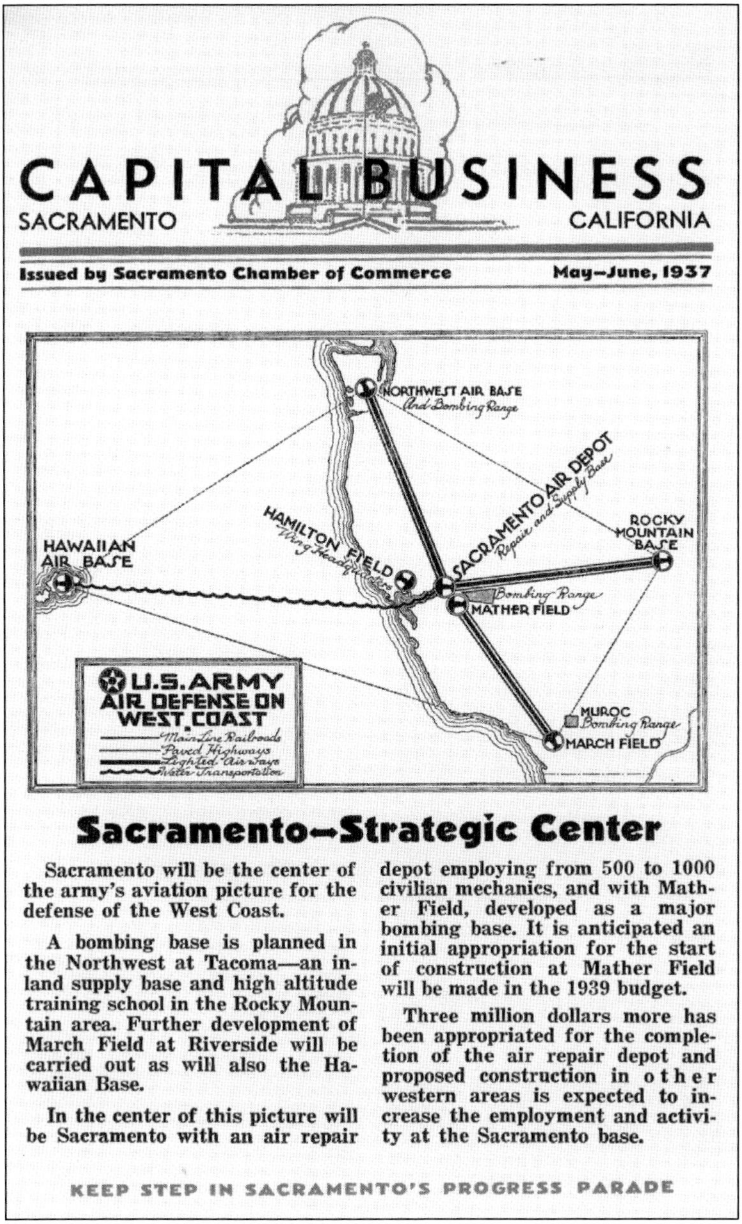

CAPITAL BUSINESS

SACRAMENTO CALIFORNIA

Issued by Sacramento Chamber of Commerce May—June, 1937

Sacramento—Strategic Center

Sacramento will be the center of the army's aviation picture for the defense of the West Coast.

A bombing base is planned in the Northwest at Tacoma—an inland supply base and high altitude training school in the Rocky Mountain area. Further development of March Field at Riverside will be carried out as will also the Hawaiian Base.

In the center of this picture will be Sacramento with an air repair depot employing from 500 to 1000 civilian mechanics, and with Mather Field, developed as a major bombing base. It is anticipated an initial appropriation for the start of construction at Mather Field will be made in the 1939 budget.

Three million dollars more has been appropriated for the completion of the air repair depot and proposed construction in other western areas is expected to increase the employment and activity at the Sacramento base.

KEEP STEP IN SACRAMENTO'S PROGRESS PARADE

The Sacramento Chamber of Commerce had connections to aviation trailing back to April 1909, when it was successful in enticing pilot Roy Knabenshue and his airship to hover above the city during the Sacramento Day celebration. When the lighter-than-air machine failed to remain aloft, the chamber had to pay damages to a farmer whose field was trampled and rutted by pedestrians and vehicles, but the public appetite for everything aerial encouraged the local business community to continue to provide more aviation events. The 1914 California State Fair featured a race between the "wizard of the air" Lincoln Beachey and the fastest man on four wheels, Barney Oldfield. The efforts of the chamber to promote aviation took root when the world went to war and planes were seen as a means of coastal defense. Mills Field, later known as Mather Field, came into being as a result of chamber actions, and the group's continued involvement brought the base back from neglect several times during the two decades between wars. (SPL.)

A routine flight above Sequoia National Park turned tragic on May 25, 1935, when a Martin B-10/B-12 bomber similar to the model shown below, one of the 14 planes cruising in tight formation, spun out of control before plummeting headlong to the ground and bursting into flames. Killed instantly were pilot 2nd Lt. Edgar W. Root, radio operator Pvt. Guy C. Porter, and two photographers from *Fox Movietone News*. The crash was caused by human error, with one of the Fox cameramen blacking out at the high altitude or accidentally jamming the controls with his equipment as he jockeyed for a shot. Red tape saved the lives of two *Sacramento Bee* employees and one of Sacramento's best-known commercial photographers when they were denied admission to the flight. The *Bee* reporter and photographer did not receive permission in time, and Harley W. Frederick Jr. (right) was practically aboard when a discrepancy in his flight permit forced him back on the runway. (Both, SPL.)

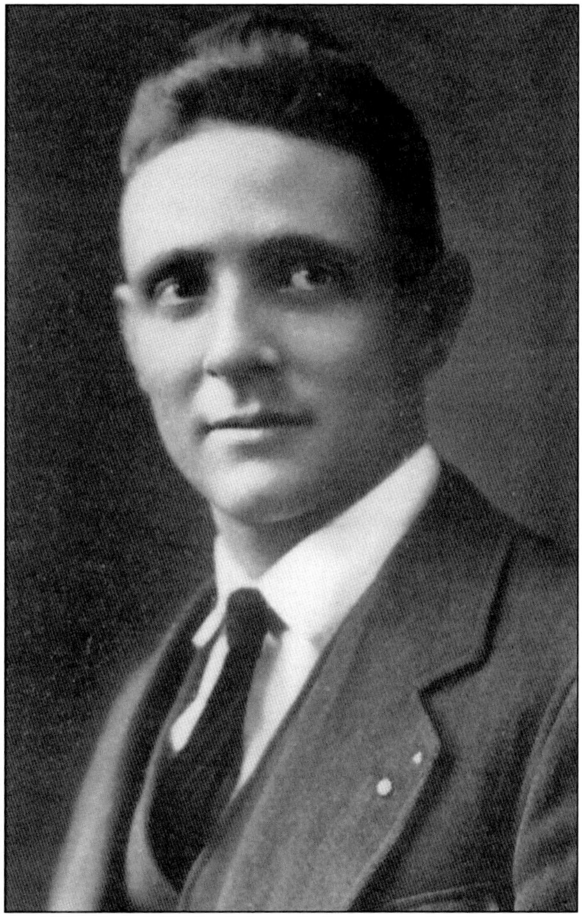

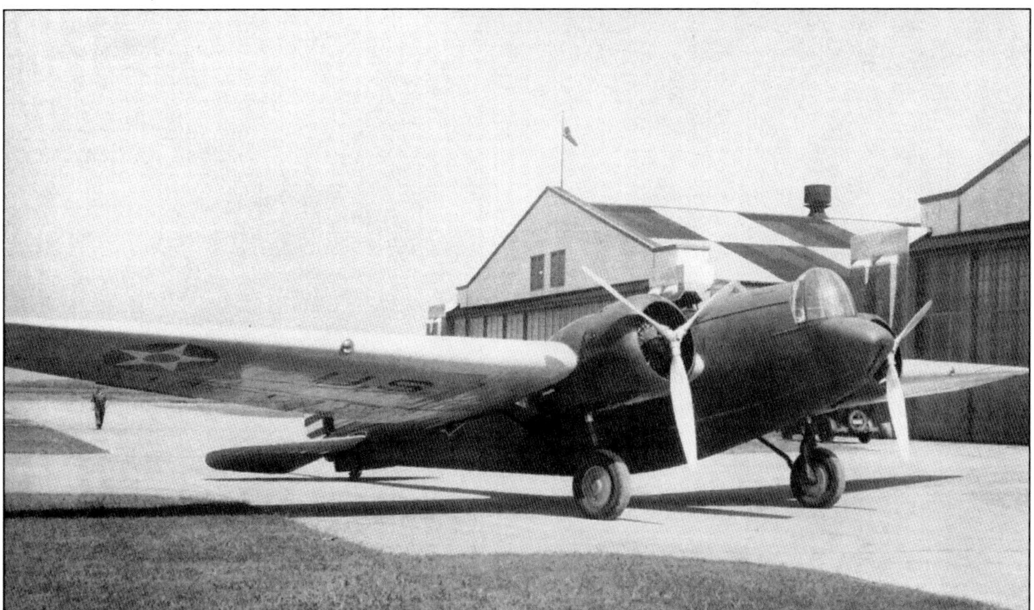

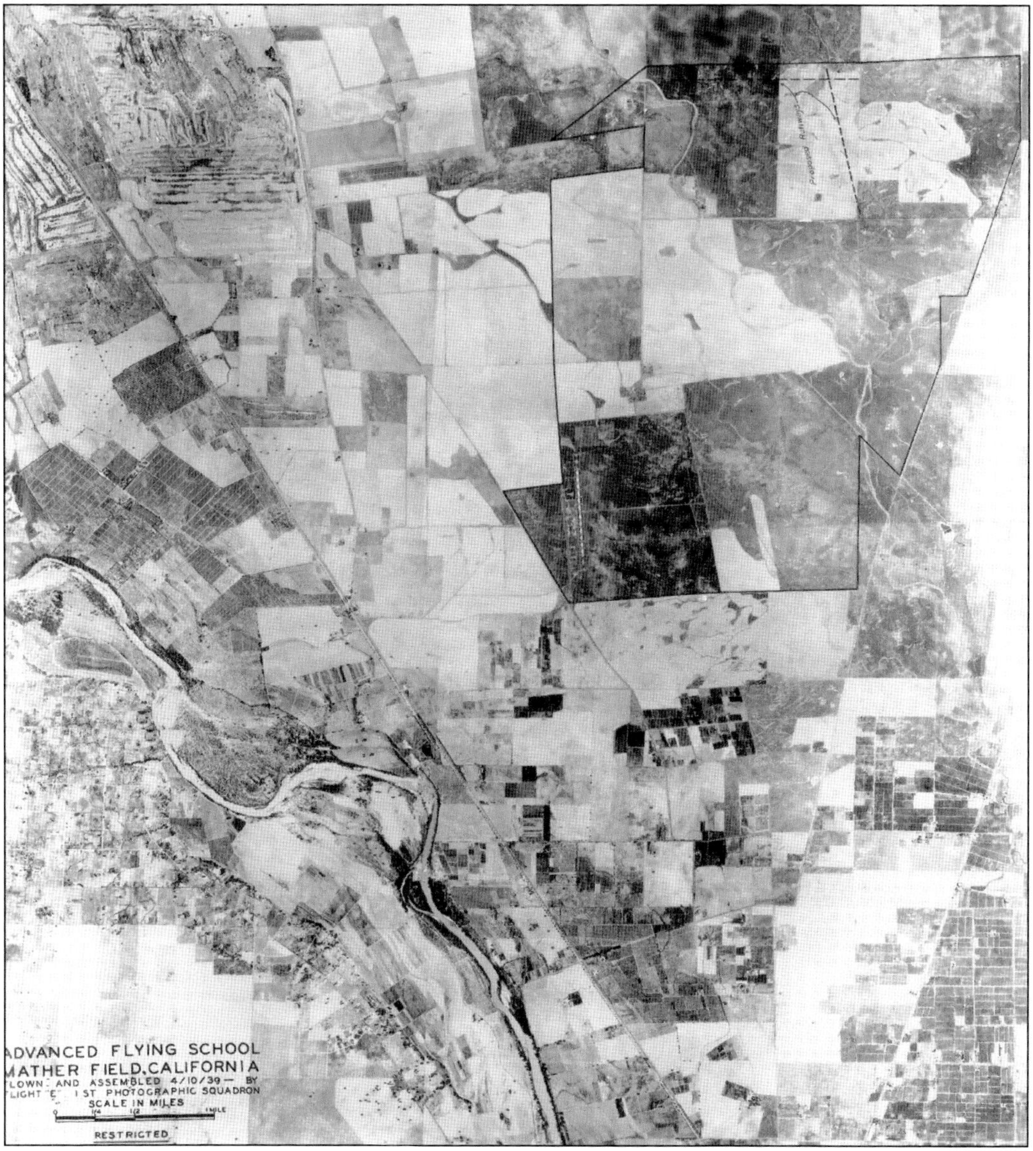

The aerial maneuvers generated from Mather Field in May 1935 were closely watched by a government eager to establish new lines of defense involving airpower despite the nation's policy of involvement at home rather than abroad. Pres. Franklin D. Roosevelt advocated the establishment of air bases near critical facilities on the West Coast, and early in June 1935, the National Air Frontier Defense Bill quickly moved through the House of Representatives. Powerful US senator Hiram Johnson of California shepherded the bill through the final phases of approval. The measure provided funding for seven army air bases on what was considered America's borders, as well as authorization for the development of supplemental support bases as needed. Mather Field was already considered an ideal location and fell midway between Canada and Mexico in flight hours. In 1939, America was just beyond the war engulfing much of the world, but after the construction of the McClellan Air Depot, Mather's reactivation was just a matter of time. (SPL.)

Four

A Reprise of War
by James Scott

Mather's World War II experience was one of stark contrasts. Just on the eve of Pearl Harbor, the base was revving itself toward war readiness with a functional collection of AT-6 Texan trainers, but it was far from fit to make war on a global scale. By conflict's end in June 1945, it was Mather that would be amassing an aerial armada of 234 B-29 Superfortress bombers, all bound for Japan.

Between December 7 and Christmas Day 1941, Sacramento, like most of the nation, was flittering about, trying to make sense of horrific dispatches from Hawaii: the Tower Bridge was under armed guard, as was the Pacific Gas and Electric steam-power station, and the fire department was distributing sand to city homes in the event of an incendiary bomb attack. At Mather, leave was cancelled, guard duty around the base's perimeter was doubled, and the grounds at both Mather and McClellan were illuminated for fear of sabotage.

As early as May 1941, Mather had been slowly resurrecting itself out of interwar mothballs and into the West Coast's first-ever navigation school, the 333rd School Squadron. In the coming months and years, the base would take on the title of the 3031st Army Air Force Base Unit, responsible as both a transitional trainer for crews of B-25 Mitchell medium bombers and as an advanced twin-engine school. The 3031st was discontinued in September 1944, only to be replaced by the 1505th and 1564th AAF Base Units, both with the primary task of serving as a point of embarkation for crews and craft heading to the Pacific theater of operations (PTO).

Conversely, Mather also acted ably as a terminus for servicemen and aircraft transitioning out of the PTO. The so-called Sunset Project was responsible for accepting 1,266 planes and 17,534 crew members stateside. Even the hero of April 1942's raid on Tokyo, Lt. Gen. Jimmy Doolittle, transited Mather in September 1945.

Also in the Pacific war's twilight, Mather experienced a potentially disastrous brush with the Manhattan Project, an appropriate happenstance for a facility on the verge of Cold War anxieties.

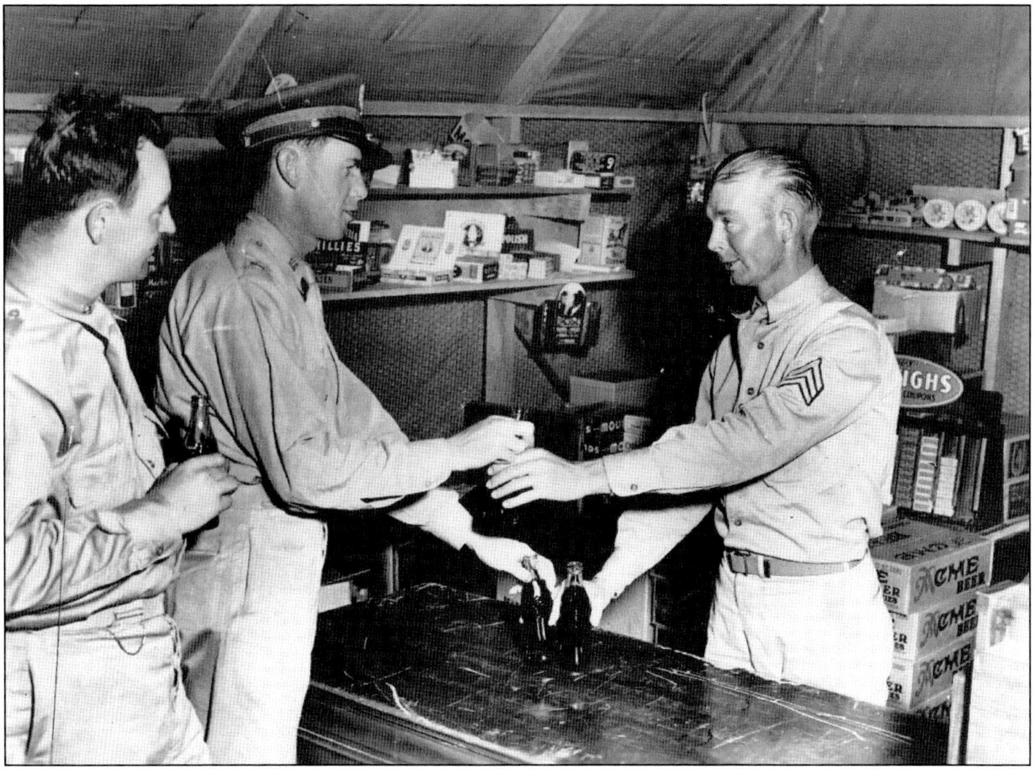

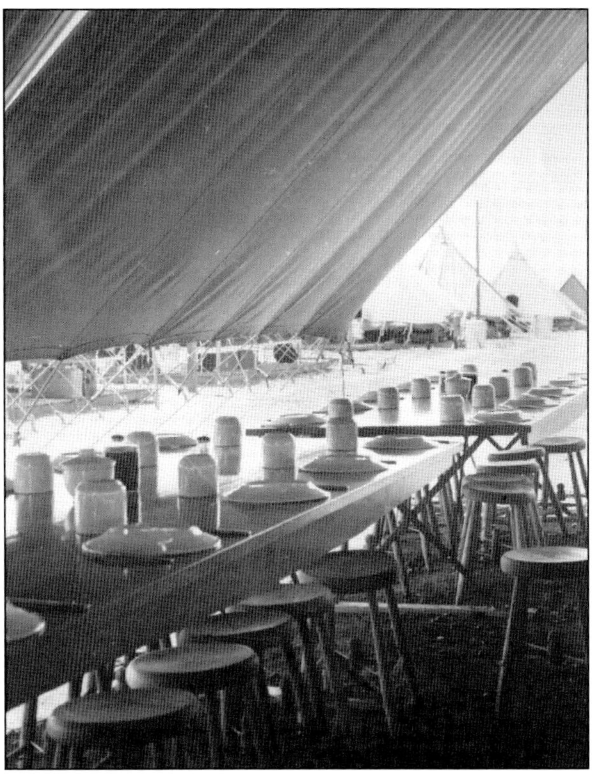

When Mather accepted its first class of World War II–era cadets in June 1941, facilities were rustic, at best. Nearly all support points were housed in tents, including, albeit rife with refreshment (fermented and nonfermented), the base's Post Exchange (PX), seen above. Within months, the formal PX would offer a barbershop with 12 chairs, as well as a café, cobbler, jewelry repair shop, and tailor. Insofar as housing, men were billeted, four apiece, in tents located on the east end of the field. Initial mess facilities, left, were spartan yet egalitarian, as all personnel dined together, regardless of rank, until separate mess halls were built. Before formal kitchens were constructed, Mather denizens were comforted with baked goods from Sacramento housewives that were accepted in the lobby of KFBK radio. By October, Mather's mess facilities were robust enough to produce nearly 10,000 meals a day. (Both, CSH.)

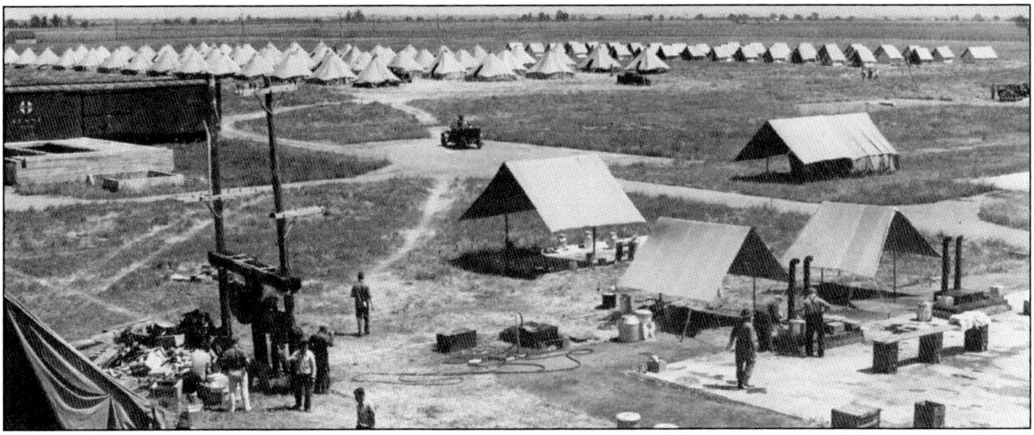

A temporary military tent village sits to Mather's east in 1941. By October, three formal mess halls had been built, feeding some 3,000 personnel. Meals consisted of meat or fish, potatoes, gravy, two vegetables, and a fruit desert. Meats included steak, meatloaf, ham, lamb, and chicken, with hot dogs being Mather's most popular food. Several civilian workers mill about the foreground with mess facilities sitting to the right. (SPL.)

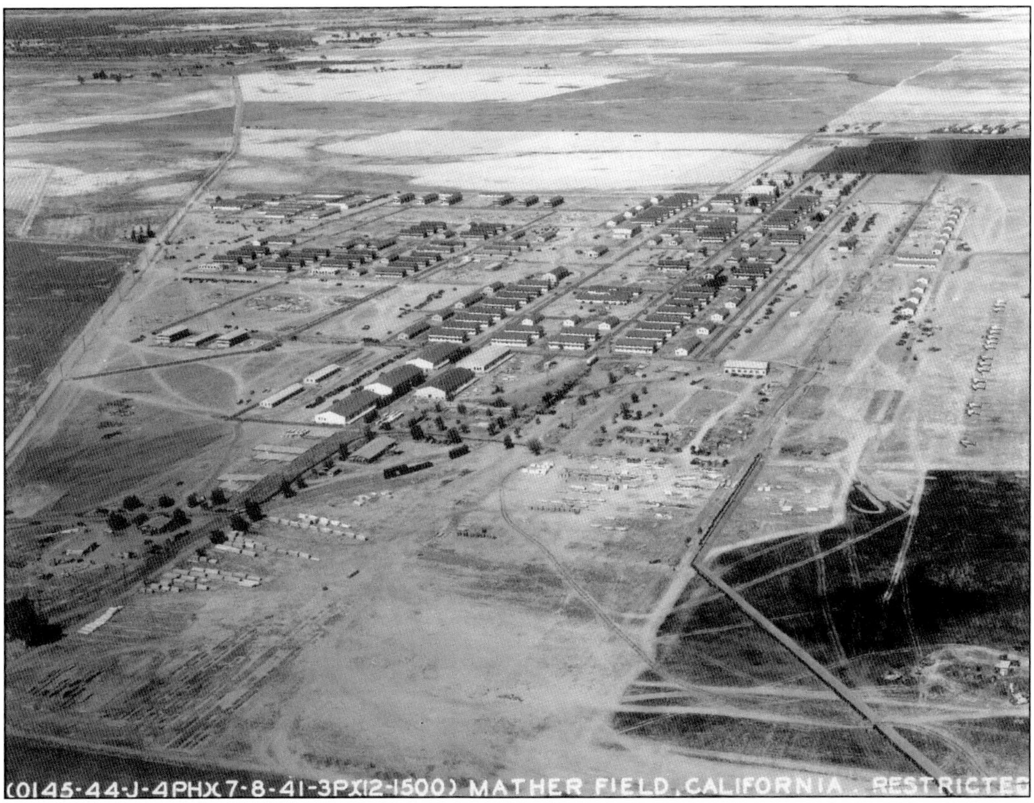

In a view from the west, this July 1941 photograph reveals a nearly reconstituted Mather. Its $4-million rehabilitation began on May 1, when 1,700 workers, representing 13 Sacramento contractors, took to the sleepy station. In three months' time, 40 buildings, comprised of 8.43 million board feet of lumber, and base roads with enough concrete to construct a 32-mile-long highway were completed. The new Mather was formally inaugurated in October 1941. (CSH.)

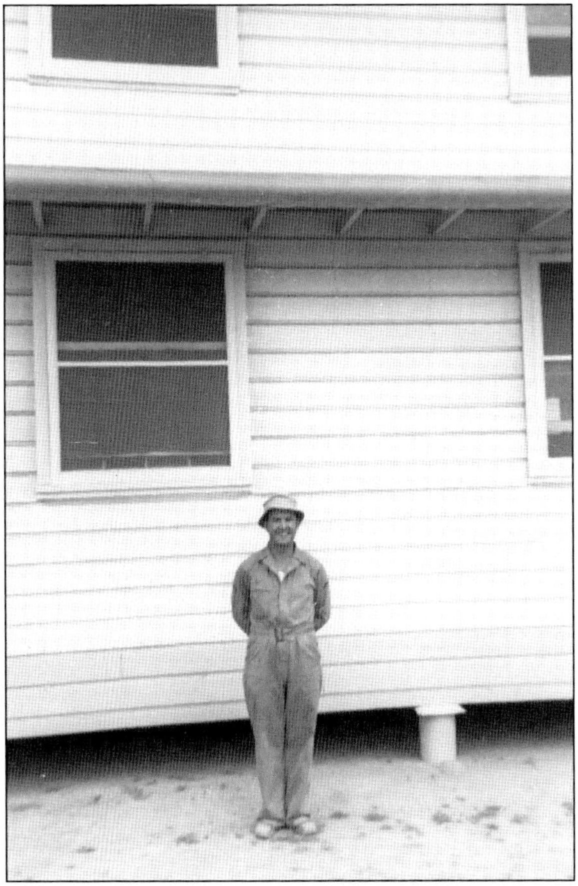

Smiling widely on December 7, 1941 (and blithely unaware of events in Hawaii) is Pvt. Bob Andrews. Most personnel spent Sundays off base, but out of money, Andrews sat relegated to Mather's Jefferson Barracks. It was while listening to the New York Symphony that he learned of the Pearl Harbor attack. Amidst the following chaos, personnel were issued World War I–era Lee-Enfield rifles, five ammunition clips, and a bayonet. (CSH.)

This Sunday, December 7, 1941, photograph looks southwesterly toward Mather's flight line and a grouping of North American AT-6 Texan trainers. By 3:00 p.m. of the day this photograph was taken (nearly four hours after first wave of attacks on Pearl Harbor), each trainer was armed with three .30-caliber machine guns, with one in the rear canopy and two near the propeller. (CSH.)

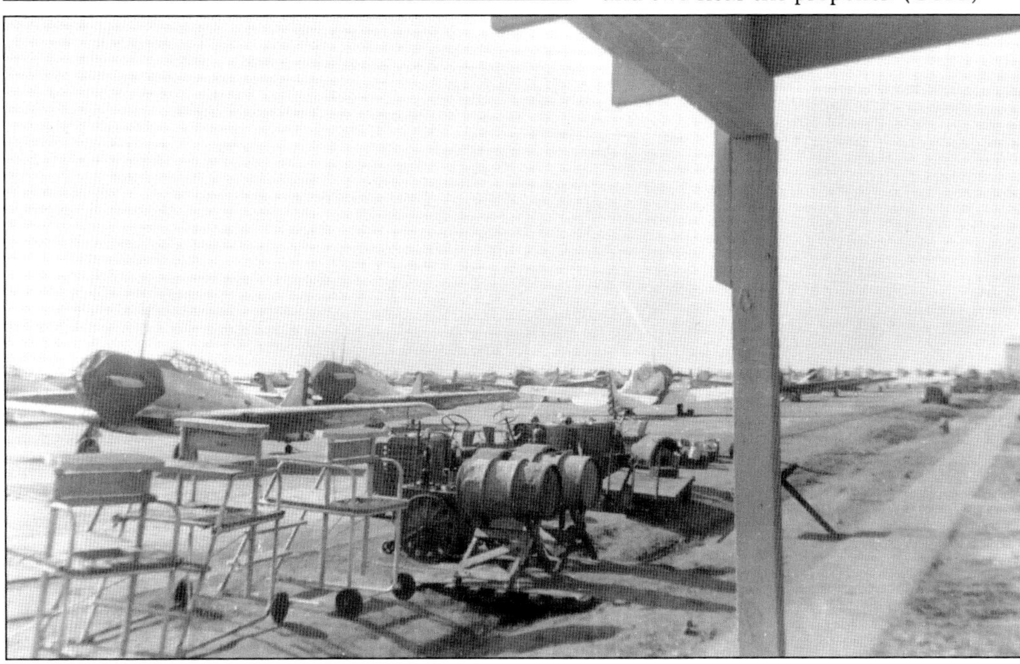

This December 1941 image shows a Bonaparte-aping Andrews, sporting his World War I–era gas mask. Throughout World War II, Mather personnel were required to wear gas masks for at least an hour a week as part of their training regimen and in the event of chemical attack. So as to maximize free time, personnel could be seen wearing masks during a game of basketball or hand of cards. (CSH.)

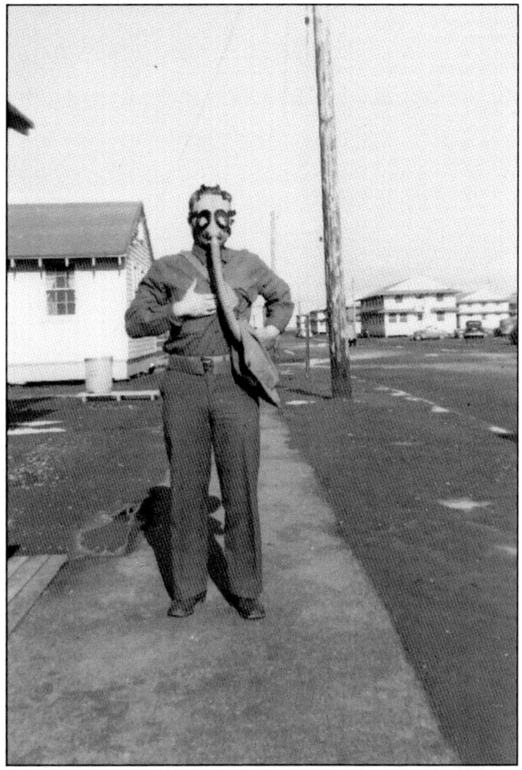

Viewed from the south in February 1942 is Mather's $835,000 runway. Built by Sacramento's Adolph Teichert and Son, it was comprised of 21,000 linear feet of concrete and included a 3,600-by-400-foot warm-up apron and a 6,500-by-400-foot ramp. The crossing strips each measured some 5,000 feet in length. To the west and south are several of Mather's signature vernal pools. (CSH.)

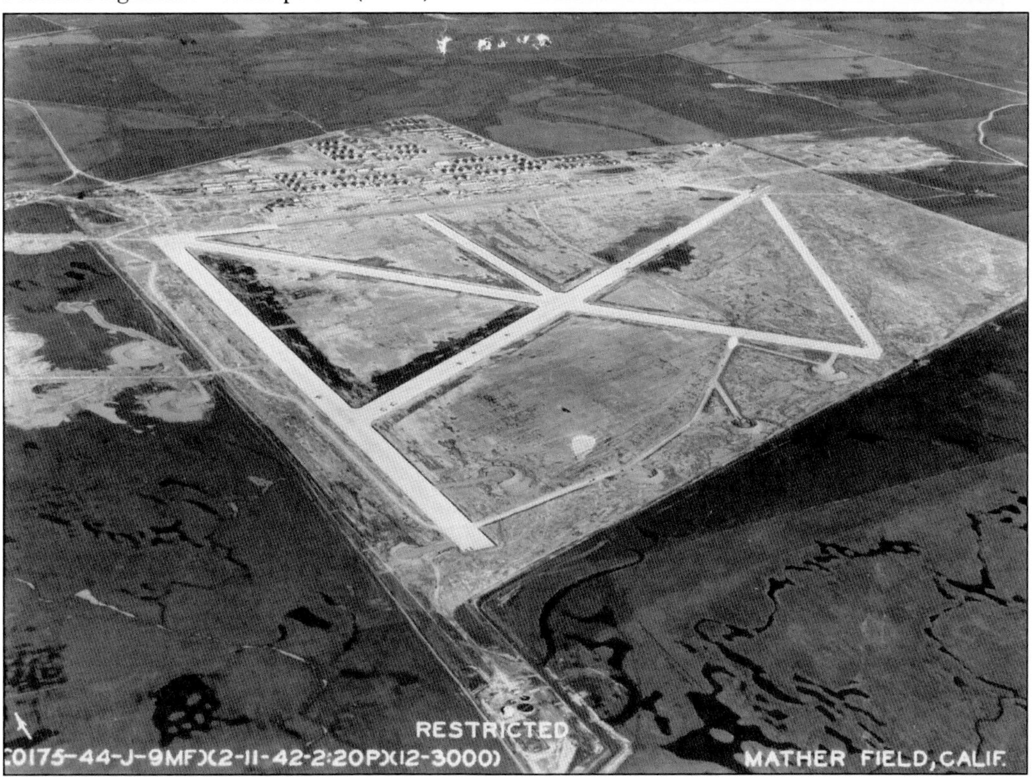

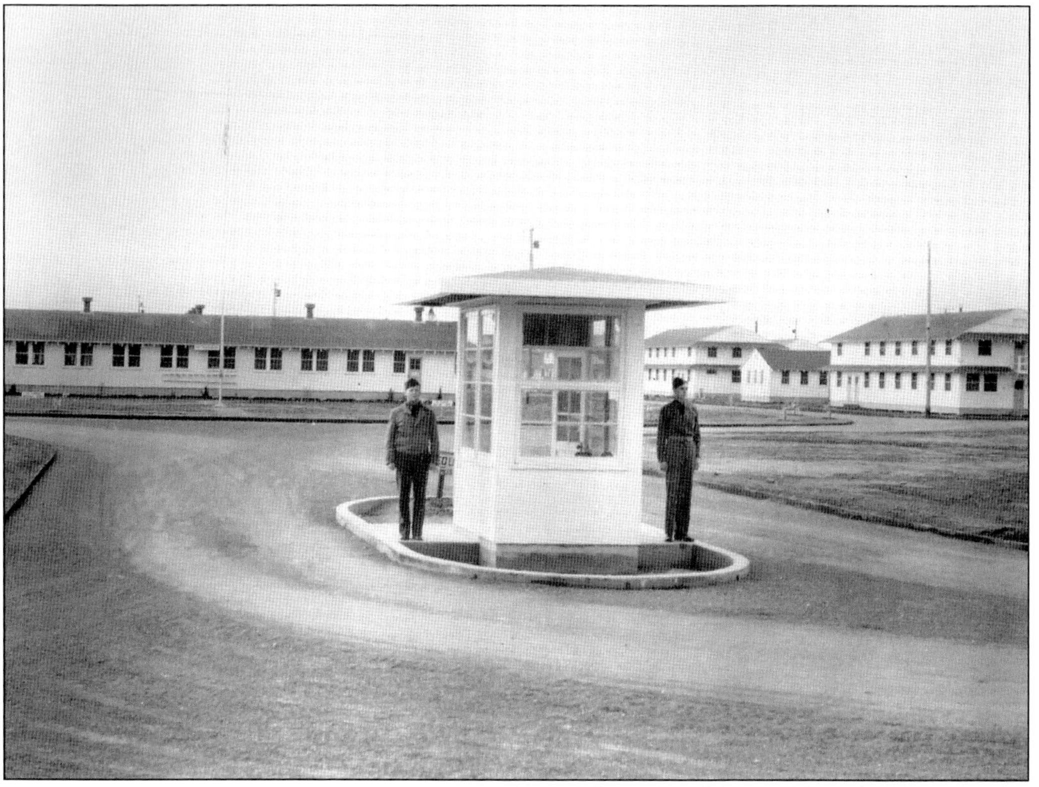

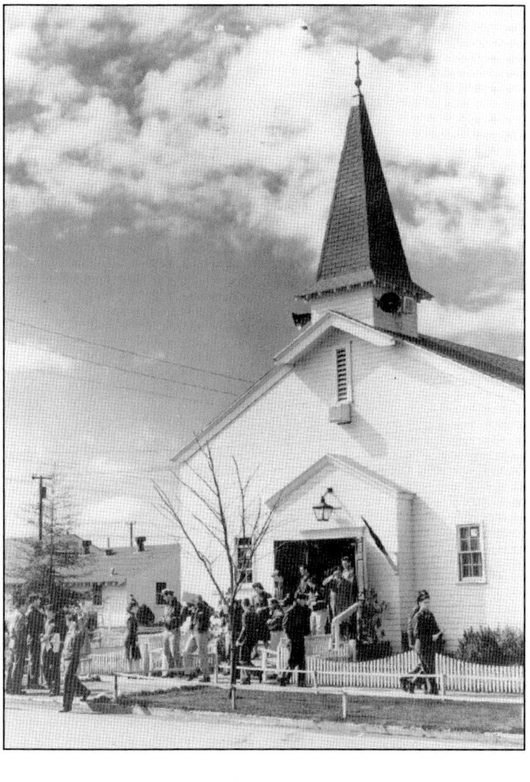

In this 1941 photograph, military policemen (MPs) of the 874th Guard Squadron occupy Mather's main gate. Trained in boxing, judo, chemical identification and decontamination, and, of course, the use of firearms (from 12-gauge shotguns to Colt .45 revolvers), Mather's war-era units proved a formidable deterrent. An MP's most typical wartime duty was perimeter defense, although special assignments, such as guarding bombsights and monitoring liberty in Sacramento, were also in play. (CSH.)

Pictured in 1944 is Mather's chapel. Servicemen exit the 400-seat structure after a devotional service for crews heading into the Pacific theater. Built in 1941, the chapel had a portable altar, pulpit, and lectern, so as to accommodate Mather's various Christian denominations. Jewish personnel were encouraged to attend the off-base Mosaic Law Synagogue or Temple B'nai Israel. During periods of special observance, Jews were granted passes for extended leave. (CSH.)

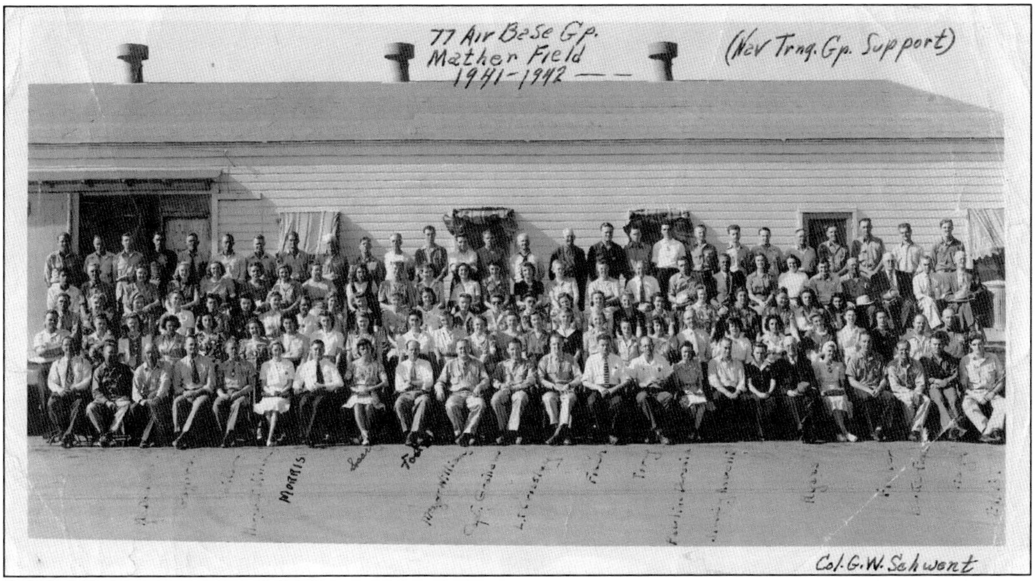

Pictured in spring 1941 are civilian support personnel for the Air Corps Advanced Flying School at Mather. At this time, the base employed upwards of 150 civilians, half of whom were women slated for clerical assignments, including stenography, typing, duplicating, and filing. In the early stages of a reconstituted Mather, support personnel worked at Sacramento's chamber of commerce, then in tents, and finally, in formal base buildings. (CSH.)

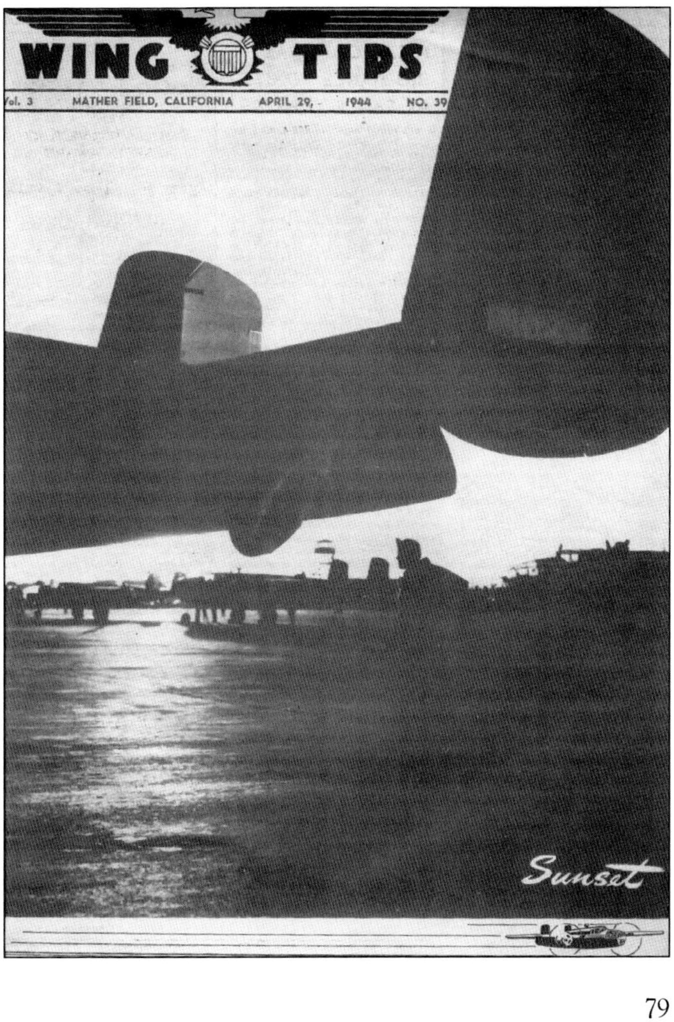

Mather's weekly newspaper, *Wing Tips*, was founded in August 1941 and ran until the base's closure in 1993. The publication's title was selected in a July 1941 contest that garnered the winner, Cpl. Seth Thornton, a prize of $10. The cover of this April 1944 issue shows the twin stabilizers of a B-25 Mitchell bomber and foretells the coming of the transitional Sunset Program, still several months away. (SPL.)

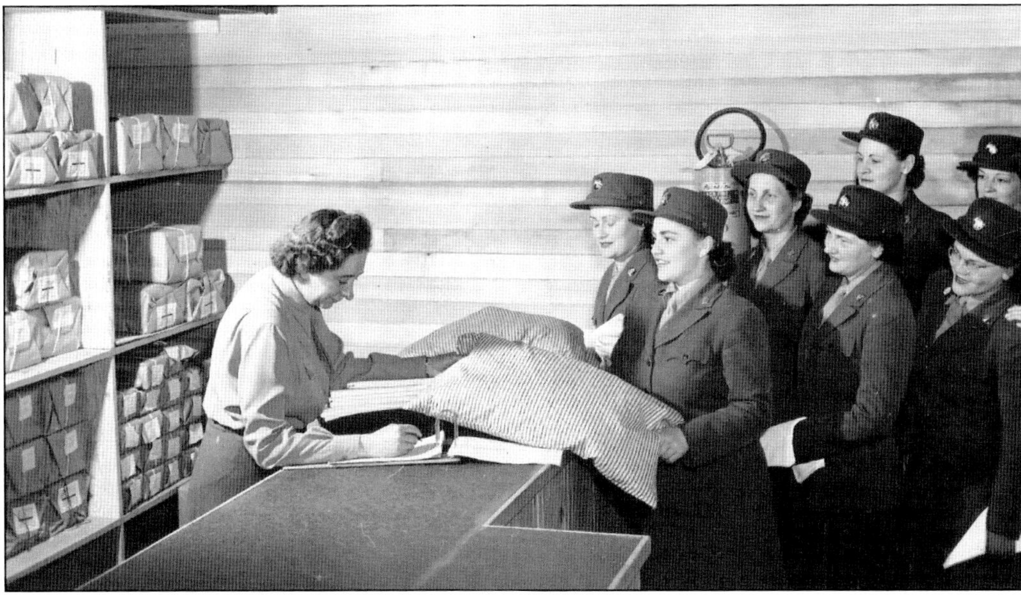

"Release a Man for Combat Duty" was the motto of the WACs, members of the Women's Army Corps, several of whom are pictured here at Mather in 1943. Mather's first WACs, a total of 165, arrived in May 1943, taking over clerical, mess, and truck-driving duties. In addition to WAC posts at Mather and McClellan Fields, Sacramento's Grant Union Junior College housed the nation's first WAC Signal Corps Training School. (CSH.)

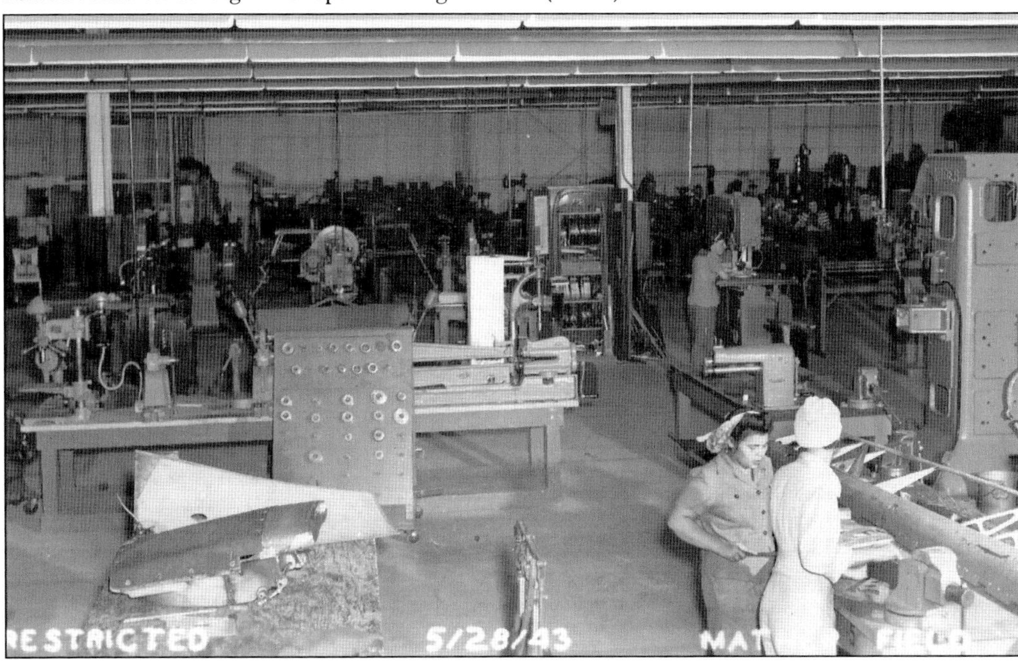

Pictured in spring 1943 is Mather's sheet-metal shop. Amongst the clutter of machines are a few female civilian workers. Between 1940 and 1950, California saw a 200-percent increase in the number of women involved in manufacturing and a 500-percent increase in female construction workers. In short order, the gender role paradigm had transformed, with America's war-making demands playing no small part in affecting as much. (CSH.)

In this 1942 photograph, a maintenance worker from Mather's 200-member 334th School Squadron works on the engine of an AT-6 Texan. In addition to general repair responsibilities, the group conducted 60-point daily inspections, 35-point preflight inspections, and inspections following every 25 and 50 hours of flight time. By 1943, the base had instituted an assembly line method of maintenance, similar to that employed by America's automobile industry. (SPL.)

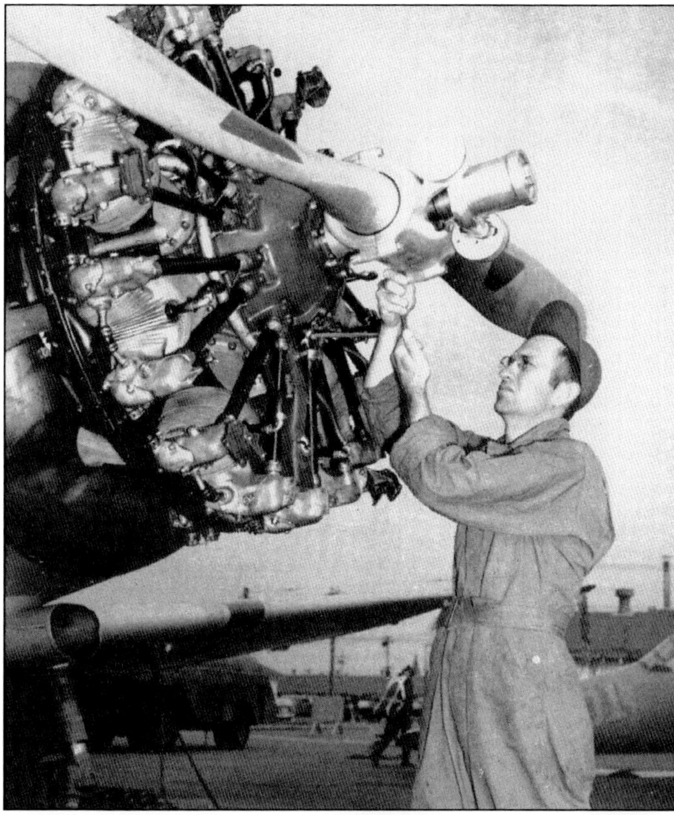

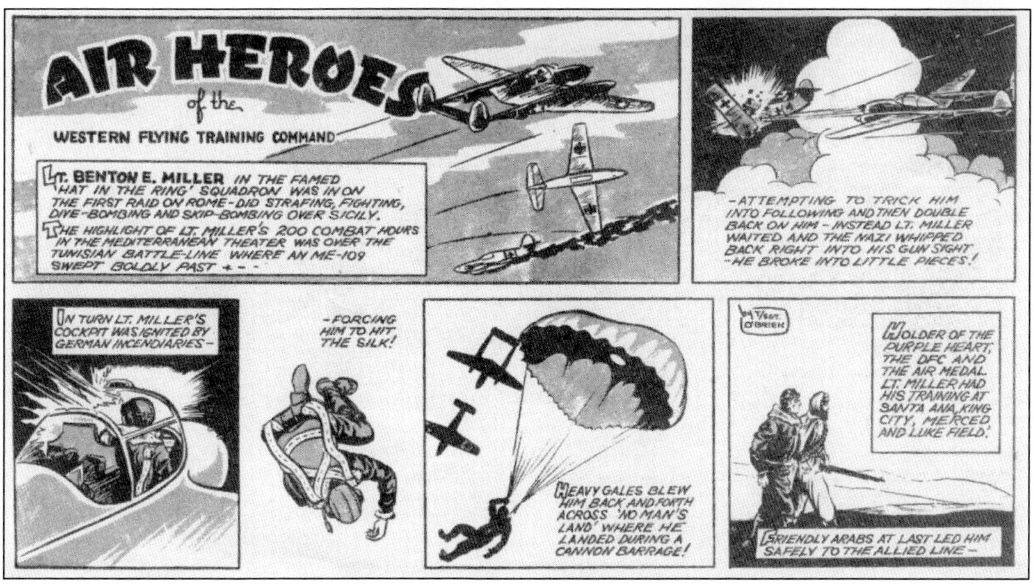

Running in the March 4, 1944, issue of Mather's *Wing Tips* was this installment of the morale-revving cartoon serial *Air Heroes of the Western Flying Training Command.* It features the North African adventure of P-38 Lightning pilot Benton Miller. The Western Flying Training Command oversaw dozens of bases, including Mather, in 11 western states, and was charged with producing one-third of the nation's aviation officers. (SPL.)

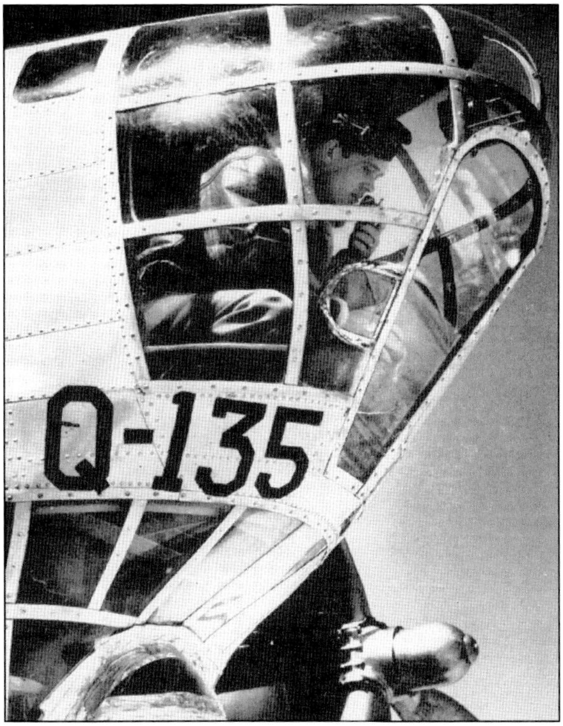

This 1942 photograph shows a Mather bombardier cadet practicing in the "greenhouse" of a Douglas B-18 Bolo bomber. The 12-week training regimen required mastery of the ultra-secretive Norden and Sperry bombsights and the many facets of bombing theory, including plane speed, height, air temperature, ordnance weight, winds, and cross drift. Practice runs were conducted day and night and involved dropping black powder–filled 100-pound bombs. (SPL.)

Mather's photography unit poses with "Nellie" in this 1942 image. Art savant Wayne Thiebaud was responsible for painting the colorful jalopy, which had been driven cross-country several times by its owner, Pvt. Sam Peruch, a resident of Connecticut and member of the photography unit from 1941 to 1945. He is positioned at the driver's seat, wearing a garrison cap. (CSH.)

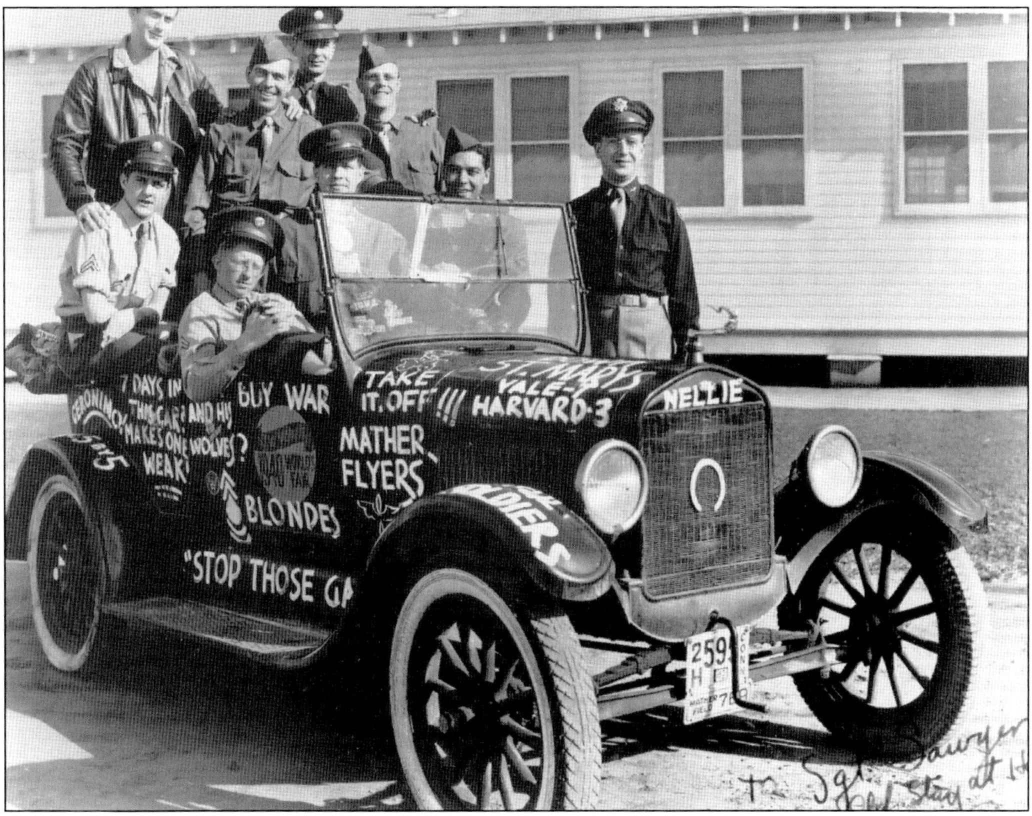

The smart scene at right was captured amidst the giddiness and glitz of the Mather Field Non-Commissioned Officers' Club's grand opening on New Year's Eve 1942. The headliner that night was the Dan Parenti Orchestra. Designed as a meeting spot for servicemen and their families, the three-story club included a dance floor, bar, and ladies' lounge, plus reading, writing, and game rooms. While accommodating all NCOs (corporals and sergeants), the club underwent a $5,000 renovation accomplished through a loan provided by Mather Field's officer corps. Below, flanked by hi-fi record player and club comforts, artwork adorns establishment walls. Closing in the late 1940s, the club occupied the Native Sons of the Golden West building at 1029 J Street. (Both, CSH.)

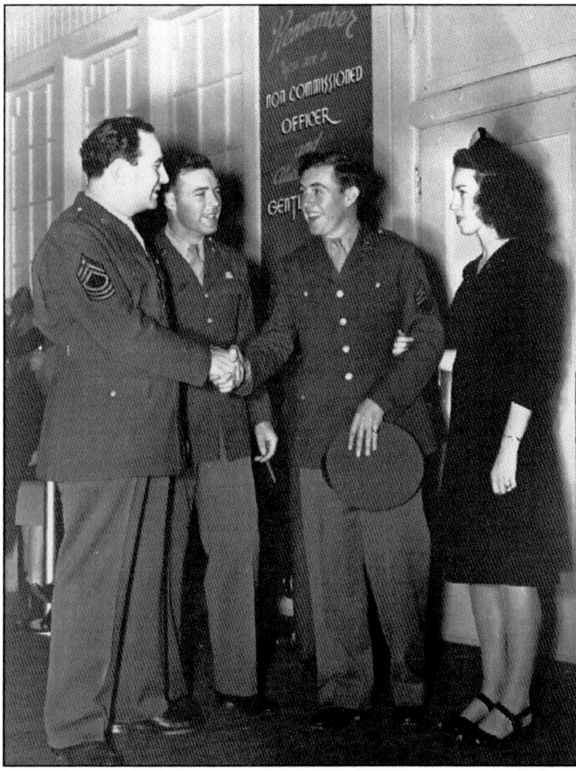

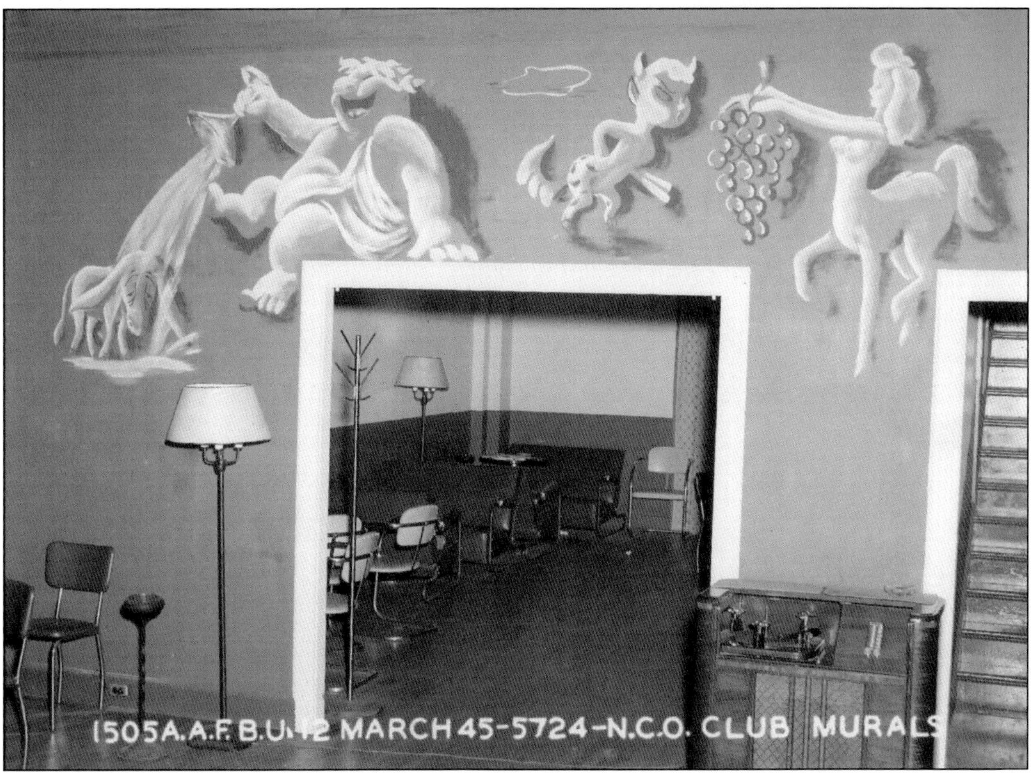

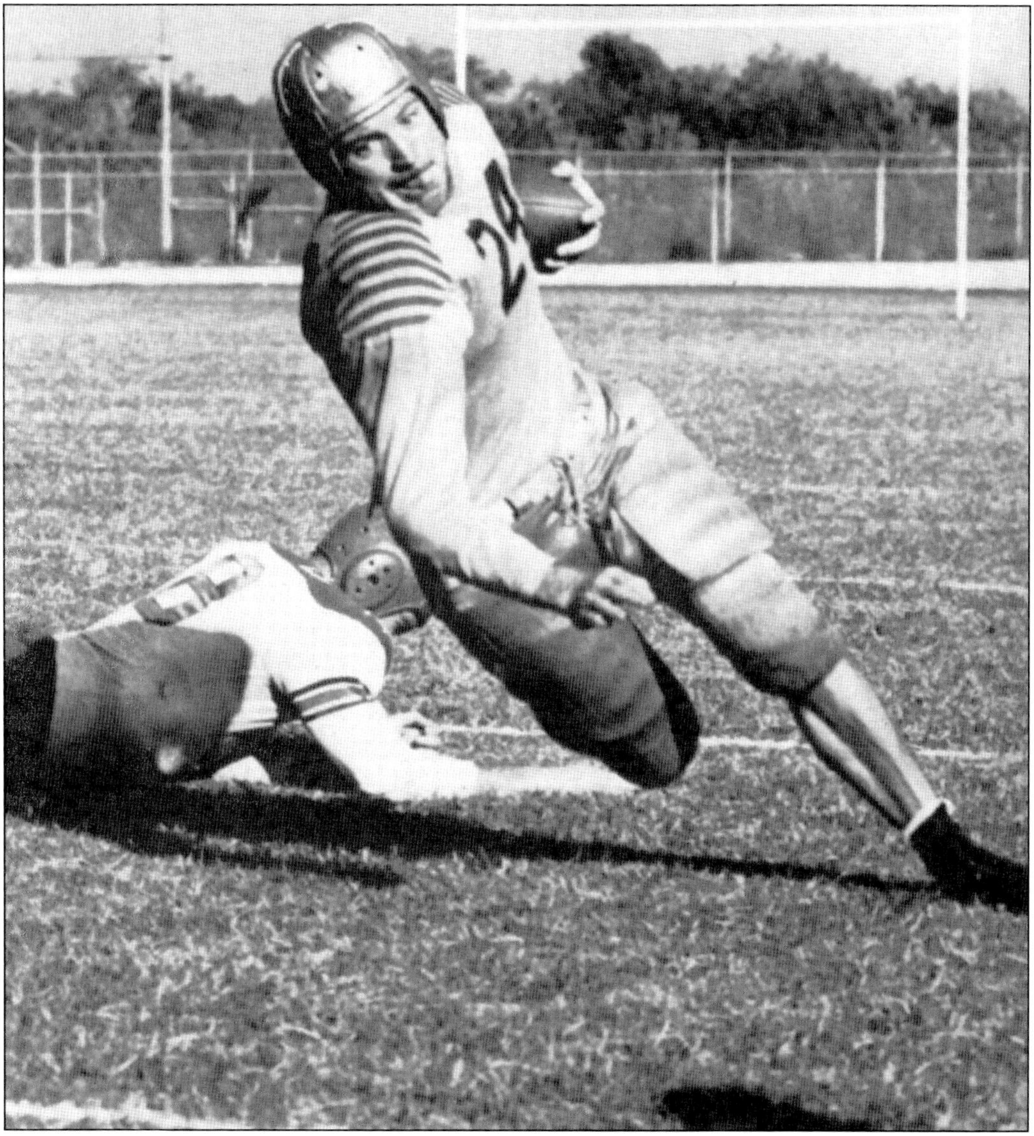

Charging around left end in 1942 is Oregon State College All-American and Mather aviator Alexander "Jim" Kisselburgh. One of Mather's finest athletic hours came on Armistice Day in 1942 when the "Matherite" footballers defeated crosstown rival McClellan Field 19-14 in front of 10,000 spectators at Sacramento Stadium. In that game, Kisselburgh took a punt back 55 yards for a touchdown. Although he was a sixth-round pick of the Cleveland Rams, duty beckoned. Kisselburgh, now a captain, went on to pilot a B-17 bomber. En route to a raid on Regensburg, Germany, in February 1944, Kisselburgh's plane was shot down and his crew captured, spending the remainder of the war at Stalag Luft 1. Kisselburgh's postwar future included a coaching stint at Oregon State, test-piloting B-36 Peacemaker bombers, flying unmarked planes over North Vietnam to drop propaganda leaflets, and commanding Ellsworth Air Force Base in South Dakota. He retired in 1974, spending much of the rest of his life in El Paso, Texas, and summering at Wallowa Lake, Oregon. He passed away in 1996 and is buried at the Fort Bliss National Cemetery. (SPL.)

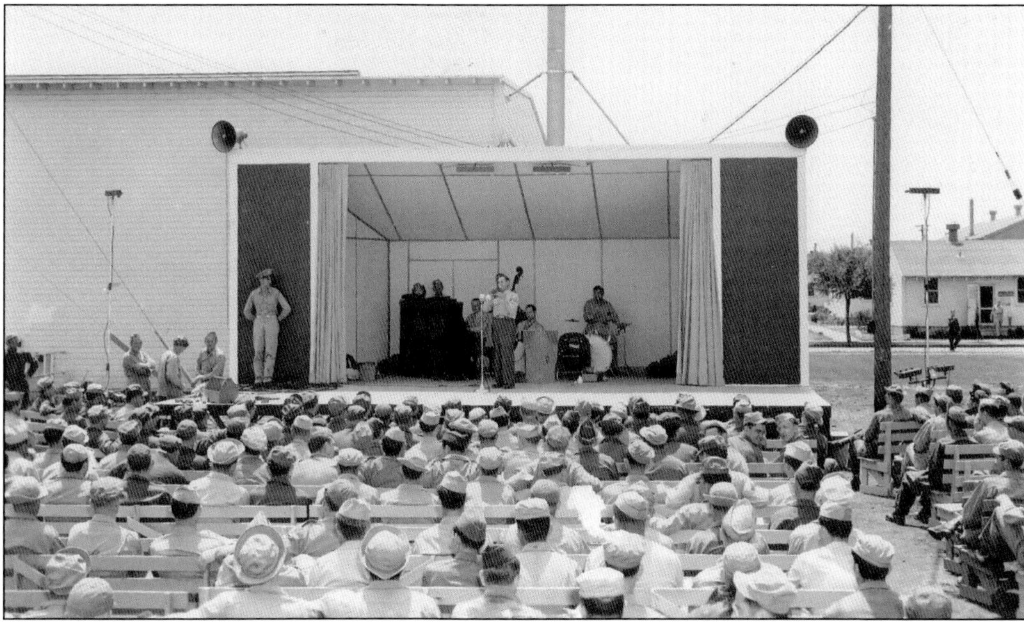

Mather's open-air theater, known also as the Mather Bowl, is pictured in 1944. While a stop on the United Service Organizations (USO) entertainment circuit with visitors like Bob Hope, Lena Horne, and Jack Benny, Mather possessed its own pool of talented live artists, including a base dance orchestra that performs here. With the removal of chairs, the venue could be converted to a dance floor, accommodating weekly dances for enlisted men. (CSH.)

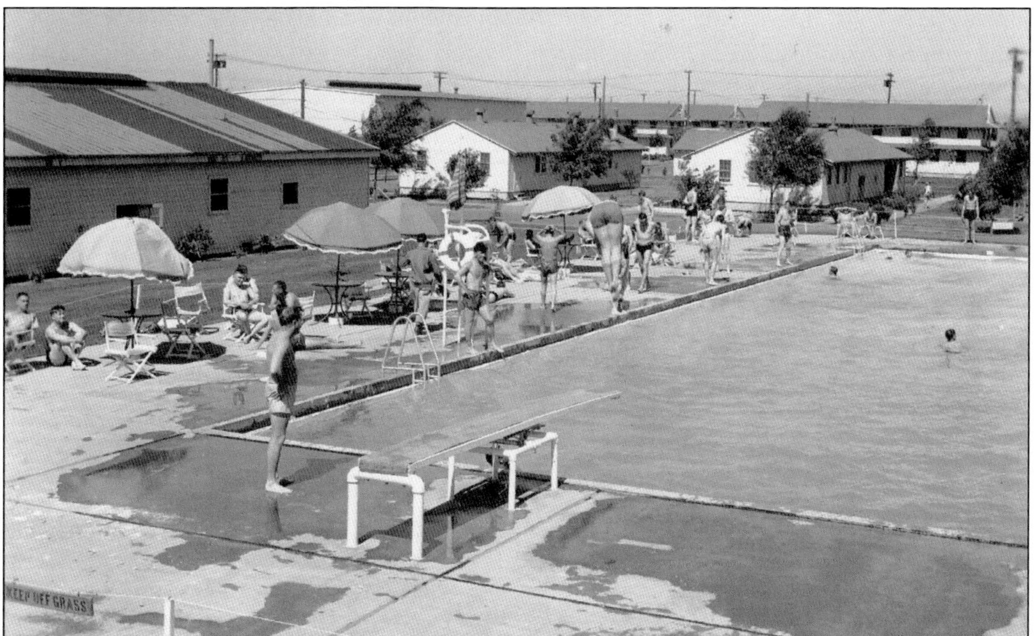

The enlisted men's and WAC pool is shown here in May 1944. Operating seven days a week, from 10:00 a.m. to 6:00 p.m., and later when the weather was warmer, the pool was a popular spot for recreation. However, for at least one hour a week, physical training was required in the pool. A separate officer's pool opened in summer 1944. (CSH.)

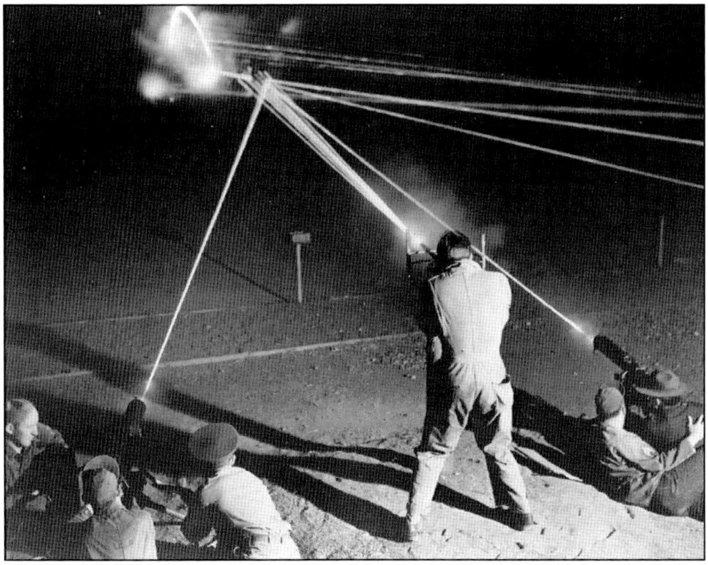

Tracers light up the night at Mather's firing range in this June 1942 photograph. To the sides, crews fire Browning water-cooled .30-caliber machine guns. With ammunition box protruding, the middle figure is firing an air-cooled Browning .50-caliber machine gun, as a waist-gunner would have done in a Mather-based B-25 and other bombers of the day. In order to avoid melting the barrel, gunners fired in 8-to-10-round bursts. (CSH.)

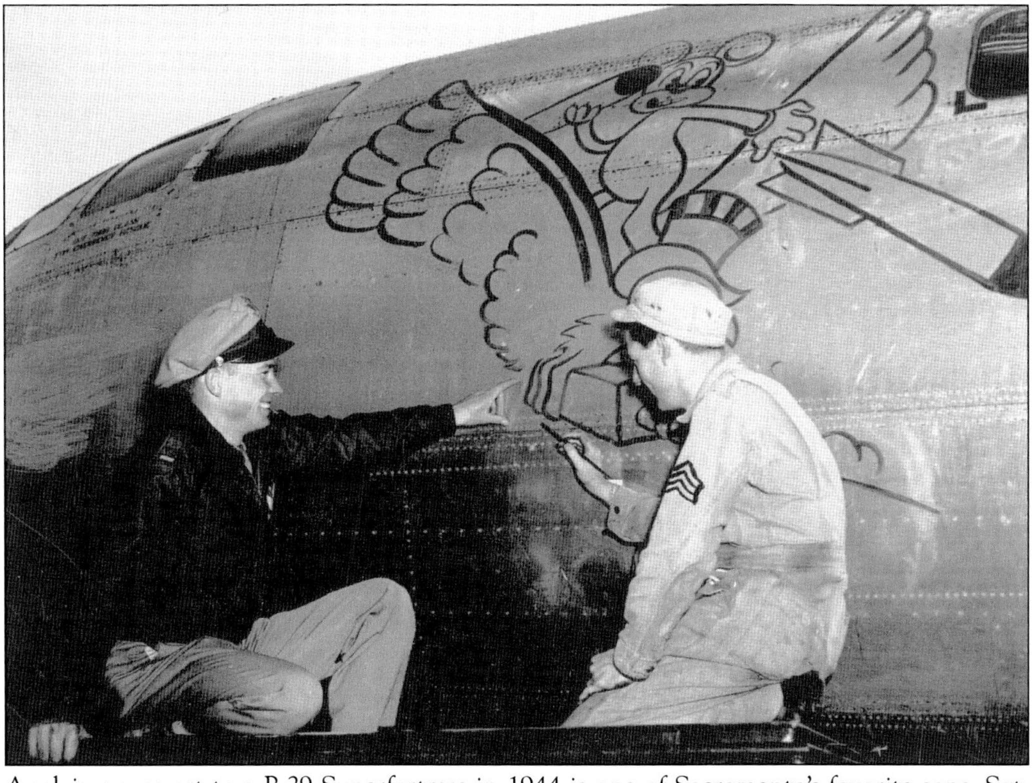

Applying nose art to a B-29 Superfortress in 1944 is one of Sacramento's favorite sons, Sgt. Wayne Thiebaud (right). From 1942 to 1945, he served at Mather as an artist. After obtaining advanced degrees in art at Sacramento State College and earning faculty status at the University of California, Davis, Thiebaud gained considerable fame through a series of iconic still lifes depicting mainstream American foods. The man on the left is unidentified. (Archives of American Art, Smithsonian Institution.)

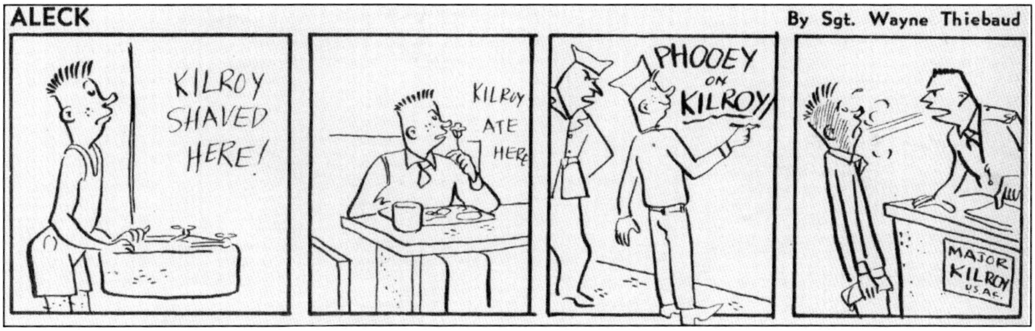

Among Thiebaud's base assignments was *Aleck*, a popular cartoon published in Mather's newsletter, *Wing Tips*. The above installment was released on July 28, 1945. Below and also drawn by Thiebaud is a humorous look at the base's Post Exchange. Released on April 22, 1944, the sketch's central feature is Mather's 50-seat Post Exchange Café. Staffed by 15 waitresses and open from 7:00 a.m. to 10:00 p.m., seven days a week, it was there that enlisted men could find much, from soft drinks to T-bone steaks. Known for its modest prices, the PX also provided a spot for purchasing toiletries, candy, souvenirs, tobacco, magazines, and newspapers. Much of the PX's profits went to funding the base's sports programs and library. (Both, SPL.)

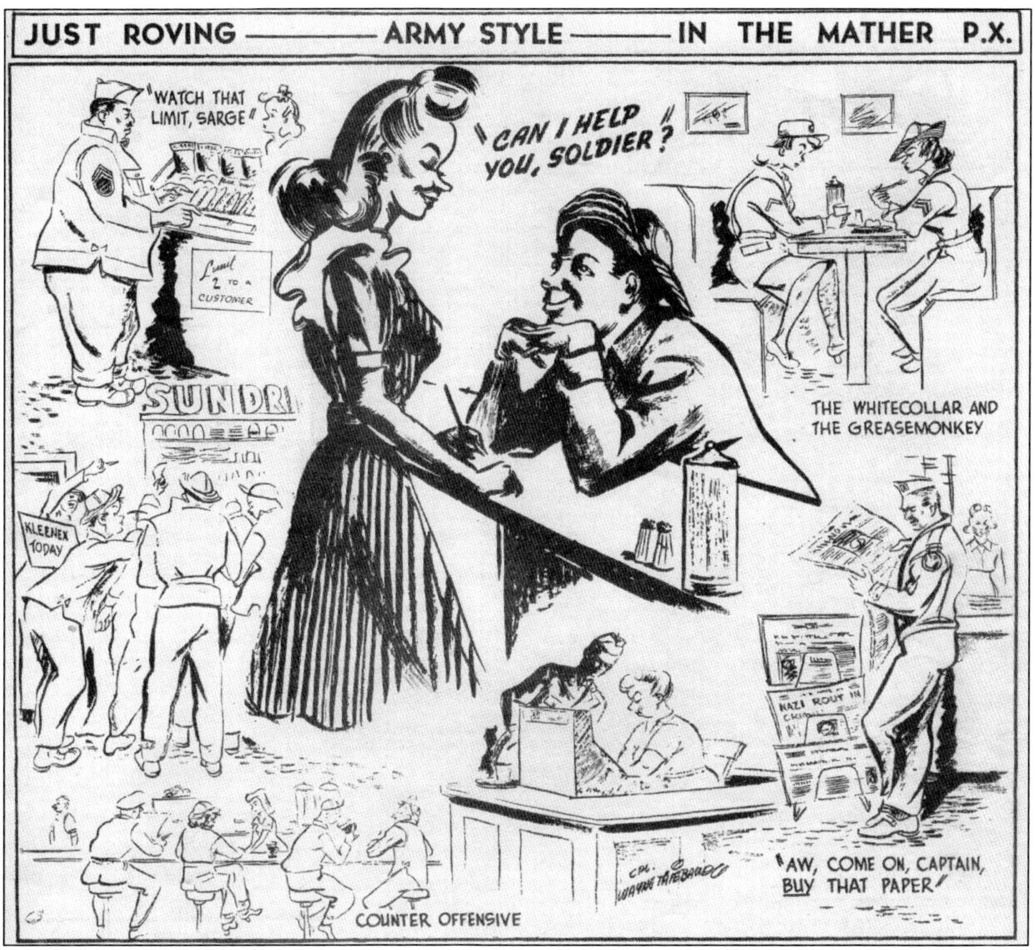

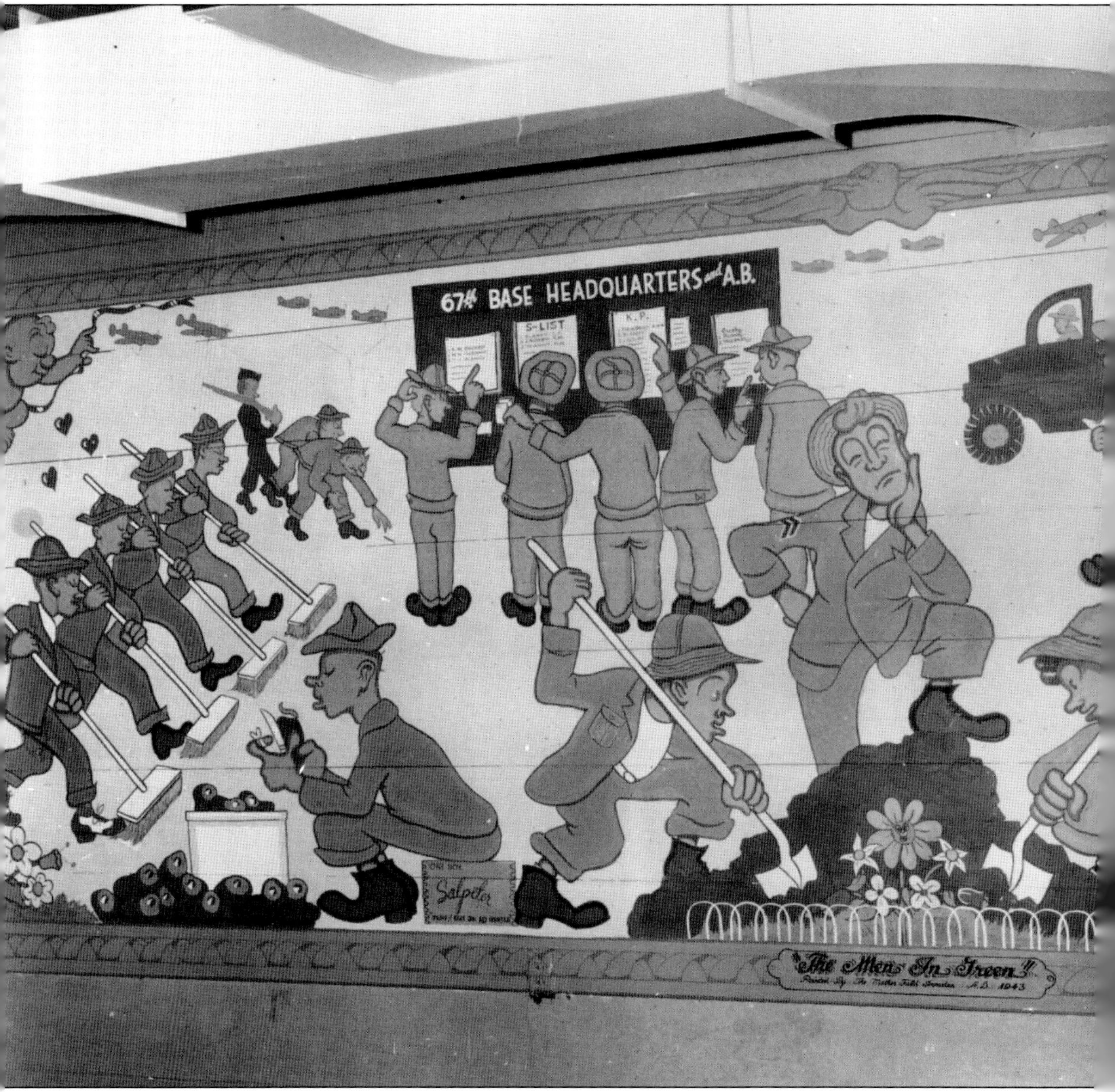

More of Thiebaud's exquisite wartime touch is exhibited in this 1943 dayroom mural, entitled *The Men in Green*. During his time with Mather's 67th Base Headquarters and Air Base Squadron, Thiebaud enjoyed the use of his own studio in the base's Special Services building and was actually furloughed for two weeks of study as a guest student at Los Angeles's prestigious Art Center College

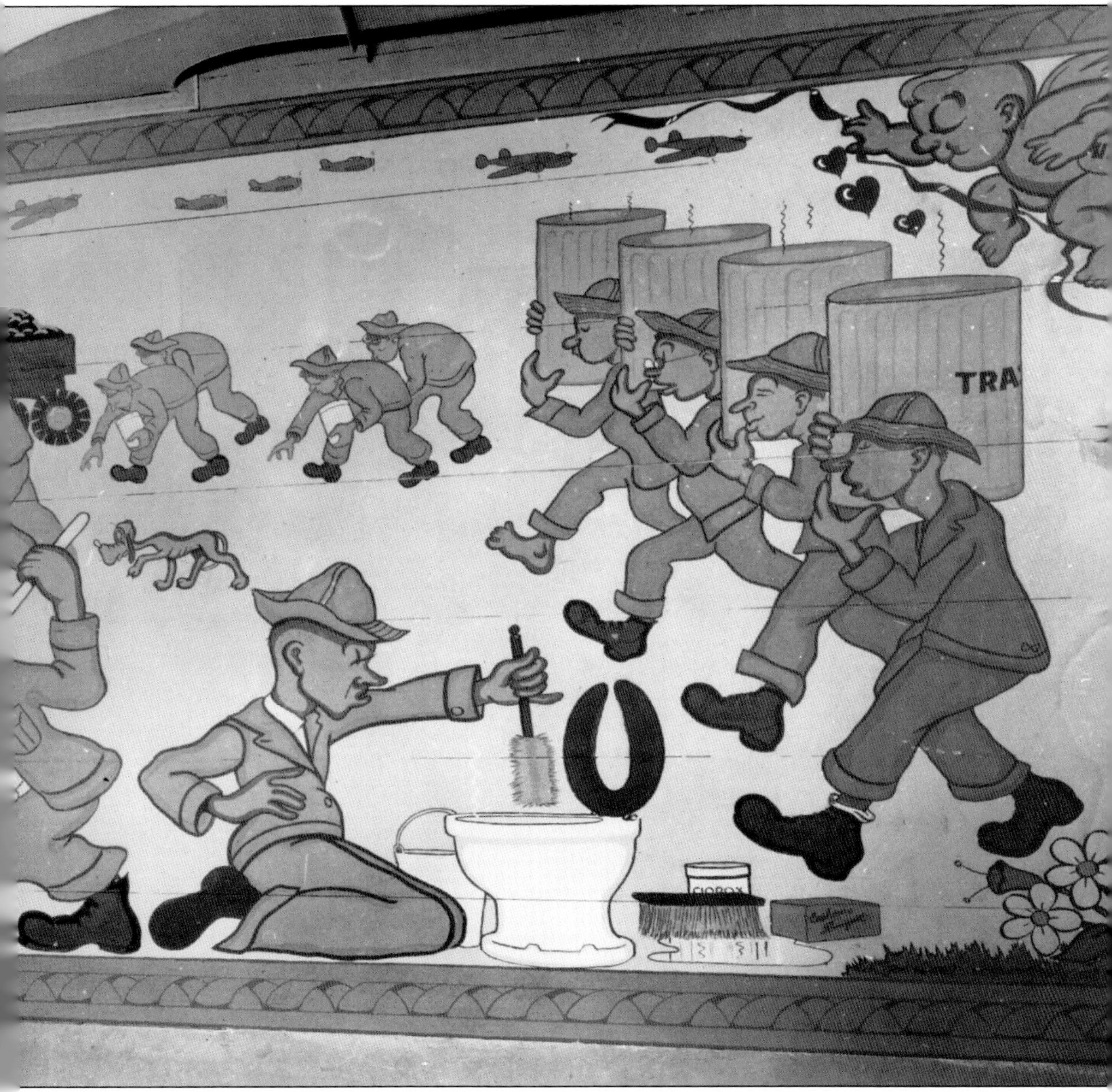

of Design. Prior to World War II, the self-taught artist worked at the Walt Disney studios. After victory over Japan, or V-J Day, he found employment as a commercial artist in Los Angeles with Rexall Drugs, eventually settling back in Sacramento in 1951. (CSH.)

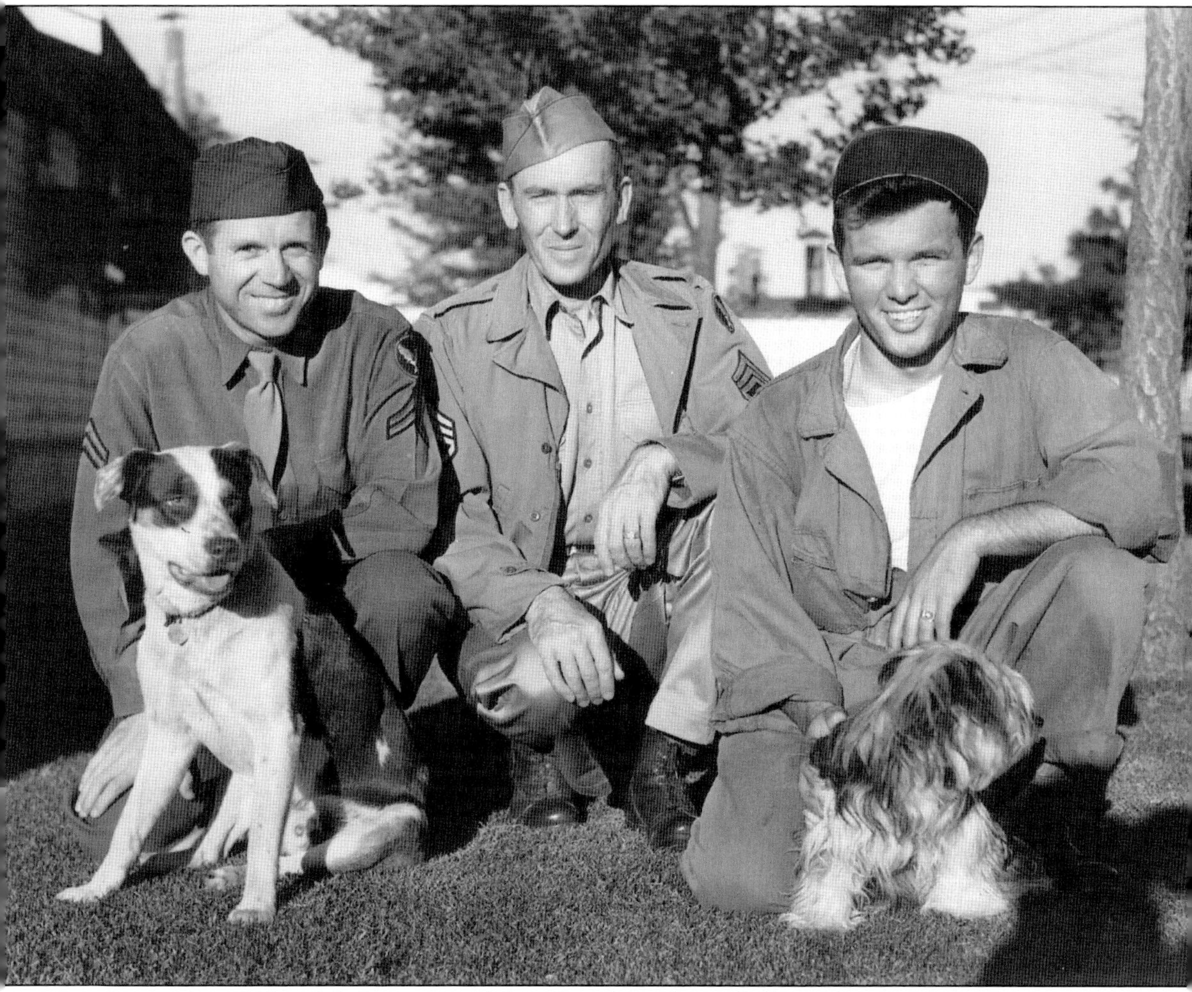

Pictured in 1945 are Mather men and dogs. Four-legged Pete (left) was known to march in step with drill formations. Canine mascots were a common sight at Mather, the sum of which was referred to as the "WAG" detachment (WAG being a play off the acronym WAC, for the Women's Army Corps). Dogs also played a role in bolstering Mather's security. Trained with their handlers at Fort Robinson, Nebraska, canines ranged typically from 12 to 18 months in age. Shifts lasted from 8 to 12 hours and, once a day, dogs were fed horse meat, corn meal, rolled oats, commercial dog food, and vegetables. Nationwide, civilian dogs found wartime work via Dogs for Defense (DFD). Started by the American Kennel Association in January 1942, DFD sought qualified dogs over a year old, over 20 inches high, and weighing over 50 pounds for use in the Army Quartermaster Corps. Sacramento candidates for DFD went to San Carlos, California, for training. (CSH.)

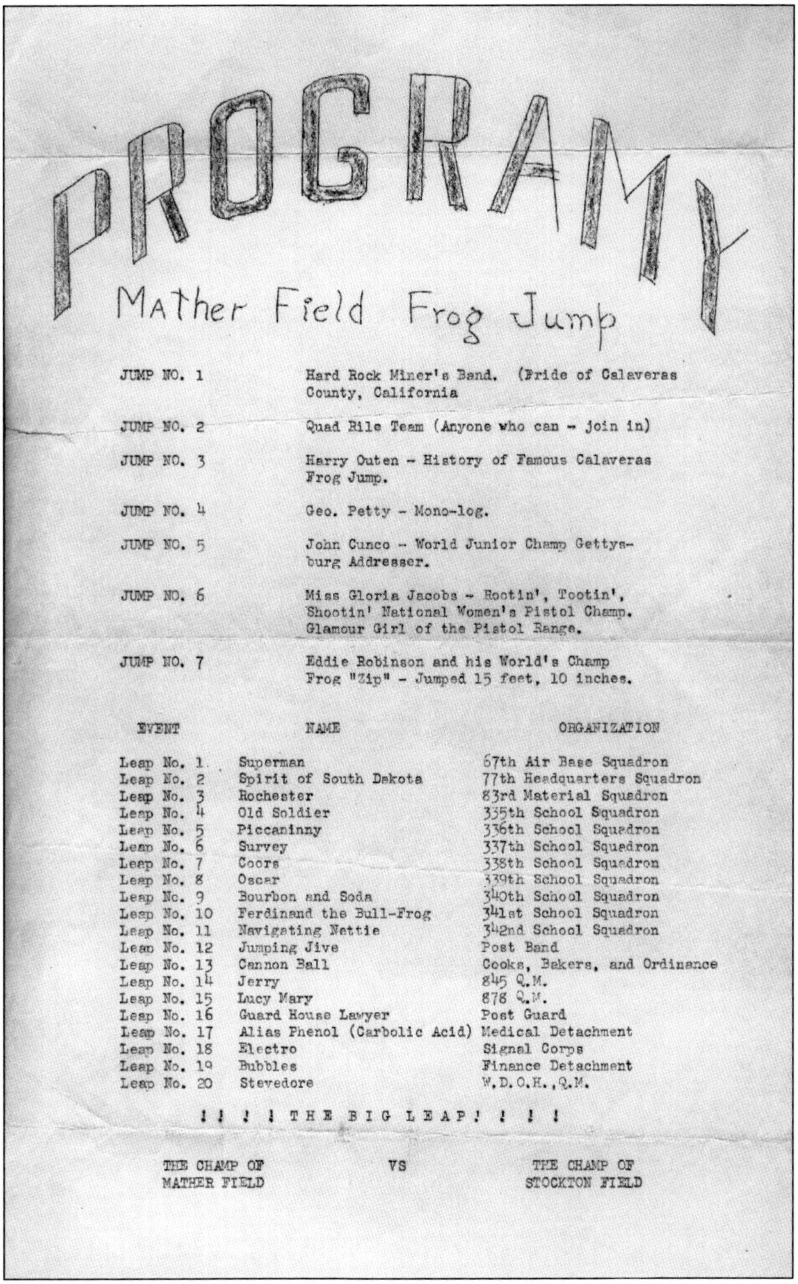

PROGRAM

Mather Field Frog Jump

JUMP NO. 1	Hard Rock Miner's Band. (Pride of Calaveras County, California
JUMP NO. 2	Quad Rile Team (Anyone who can - join in)
JUMP NO. 3	Harry Outen - History of Famous Calaveras Frog Jump.
JUMP NO. 4	Geo. Petty - Mono-log.
JUMP NO. 5	John Cunco - World Junior Champ Gettysburg Addresser.
JUMP NO. 6	Miss Gloria Jacobs - Rootin', Tootin', Shootin' National Women's Pistol Champ. Glamour Girl of the Pistol Range.
JUMP NO. 7	Eddie Robinson and his World's Champ Frog "Zip" - Jumped 15 feet, 10 inches.

EVENT	NAME	ORGANIZATION
Leap No. 1	Superman	67th Air Base Squadron
Leap No. 2	Spirit of South Dakota	77th Headquarters Squadron
Leap No. 3	Rochester	83rd Material Squadron
Leap No. 4	Old Soldier	335th School Squadron
Leap No. 5	Piccaninny	336th School Squadron
Leap No. 6	Survey	337th School Squadron
Leap No. 7	Coors	338th School Squadron
Leap No. 8	Oscar	339th School Squadron
Leap No. 9	Bourbon and Soda	340th School Squadron
Leap No. 10	Ferdinand the Bull-Frog	341st School Squadron
Leap No. 11	Navigating Nettie	342nd School Squadron
Leap No. 12	Jumping Jive	Post Band
Leap No. 13	Cannon Ball	Cooks, Bakers, and Ordinance
Leap No. 14	Jerry	845 Q.M.
Leap No. 15	Lucy Mary	878 Q.M.
Leap No. 16	Guard House Lawyer	Post Guard
Leap No. 17	Alias Phenol (Carbolic Acid)	Medical Detachment
Leap No. 18	Electro	Signal Corps
Leap No. 19	Bubbles	Finance Detachment
Leap No. 20	Stevedore	W.D.O.H.,Q.M.

! ! ! ! THE BIG LEAP ! ! ! !

THE CHAMP OF MATHER FIELD VS THE CHAMP OF STOCKTON FIELD

This May 1942 flier provides the itinerary for Mather Field's Frog Jump and an eventual showdown with the champion of Stockton Field. Mather's winner also qualified to participate in the annual frog-jumping contest at Angels Camp in Calaveras County. At the outset of World War II, the War Department devised a morale branch, whose goal it was to maintain an elevated sense of well-being in troops by creating and promoting a healthy number of diversions. Athletics, drama, music, and a library—an actual branch of the Sacramento City Library—were a few of Mather's most common extracurricular offerings. The base also included a sizable athletic field and two large indoor recreation centers. Both recreation buildings were fit with stages, movie screens, and projection equipment. (CSH.)

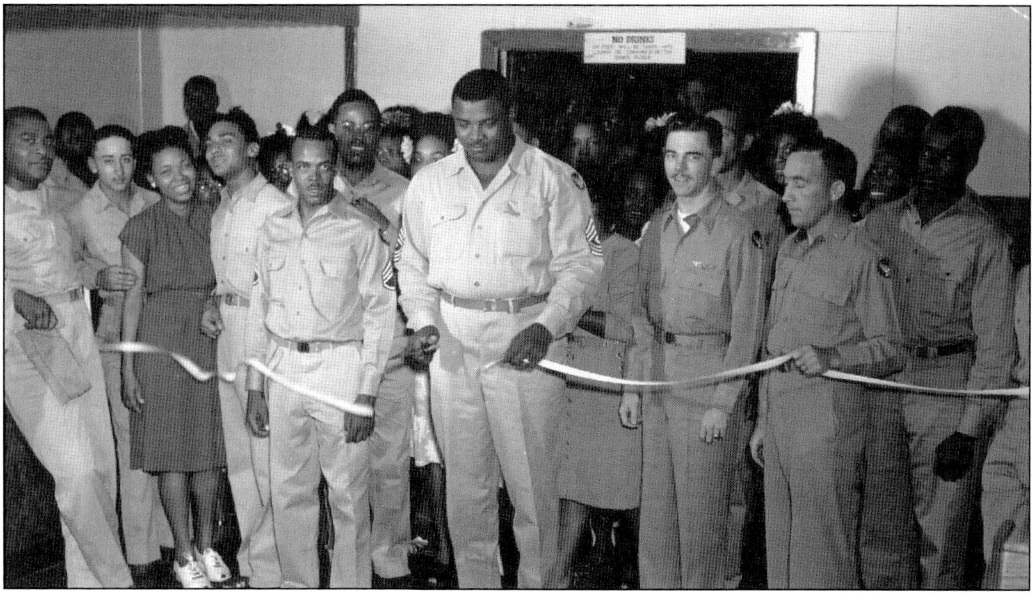

This June 29, 1945, image above captures the opening of the all–African American Squadron F's newest recreation spot, the Bar Lounge. The venue was officially christened on the evening of July 18 with the appearance of the US Navy's 21-piece Camp Shoemaker Orchestra. The event saw a record number of hostesses brought in from Sacramento, with Coca-Cola and cold beer pouring freely. Pictured below in 1944, a throng of enlisted men and NCOs take a moment to enjoy lager. Although questioned by many, it was the conviction of Secretary of War Henry Stimson that the on-base sale of alcohol was a healthy practice, creating "a degree of temperance among Army personnel which is not approachable in civil communities now" by encouraging soldiers "to remain on the reservation (their home) and enjoy refreshment under conditions conducive of temperance." (Both, CSH.)

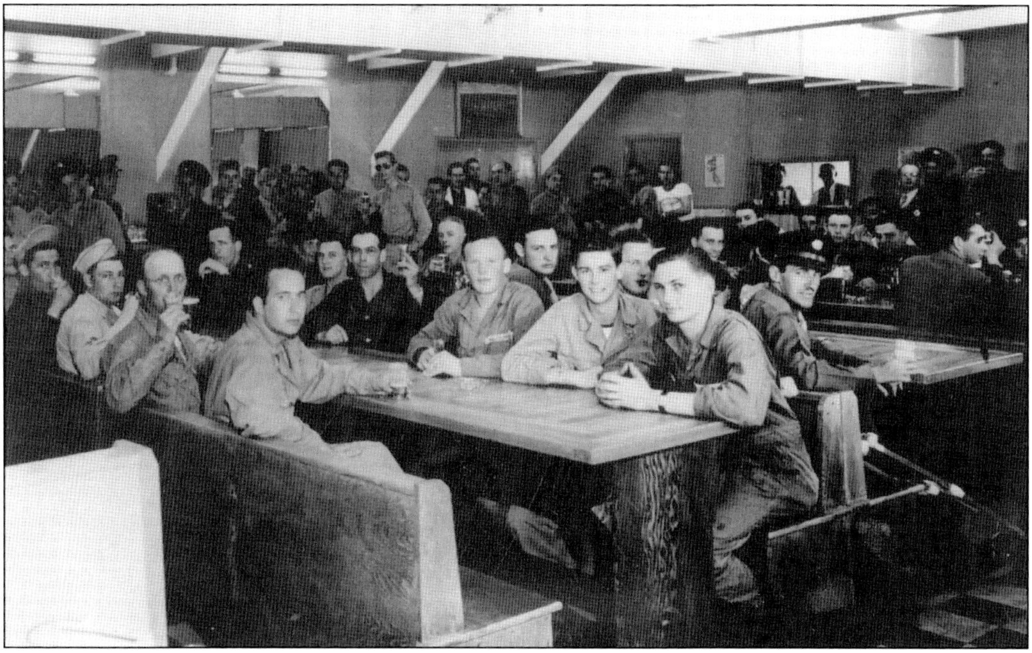

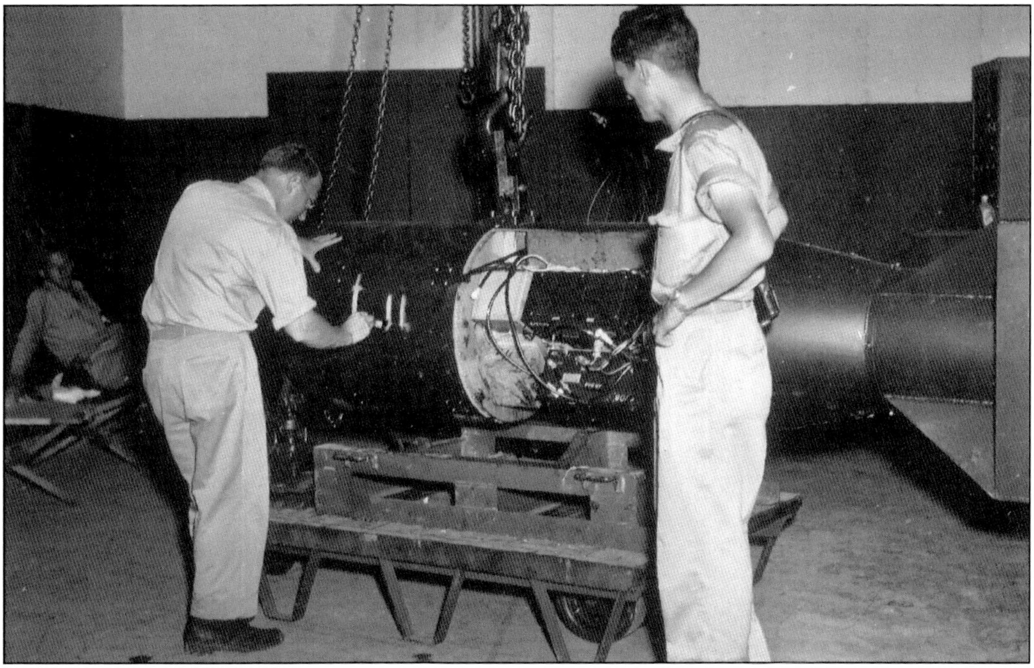

Pictured above on Tinian Island is the atomic bomb known as "Little Boy." The disassembled A-bomb nearly left a disastrous mark at Mather Field, a refueling point along its transit to Hawaii and beyond. Little Boy was brought to Mather on a B-29 Superfortress that was named the *Laggin' Dragon*, as seen below. During a hurried takeoff and at a mere 50 feet above the ground, a hinged door accidently opened, sending a life raft astern, where it wrapped itself around the plane's right stabilizer, sending the B-29's nose downward and blocking any elevator movement. Pilots Edward Costello and Harry Davis fought to turn the plane by 10 degrees, thus dislodging the raft and helping the plane land safely. Within a week of the incident, Little Boy had been dropped on Hiroshima. (Above, National Archives; below, National Air and Space Museum.)

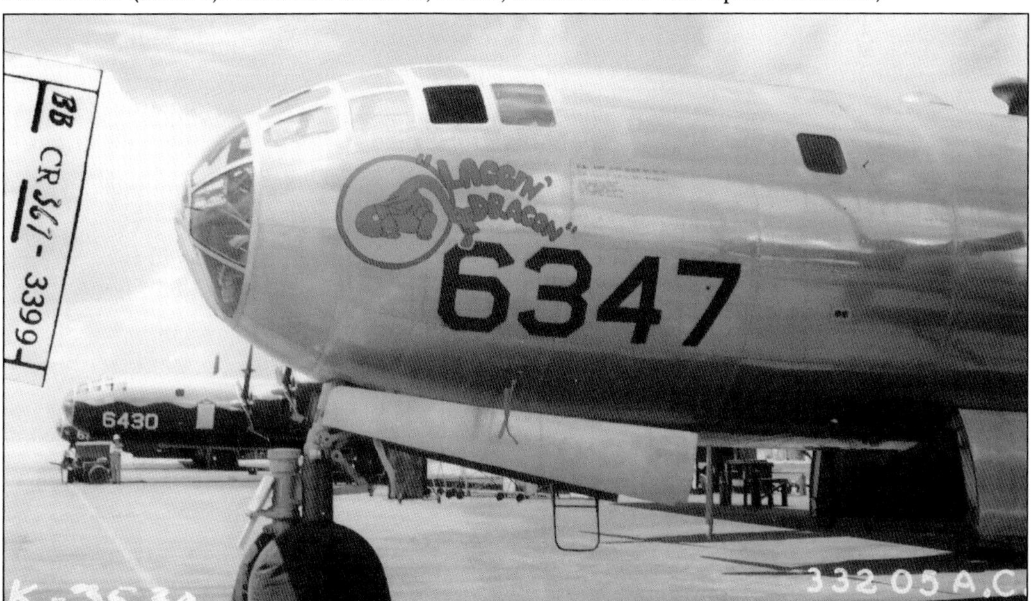

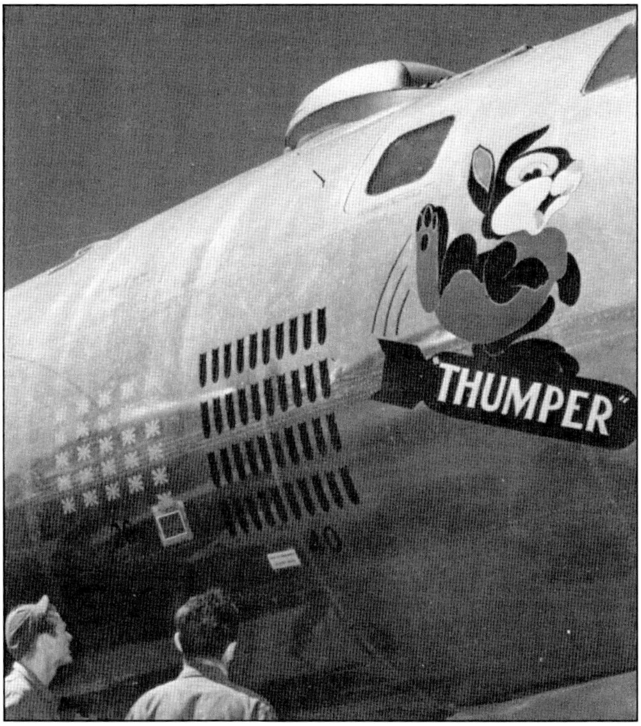

This 1945 photograph shows *Thumper*, one of the many B-29s going full circle at Mather. Starting in October 1944, the base became the point of embarkation for all B-29s headed to the Pacific. However, as the war ended, it was Mather that welcomed those same B-29s home. As a member of the 497th Bomb Group, in over eight months of service, *Thumper* completed 40 missions and shot down 26 enemy planes. (SPL.)

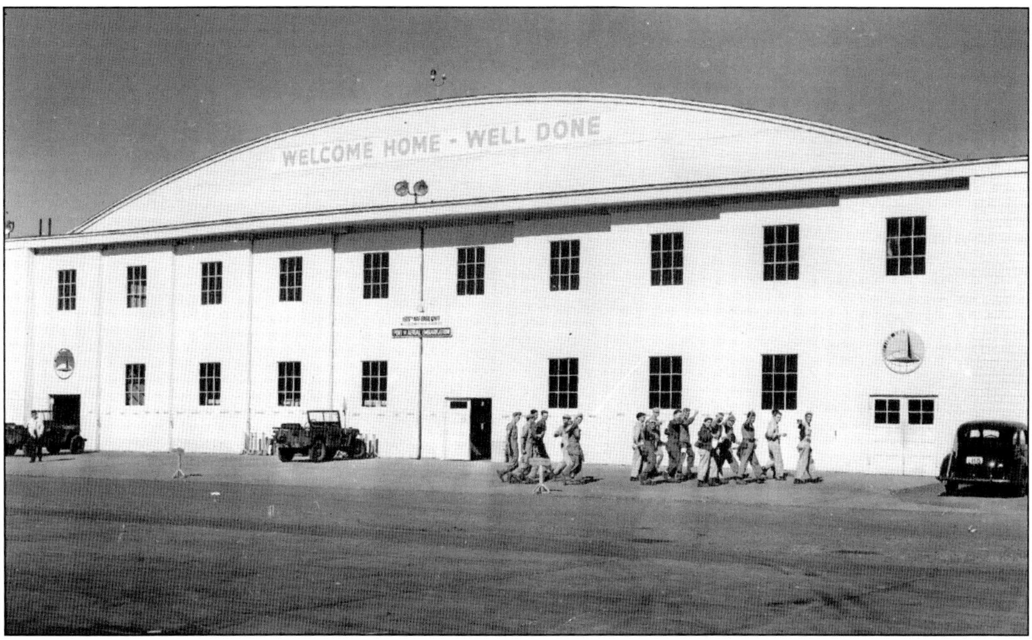

In this 1945 photograph, a hearty "Welcome Home—Well Done" greets servicemen returning from the Pacific Theater of Operations. On October 1, 1945, Mather became the terminus for servicemen and aircraft transitioning out of the PTO. Between early October and mid-November, the Sunset Project returned 1,266 planes and 17,534 crew members stateside. By December 1945, Mather was transferred to the Air Training Command, an association that would last for decades to come. (CSH.)

Five

Mather and the Cold War

by James Scott

VJ Day in Sacramento was nothing short of grand: firecrackers snapped throughout the West End, ersatz confetti rained down upon the throngs occupying a sealed-off K Street, and Mather-based B-29 crews reveled in the cancellation of Pacific-bound missions.

Within a few years, however, Mather was poised for rededication. *Jane's Naval Intelligence* reported a Soviet army "already far in excess of the normal requirements of defense," the Atomic Energy Commission admonished vigilance with the Soviet drive to accelerate its nascent atomic arsenal, and Congress passed the Civil Defense Act of 1950 in preparation for "atomic attack." Just as the geopolitical game was changing, Mather slowly regained both the persona of a teaching installation and an edge, with base publications freely using the pejorative "Reds."

In October 1958, Mather stepped boldly into the nuclear age with units of Gen. Curtis Lemay's Strategic Air Command (SAC)—the 4134th Bombardment Wing—arriving at the base before thousands of cheering Sacramentans. They landed on a new runway 11,300 feet long and composed of 300,000 cubic yards of concrete; it was long enough and thick enough to accommodate the most enduring symbol of the Cold War, America's B-52 Stratofortress.

Mather's instructional mission widened in 1947 with the Aircraft Observer Bombardment program, only to be extended by the 1961 arrival of Electronic Warfare Officer training and the 1965 acquisition of the Undergraduate Navigator Program. Postwar housing shortages, exacerbated by the surge of personnel at Mather, eased as residential building programs were completed in 1950 and the early 1960s. By 1983, base housing totaled nearly 1,100 units and a "city within a city" was burgeoning under the dictates of deterrence and in spite of the rising tide of peace activism.

By 1989, the Soviet bear was retreating. Eastern European frontiers were pierced not by tanks, but by a fiery populism that had four decades to incubate itself toward action. With the Cold War thawing, one question lingered: would Mather's exemplary heritage of service and annual expenditure of $1 billion within the Sacramento region be enough to sustain the venerable base into a new century?

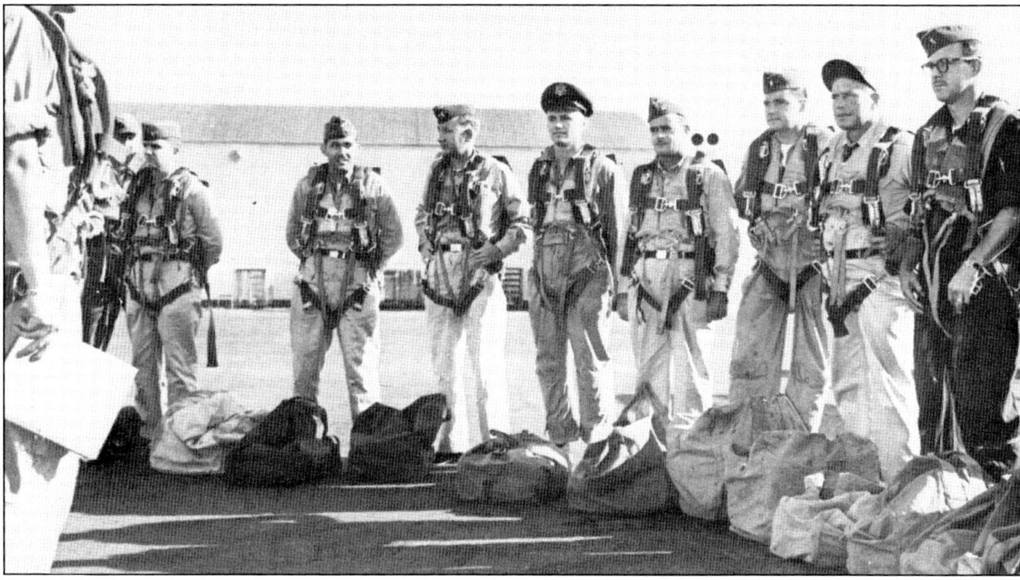

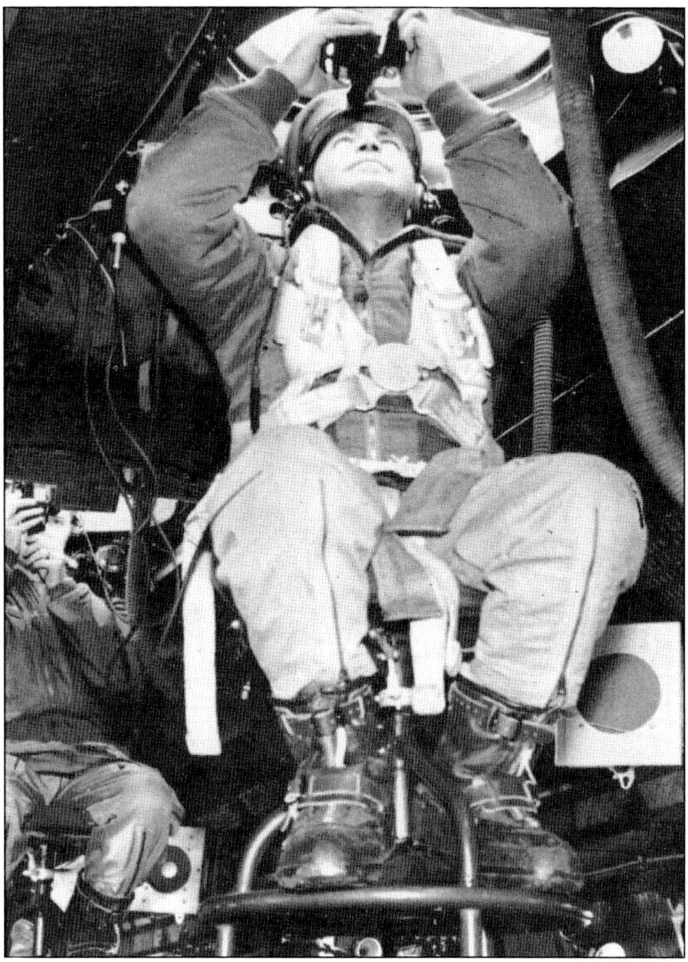

Above, cadets absorb a preflight briefing in 1952. By this time, Mather's mission and curriculum had entered a brave new phase of development with the advent of the Observer, a three-headed monster combining the tasks of a navigator, bombardier, and radar operator. It was also at this time that specialized coursework was added to accommodate both the demands of the Korean War and the need for greater surveillance of Soviet military activity. The origins of this interdisciplinary regimen began in 1947 with the arrival of the Aircraft Observer Bombardment, or AOB, training program. At left, AOB students "shoot the sun" in a TC-54 flying classroom. Being the first of its kind, Mather's AOB curriculum produced thousands of crewmen to accommodate the demands of SAC's buildup in the 1950s and 1960s. (Both, SPL.)

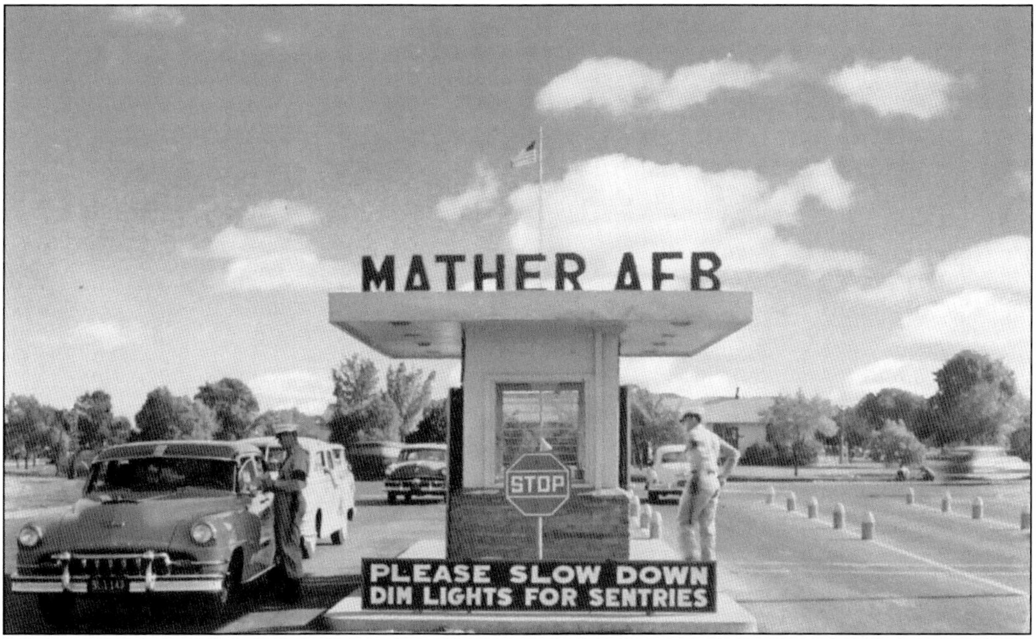

Pictured in 1955, members of the 3535th Air Police Squadron monitor Mather's main entrance. Base security had evolved markedly since the 1918 placement of fencing to keep an adoring public at bay, and in June 1941, when base MPs, fearing sabotage, borrowed sawed-off shotguns from the Sacramento Police Department. By 1985, Mather's speculated 210-unit nuclear arsenal and 14 B-52Gs were under the watchful eye of two Security Police squadrons. (CSH.)

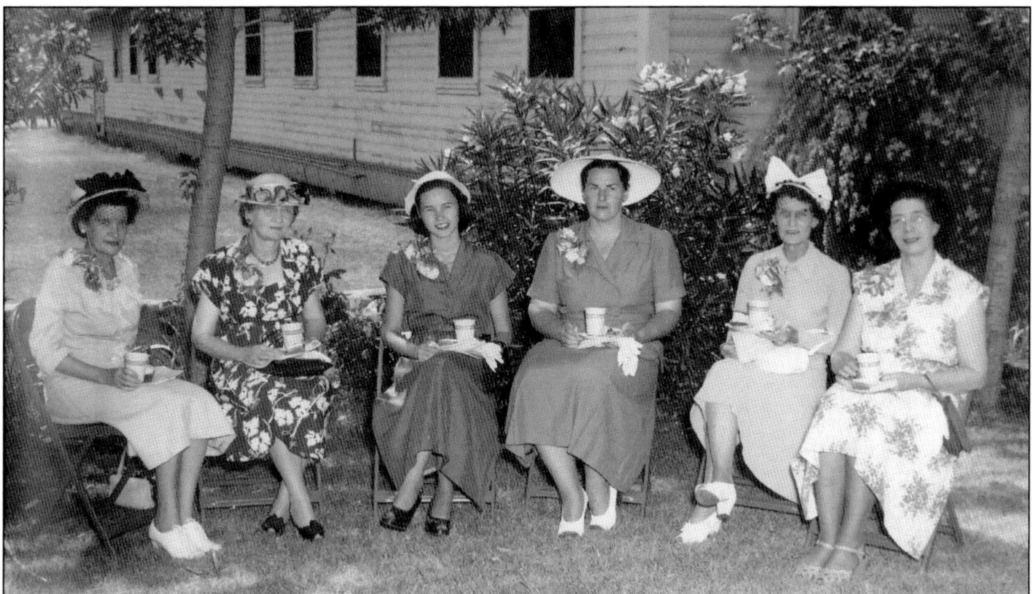

Fancy hats and corsages were in style for this 1949 tea, held by Mather Field School teachers. Kay Wood (third from left) was recently married when she joined her colleagues teaching first through third grades in a schoolhouse behind the barracks. She left Mather after two years and eventually became a noted travel agent. Also identified is kindergarten teacher Margaret de Rosa (fourth from left). The other women are unidentified. (Kay Wood.)

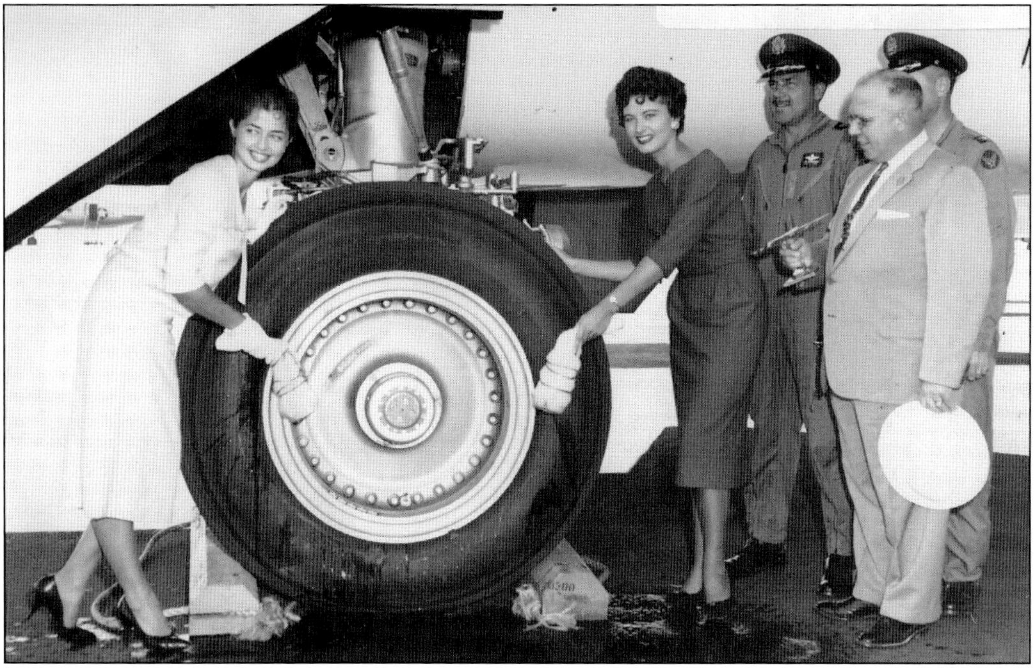

Shown above on October 3, 1958, is the formal christening of the *City of Sacramento*, the first B-52F Stratofortress to arrive at Mather as part of SAC's 4134th Bombardment Wing. Pictured are, from left to right, the champagne-wielding Miss Sacramento, Sandra Soliday, and Miss Sacramento County, Judy Bassinelli; Brig. Gen. Charles Eisenhart, commander of SAC's 14th Air Division; and the bespectacled mayor of Sacramento, Clarence Azevedo. Col. Frank Amend, commander of bombardment wing, is out of view. The wing was received in tandem with both an air show and a gala celebrating Mather's 40th anniversary. Below, some of the 2,000 Strategic Air Command (SAC) and Air Training Command airmen on parade make their way past the $8 million *City of Sacramento*. The wing's accompanying KC-135 jet tankers would arrive in June 1959, with the first to touch down christened *Capital City*. (Both, CSH.)

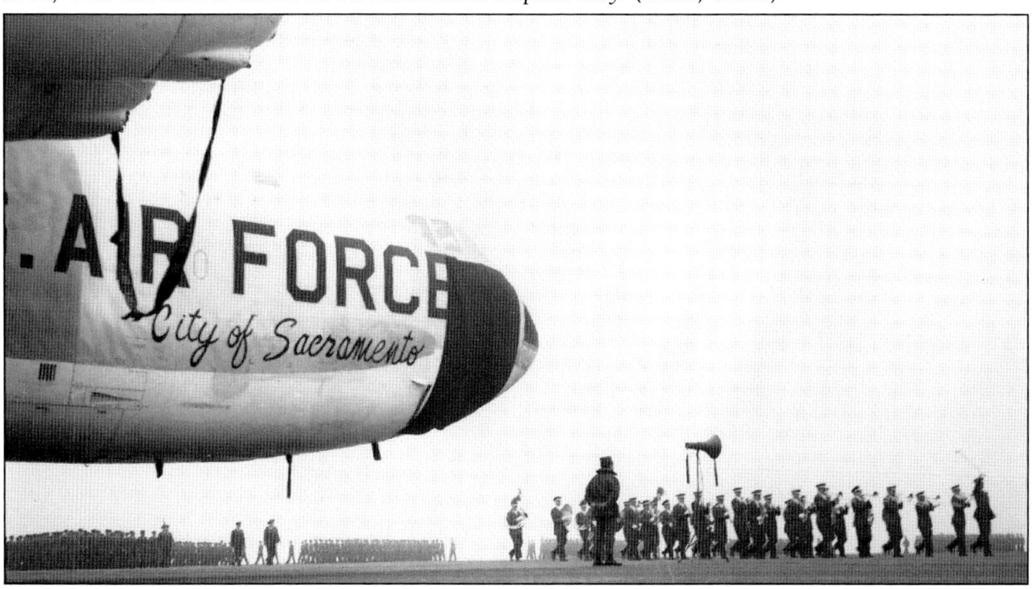

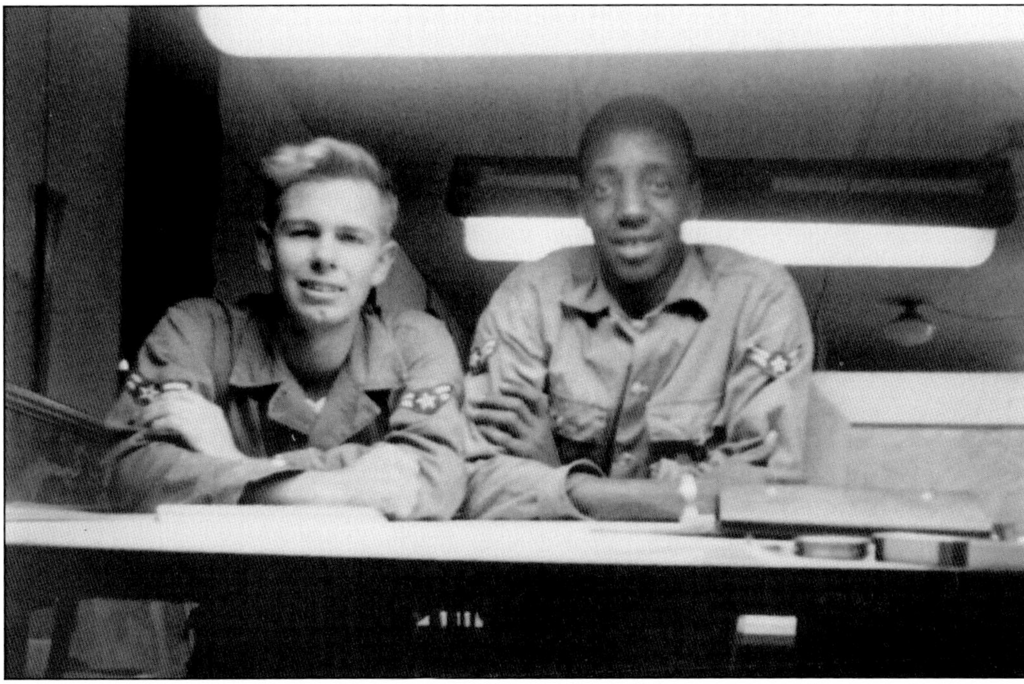

Pres. Harry Truman's July 1948 integration of the US Armed Forces was emblematic of a changing nation, with Mather Field reflecting as much. By May 1950, African Americans made up 7.1 percent of the US Air Force's force strength; by 1981, the percentage had surged to 14.4 percent, with African Americans comprising 4.8 percent of the officer corps. Pictured above in 1953 is the smiling duo of A2c. Richard Pierson (left) and A2c. L. Stuckey operating in the Graphics Section of the Training Aids Department for Mather's 3535th Observer Training Wing. Below, airmen make a harried and rain-soaked effort to refuel a plane on Mather's flight line. (Both, CSH.)

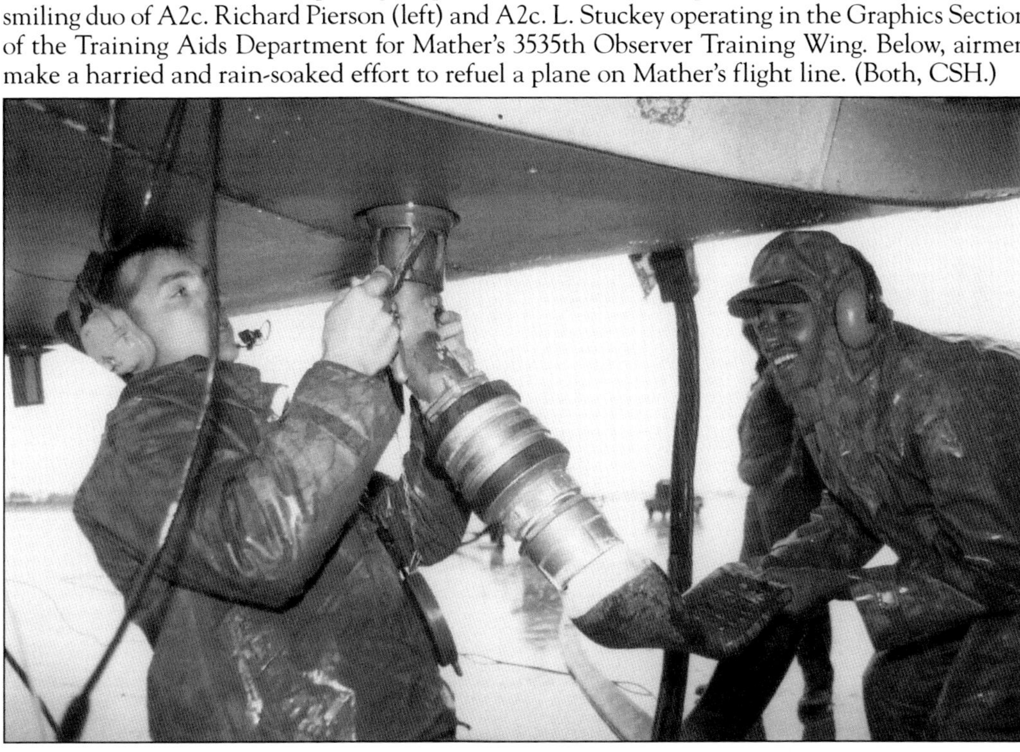

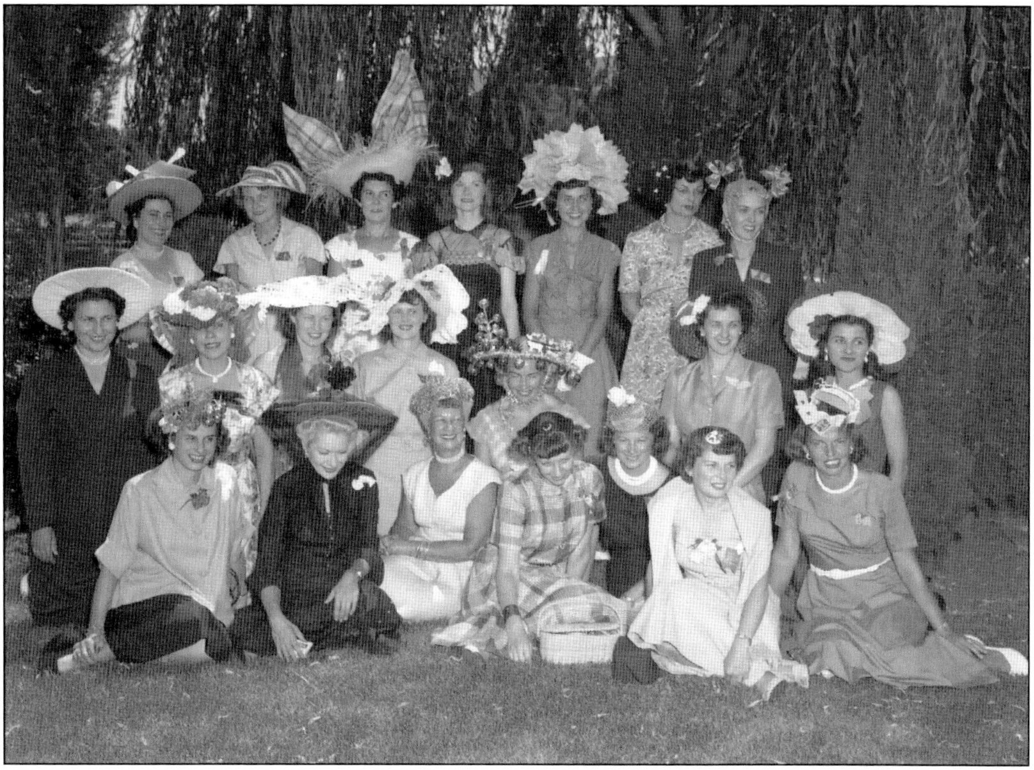

Pictured in June 1951, members of Mather's Officer's Wives Club happily model their entries for the group's annual hat show. Founded in 1949, the club served as a social, philanthropic, and educational outlet for hundreds of base wives. Notable activities included golf lessons, Sunday cocktail parties, lectures on local history, and teas for various civic leaders, including Sacramento mayor Belle Cooledge in November 1949. (CSH.)

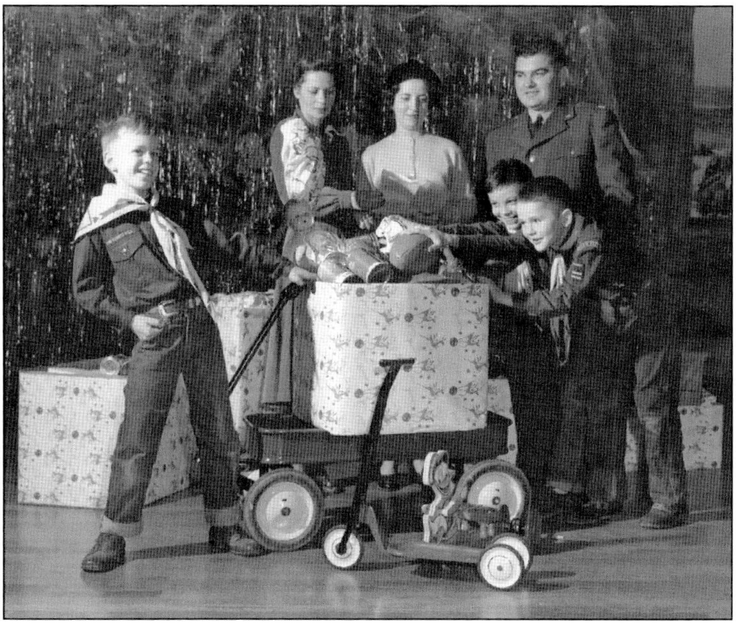

Identified from left to right in the foreground, Mather Cub Scouts Ken Lacey, John Holloway, and Steve Schmucker light up this December 27, 1950, photograph. Under the supervision of the Officer's Wives Club and base chaplains, Mather collected food, clothing, and toys for needy families in the Sacramento area. In the background are, from left to right, club members J.K. Lacey and Josephine Cross and Chaplain Thomas Myers. (CSH.)

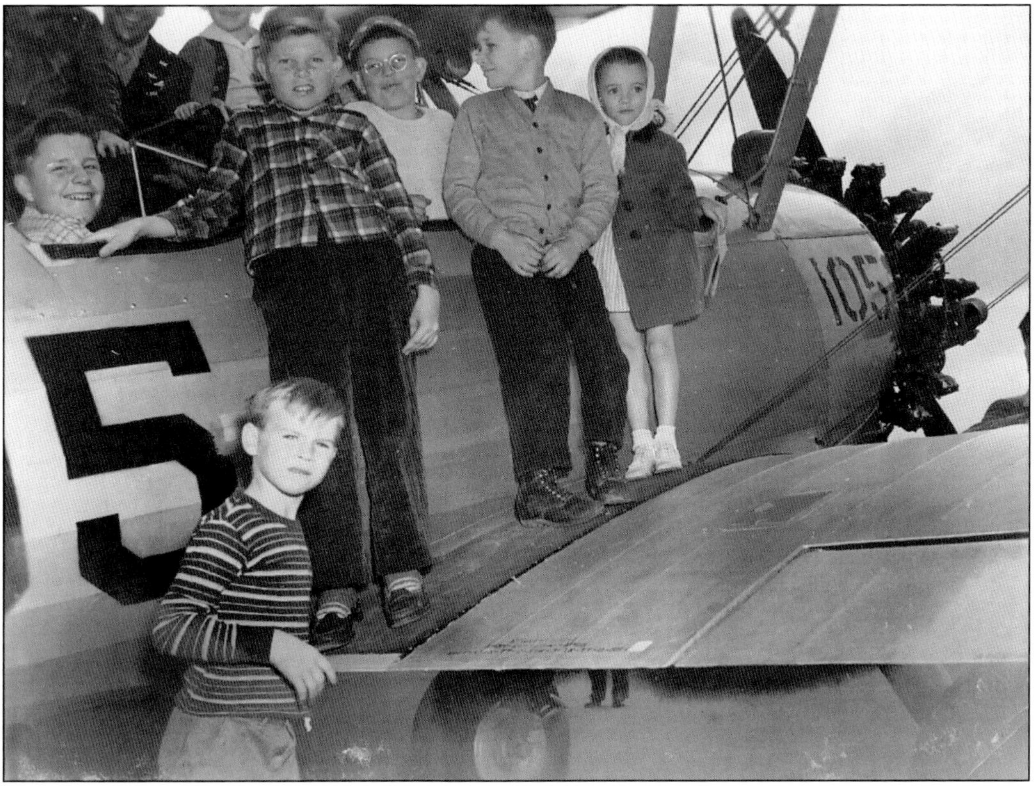

Starting with a May 1943 visit from several Sacramento High School students, Mather sought to enhance its public image through a series of Community Guest Days, each providing the general public with a chance to better comprehend the base's mission. The 1946 photograph above captures a gaggle of children around and in the fuselage of a Boeing Stearman PT-17/N2S3 trainer, which would have been used during the interwar period. Below, a May, 3 1969, photograph shows a technical sergeant orienting members of Rancho Cordova's Cub Scout Pack 17 with base firefighting equipment. Perhaps the highest-profile cancellation of Guest Day came in 1987 when Mather deemed a "dicey global climate" inappropriate for the event. (Both, CSH.)

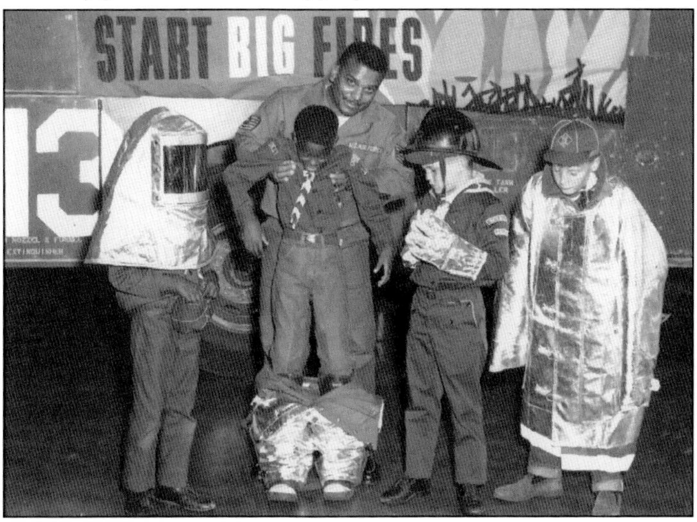

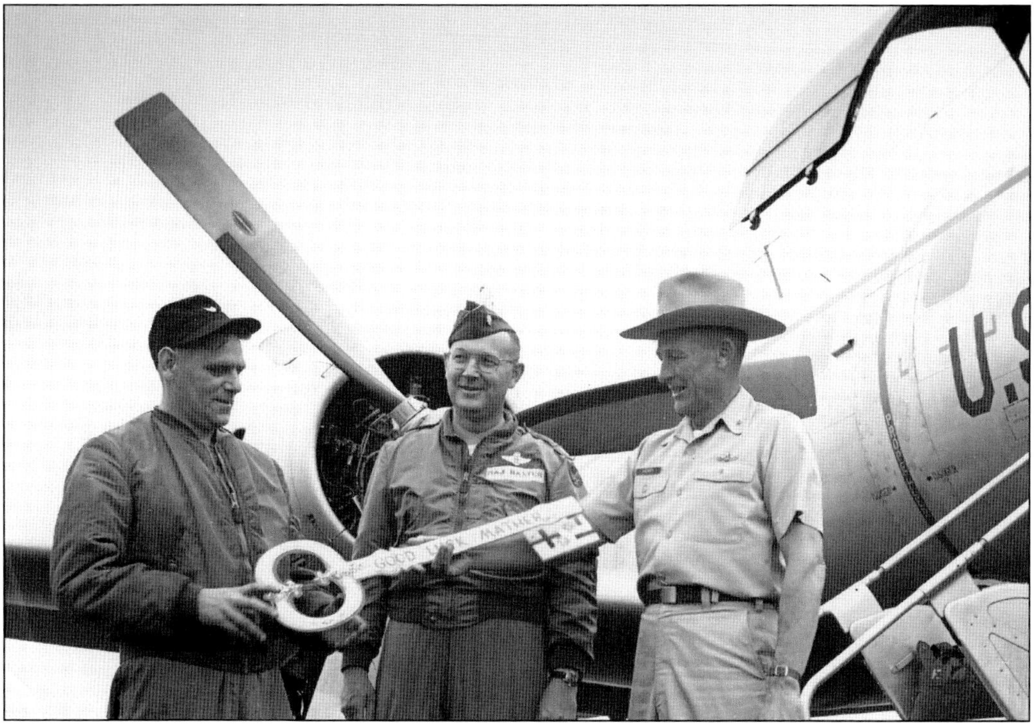

In 1964, the Air Force decided to centralize both basic and specialized navigator-training programs at Mather. Above, the Stetson-wearing commander of Mather's 3535 Navigator Training Wing, Col. Steve Henry, accepts the key to the Undergraduate Navigator Training program from Maj. John A. Baxter of Connally Air Force Base in Waco, Texas. The crew chief of the plane, a Convair T-29C, is in the background. Mather received 62 of the planes in the 1964 transfer. For decades, the T-29 series, pictured below at Mather, served as an educational mainstay for navigation, navigator-bombardier, and electronic warfare officer training. Between 1950 and 1975, the plane was responsible for training some 46,298 navigators alone, easily placing it amongst the most productive planes in modern Air Force history. (Both, CSH.)

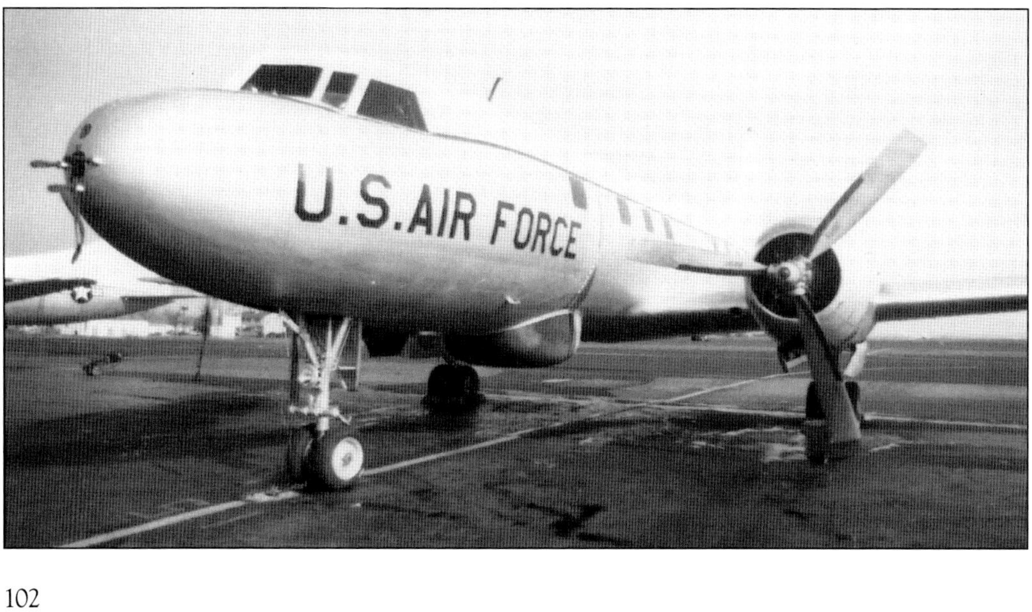

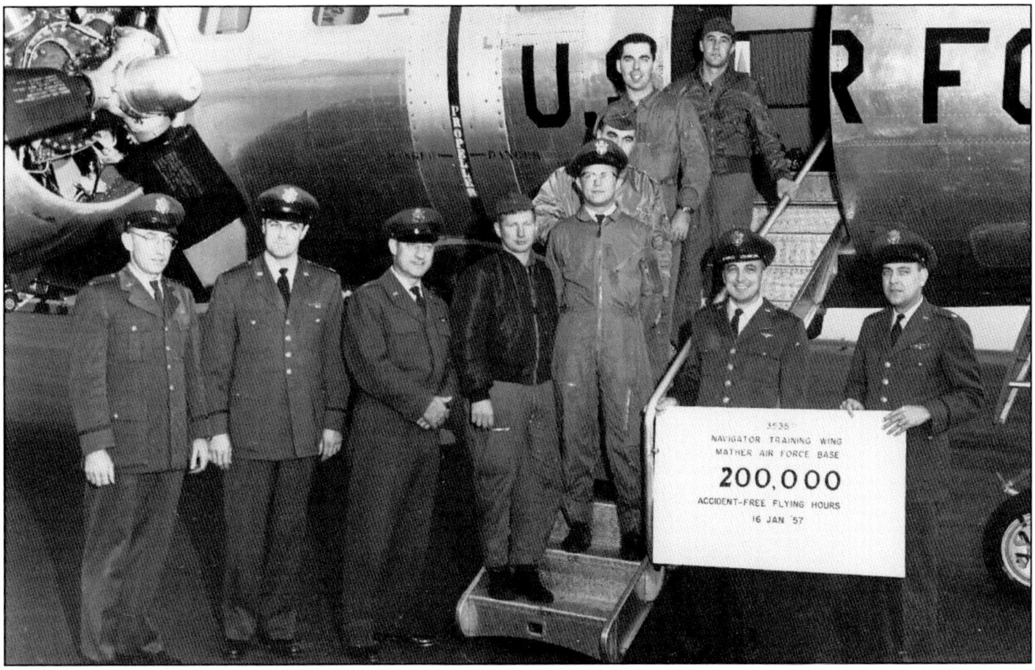

A T-29C crew and base officers pose for this 1957 photograph, recognizing Mather's completion of 200,000 accident-free flying hours. Holding the sign are Col. Peter Dawson (left), training group commander, and Lt. Col. Robert Carlson, training group operations officer. Although suffering its share of accidents, in 1948 Mather grabbed both the top safety ranking of 78 continental Air Force installations and the coveted Green Pennant for exemplary safety for its B-25 radar and bombardier-training course. (CSH.)

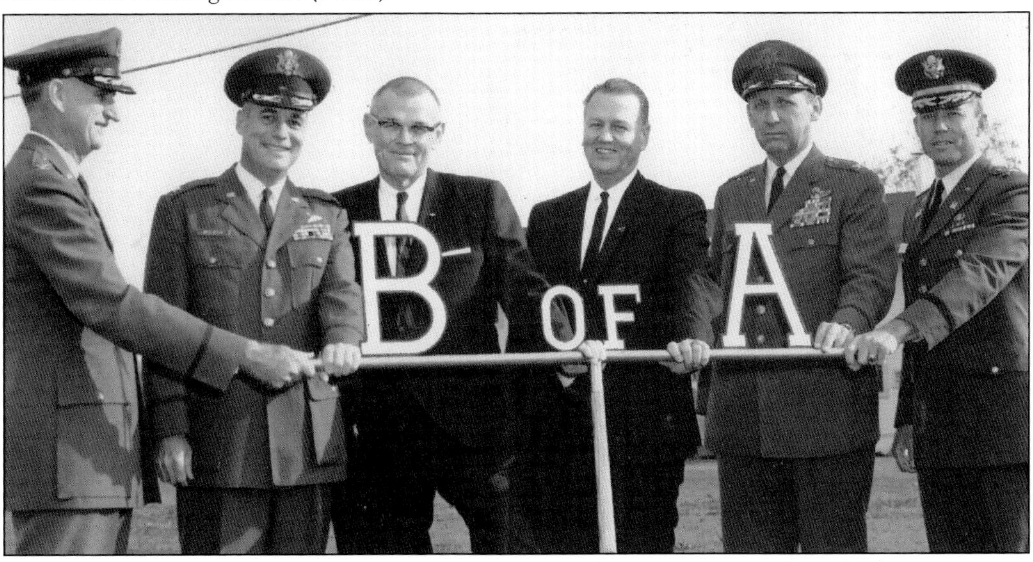

In this March 15, 1969, photograph, Mather officials and representatives of Bank of America pose at ground-breaking ceremonies for a new branch along Mather's C Street. As early as February 1943, Bank of America had carved out a relationship with the Army Air Corps, providing services to personnel at Mather, McClellan Field, and Camp Kohler, the latter two located in Sacramento County's North Highlands area. (CSH.)

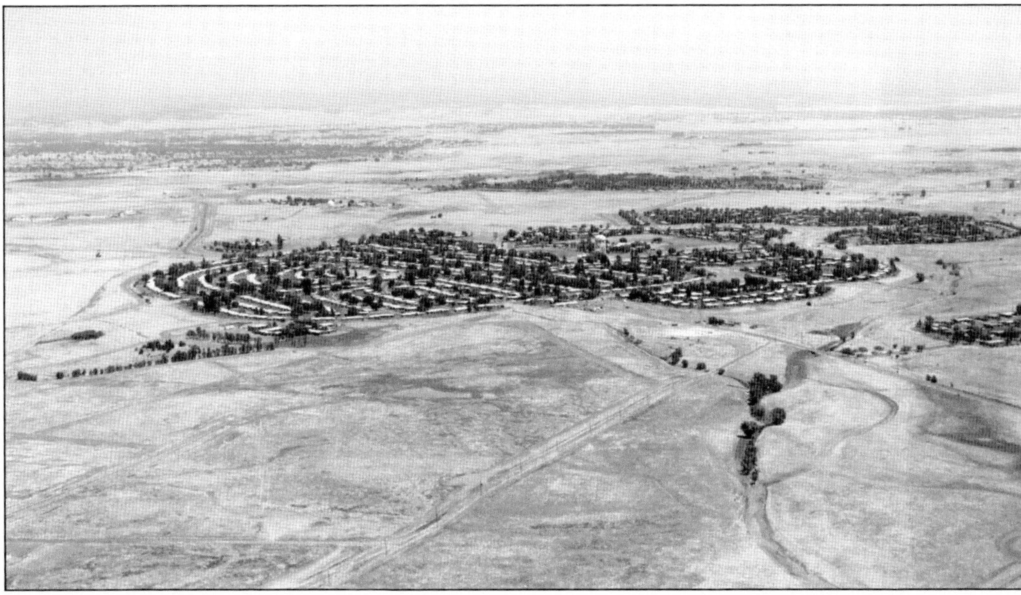

The oasis-like Mather Heights neighborhood is shown in 1980. Tucked into the base's southeastern corner, it was divided into Wherry and Capehart modules. The former, a 700-unit, $7 million village, was built in 1950, pursuant to legislation sponsored by Nebraska senator Kenneth Wherry. Wherry's structures were known for their Basalite blocks and lack of air-conditioning. The newer wood-framed and stuccoed Capehart homes were added in the 1960s. (CSH.)

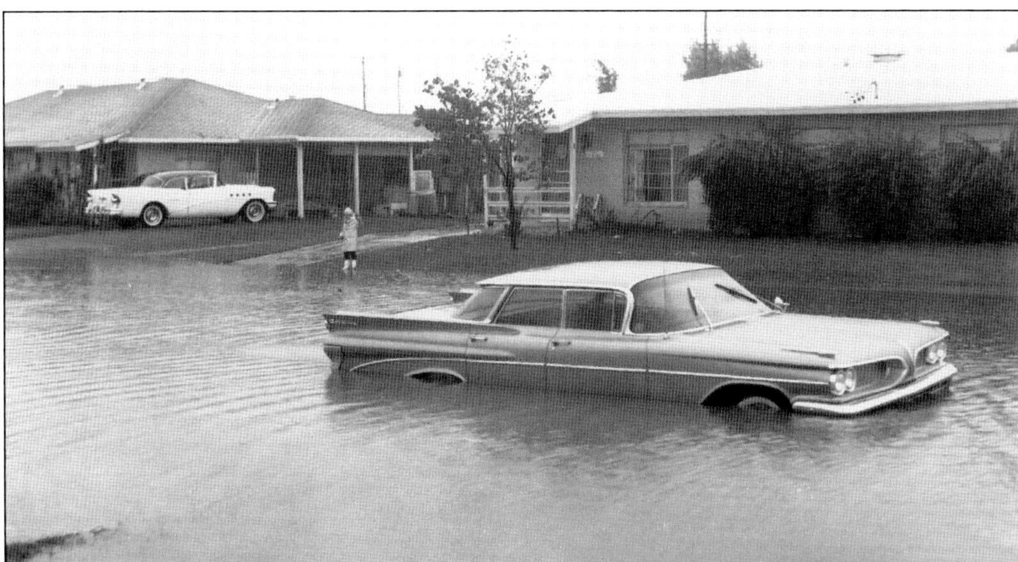

This soggy scene was captured in Mather's Wherry housing section during the blustery and tense Cuban Missile Crisis days of October 1962. The storm, hitting on October 12, yielded 12 inches of rainfall and unleashed winds surging upward to 75 miles per hour. Located within the Morrison Creek watershed, Mather's natural surface drainage flow was hindered by the construction of the airfield and its support structures, including the Wherry and Capehart housing developments. (CSH.)

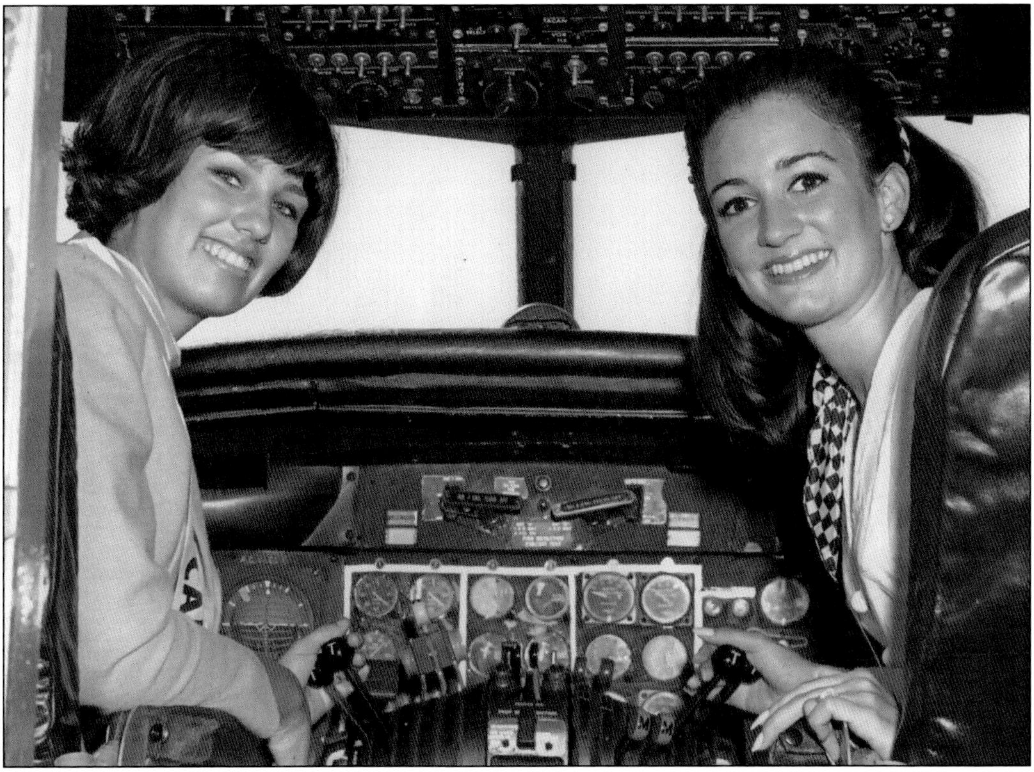

By summer 1968, high-profile assassinations, an unpopular war, and racial tension had sent over 100 American cities into riotous discontent. However, at Mather, it was all smiles. This September 8, 1968, photograph shows two finalists for the California State Fair's Miss Maid of California beauty pageant posing in the cockpit of a T-29 flying classroom. Not pictured is 1968's pageant winner, Jerri Lyn Milliken of Tulare County. (CSH.)

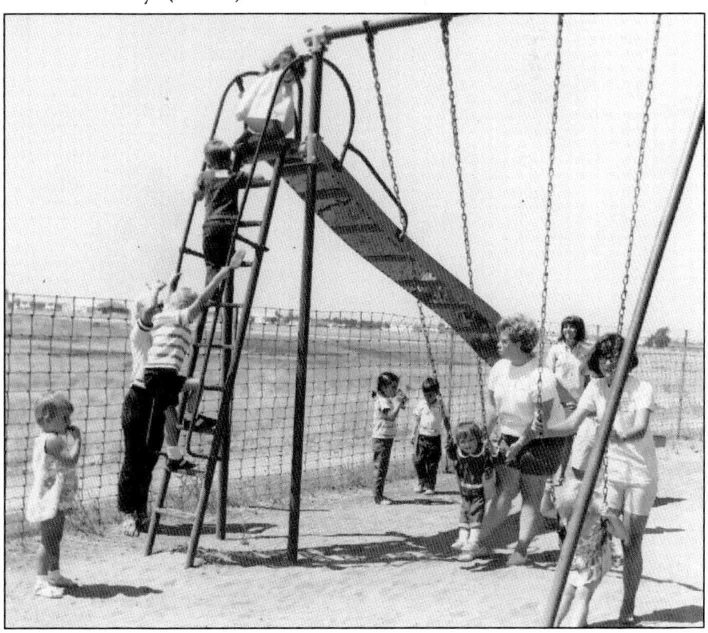

Pictured in August 1968 are Mather dependents taking in a sun-drenched base playground. Families could access multiple base benefits, including the Family Services Center. In addition to facilitating family transfers to Mather, the office offered a lending policy for assorted domestic items, such as cribs, pots and pans, and bedding; a list of babysitters and housecleaners; and courses on medical care, legal aid, survivor benefits, and military retirement. (CSH.)

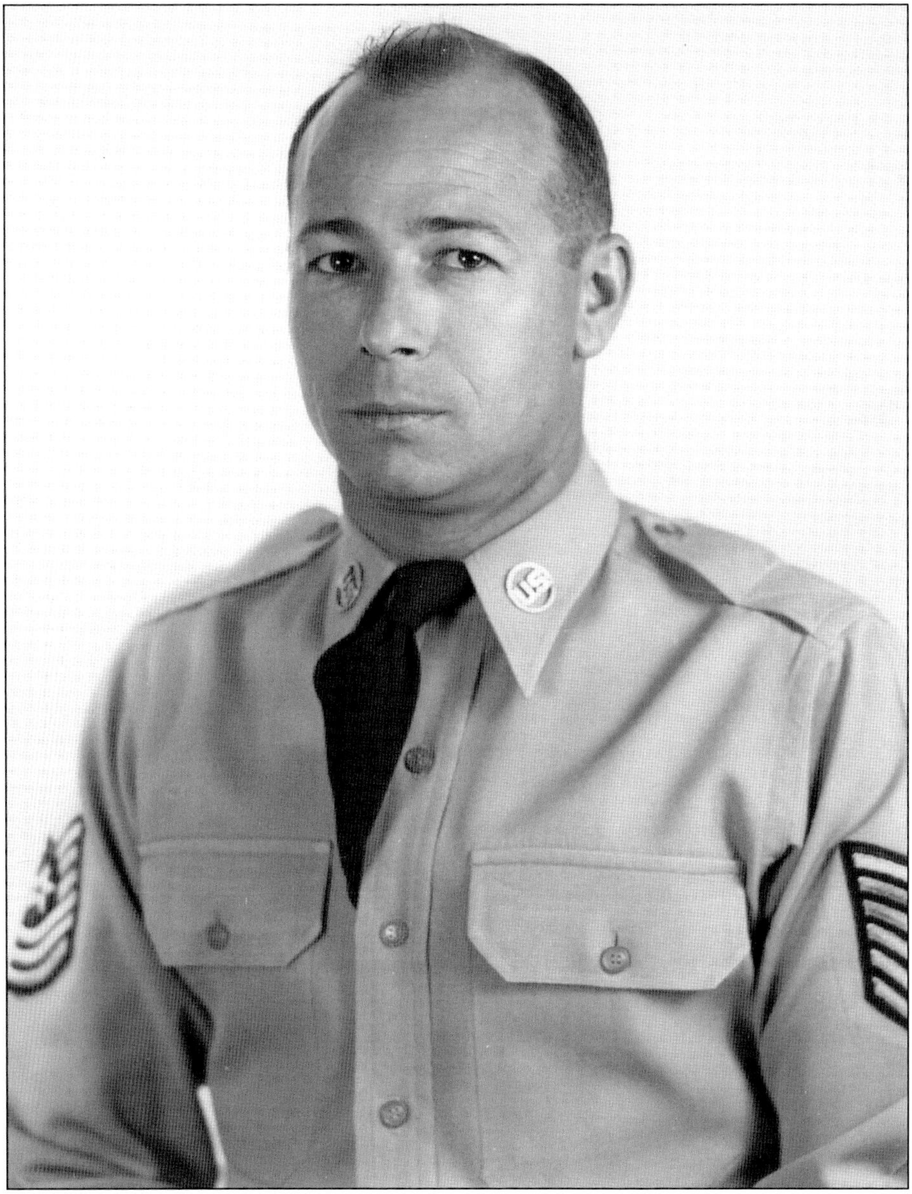

Pictured around 1955 is MSgt. Grant Ward. In hopes of broadening his horizons, the Utah native joined the Army in November 1941. Just prior to being sent to the Philippines, Ward broke his leg jumping from a plane. Little did he know that the brief humiliation would save him from the epic horrors of Bataan. Once back on his feet, Ward served in the China-Burma-India theater, often flying over the Himalayas—more commonly known as going "over the hump"—and assisting the Chinese against Imperial Japan. After World War II, Ward served as an administrator in the new Air Force, living in Brazil, Germany, and the Benelux region and holding communications positions with NATO (North Atlantic Treaty Organization), SHAPE (Supreme Headquarters Allied Powers Europe), and AFCENT (Allied Forces Central Europe). In 1966, Ward was transferred to Mather as a commanding member of the 323rd Flying Training Wing. Joining him and his wife, Jane, were their three children—John, Gerry, and Ruth—and all the makings of a typical Mather family. (Gerald Ward.)

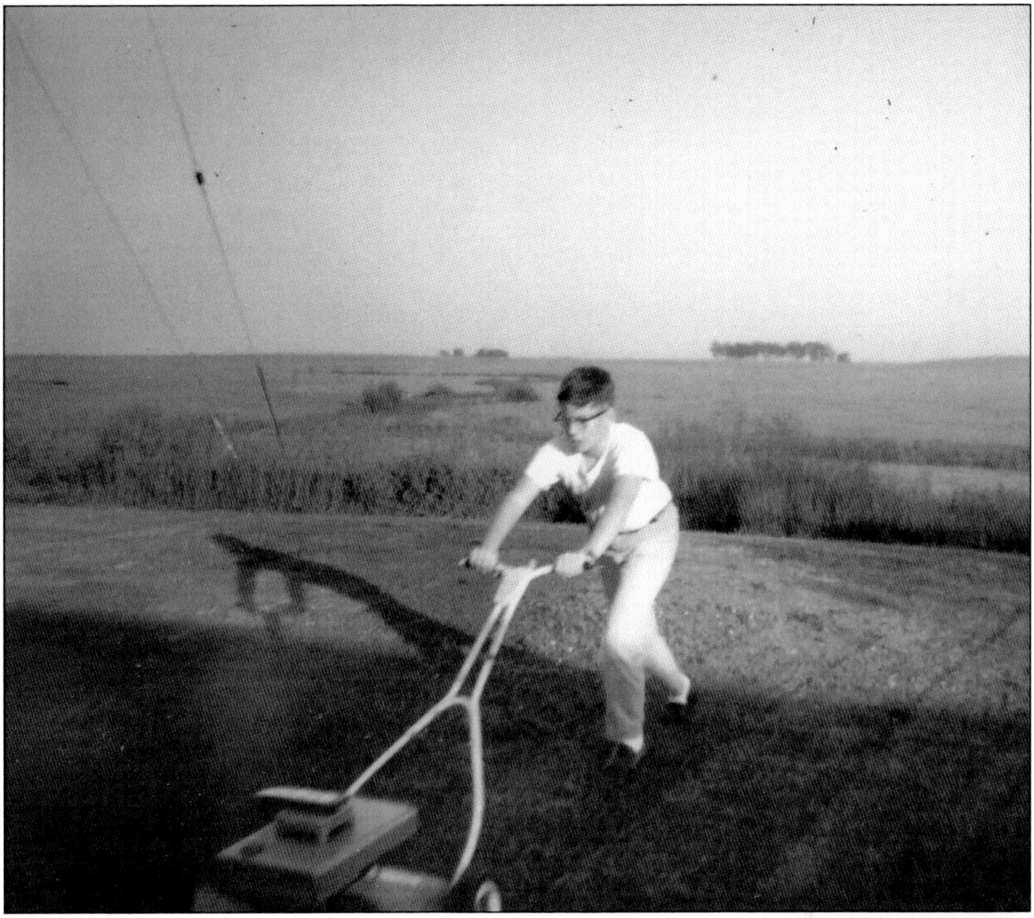

The Ward family took up residence in the Capehart section of Mather Heights in 1966. Above, 13-year-old Gerry mows the lawn. The cluster of trees in the distance marks Kiefer Road, and Morrison Creek runs just yards beyond the property line. The semirural neighborhood offered a child's paradise of open fields in three directions and Morrison Creek for scouting coyotes, jackrabbits, king snakes, and frogs. The prairie idyll sometimes faded with the Sacramento Raceway firing up its engines, Aerojet and McDonnell Douglas testing their rockets, and Mather Field scrambling its B-52Gs. Mather would be the last stop for the globe-hopping Wards. Gerry, on the left in the image at right, went on to be a reference librarian and theologian, while his brother John, on the right, became a medical librarian and linguist. Their sister Ruth, who is not pictured, became a mother and homemaker. (Both, Gerald Ward.)

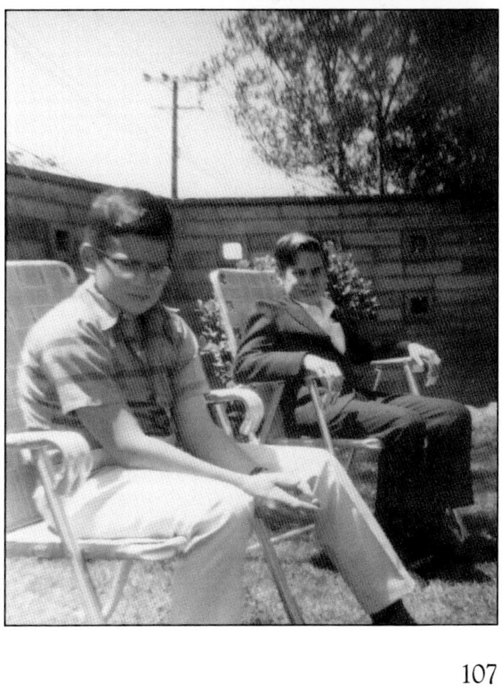

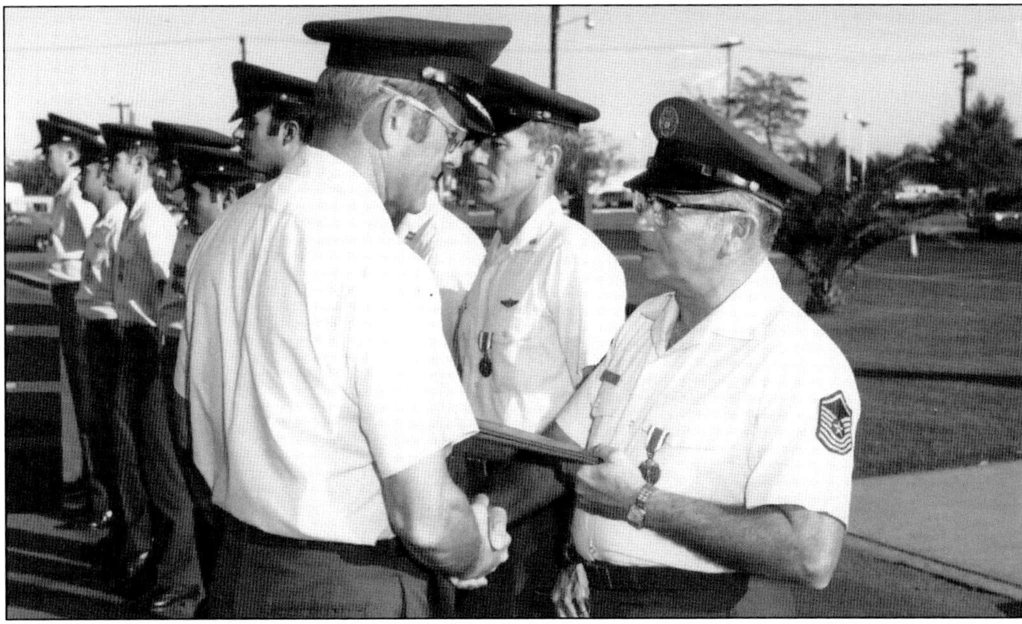

Wing Sergeant Major Ward is shown accepting congratulations during retirement and commendation ceremonies in front of Mather's headquarters building in 1973. After a 30-year stint in the Air Force, Ward went on to pursue a lifelong passion: American history. In doing so, he became a full-time student at Sacramento State University and took classes with his son Gerry. Grant passed away in 1987. (Gerald Ward.)

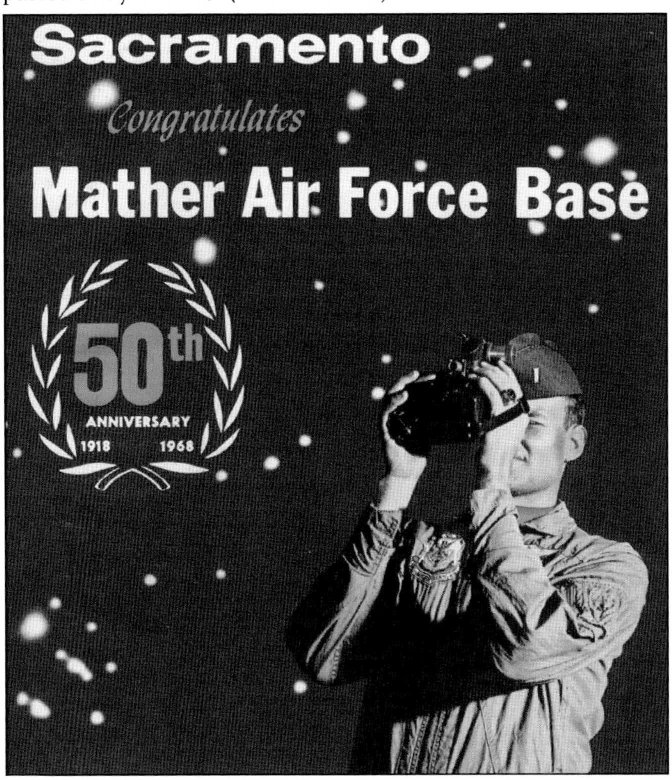

Mather's 1968 directory provides a window into the modern base's most defining image and legacy: the young navigator with sextant in hand. Concurrent to the publication's release, hundreds of Mather-trained navigators were with troop and cargo carriers operating to and from Vietnam, as well as with in-country missions aboard B-52s, B-57s and F-4Cs. This doesn't include the multitude of Mather-schooled Electronic Warfare Officers, or Ravens, operating throughout Southeast Asia. (SPL.)

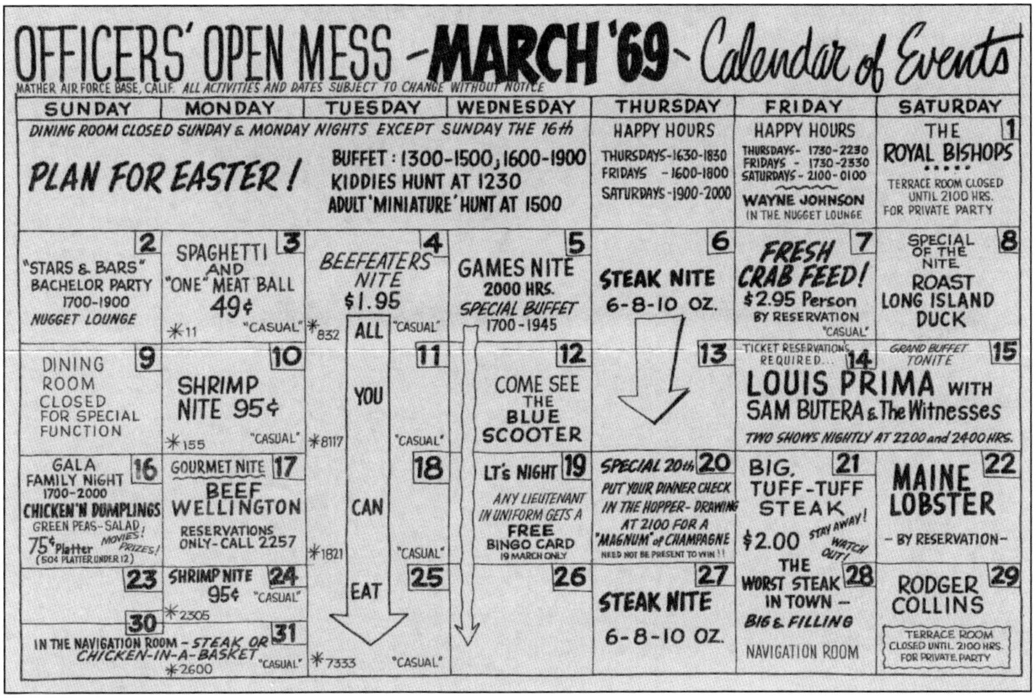

OFFICERS' OPEN MESS - MARCH '69 - Calendar of Events

MATHER AIR FORCE BASE, CALIF. ALL ACTIVITIES AND DATES SUBJECT TO CHANGE WITHOUT NOTICE

SUNDAY	MONDAY	TUESDAY	WEDNESDAY	THURSDAY	FRIDAY	SATURDAY
DINING ROOM CLOSED SUNDAY & MONDAY NIGHTS EXCEPT SUNDAY THE 16th PLAN FOR EASTER! BUFFET: 1300-1500, 1600-1900 KIDDIES HUNT AT 1230 ADULT 'MINIATURE' HUNT AT 1500				HAPPY HOURS THURSDAYS-1630-1830 FRIDAYS -1600-1800 SATURDAYS-1900-2000	HAPPY HOURS THURSDAYS- 1730-2230 FRIDAYS - 1730-2330 SATURDAYS - 2100-0100 WAYNE JOHNSON IN THE NUGGET LOUNGE	1 THE ROYAL BISHOPS TERRACE ROOM CLOSED UNTIL 2100 HRS. FOR PRIVATE PARTY
2 "STARS & BARS" BACHELOR PARTY 1700-1900 NUGGET LOUNGE	3 SPAGHETTI AND "ONE" MEAT BALL 49¢ *11 "CASUAL"	4 BEEFEATERS NITE $1.95 ALL YOU CAN EAT *832 "CASUAL"	5 GAMES NITE 2000 HRS. SPECIAL BUFFET 1700-1945	6 STEAK NITE 6-8-10 OZ.	7 FRESH CRAB FEED! $2.95 Person BY RESERVATION "CASUAL"	8 SPECIAL OF THE NITE ROAST LONG ISLAND DUCK
9 DINING ROOM CLOSED FOR SPECIAL FUNCTION	10 SHRIMP NITE 95¢ *155 "CASUAL"	11 *8117 "CASUAL"	12 COME SEE THE BLUE SCOOTER	13	14 TICKET RESERVATIONS REQUIRED... LOUIS PRIMA WITH SAM BUTERA & The Witnesses TWO SHOWS NIGHTLY AT 2200 and 2400 HRS.	15 GRAND BUFFET TONITE
16 GALA FAMILY NIGHT 1700-2000 CHICKEN'N DUMPLINGS GREEN PEAS-SALAD; MOVIES! PRIZES! 75¢ Platter (50¢ PLATTER UNDER 12)	17 GOURMET NITE BEEF WELLINGTON RESERVATIONS ONLY-CALL 2257	18 *1821 "CASUAL"	19 LT's NIGHT ANY LIEUTENANT IN UNIFORM GETS A FREE BINGO CARD 19 MARCH ONLY	20 SPECIAL 20th PUT YOUR DINNER CHECK IN THE HOPPER- DRAWING AT 2100 FOR A "MAGNUM" of CHAMPAGNE NEED NOT BE PRESENT TO WIN!!	21 BIG, TUFF-TUFF STEAK $2.00 STAY AWAY! WATCH OUT!	22 MAINE LOBSTER - BY RESERVATION -
23	24 SHRIMP NITE 95¢ "CASUAL" *2305	25 *7333 "CASUAL"	26	27 STEAK NITE 6-8-10 OZ.	28 THE WORST STEAK IN TOWN - BIG & FILLING NAVIGATION ROOM	29 RODGER COLLINS TERRACE ROOM CLOSED UNTIL 2100 HRS. FOR PRIVATE PARTY
30 IN THE NAVIGATION ROOM - STEAK OR CHICKEN-IN-A-BASKET "CASUAL" *2600	31					

The March 1969 social calendar is shown for the Officers' Open Mess, which consisted of three bars (Stag, Nugget, and Casual), the Navigation Room Cafeteria, and the Terrace Dining Room. Although strict dress codes were observed, on-alert SAC personnel were allowed to use the entire mess hall while in flight clothes. Mather had two other clubs: the Non-Commissioned Officers' Open Mess and Denker Hall, the latter for airmen and dependents. (SPL.)

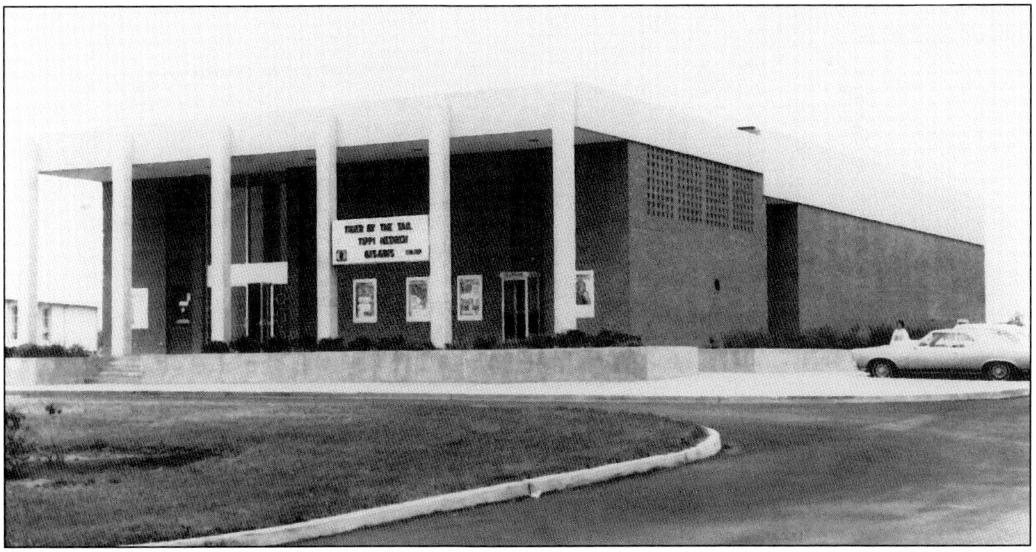

The Mather Field Theater opened late in 1941. Military personnel were offered first-run movies with five program changes weekly and shows twice a night for 20¢. Until the early 1960s, admission for base children was 10¢, with popcorn and candy costing the same price. The national anthem preceded newsreels and the feature film. Above is the remodeled theater in 1969, running two shows nightly and matinees on weekends. (CSH.)

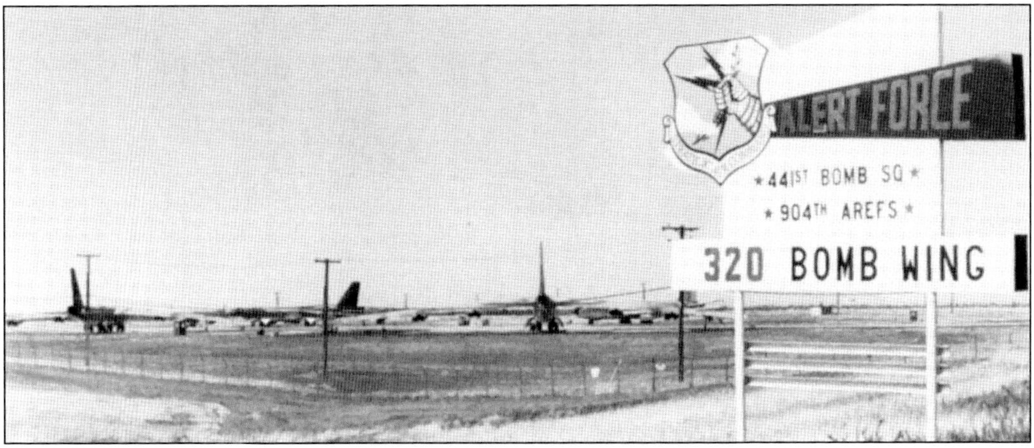

Pictured in 1974 is Mather's elite 320th Bombardment Wing. In 1965, its B-52Gs were the first strategic bombers committed to Arc Light operations in Vietnam. In 1969, it became the first wing in SAC history to score perfectly in an Operational Readiness Inspection Test. In 1976, the 320th won two of three possible trophies—Blue Steel (bombing/navigation) and Camrose (best crew)—in the Royal Air Force bombing competition. (SPL.)

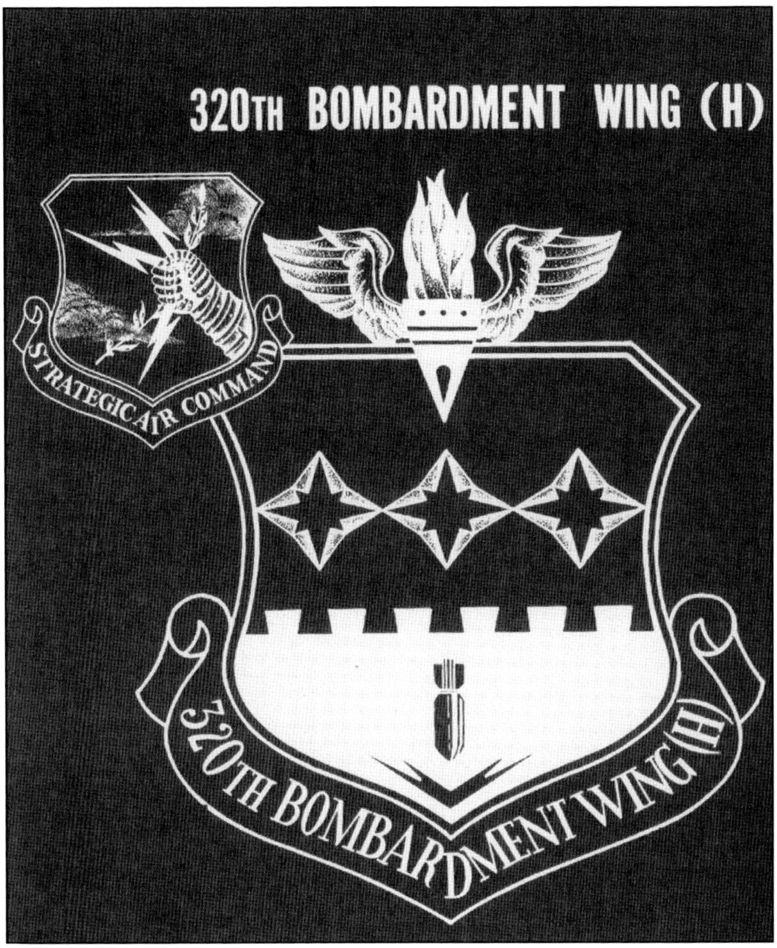

Emblems of both the 320th Bombardment Wing and the Strategic Air Command are shown. Activated in 1952, the 320th's Mather stint began in 1963. Known as the "Iron Dukes," the 320th held firm to the motto "Strength Through Awareness." The symbolism in SAC's emblem is interpreted with the armored arm representing strength while the olive branch and lightning flashes symbolize peace and speed/power, respectively. (SPL.)

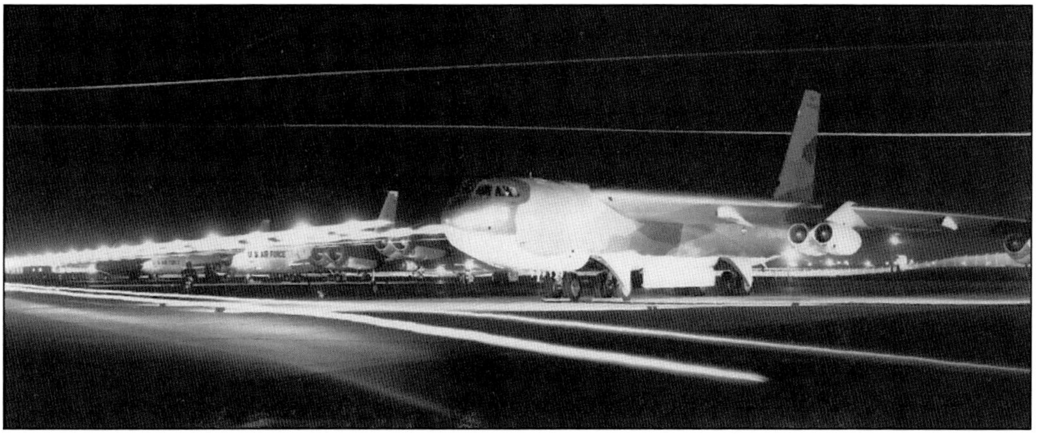

This evening photograph taken in 1975 captures an illuminated flight line at Mather. Most prominent is a B-52G of the 320th Bombardment Wing. Until October 1988, the wing was on 24-hour sitting alert. Many of the aviators who flew the plane affectionately referred to it as the "BUFF," which stood for "Big Ugly Fat Fellow"; however, the term *fellow* was often replaced. To the left are three companion KC-135 tankers. (CSH.)

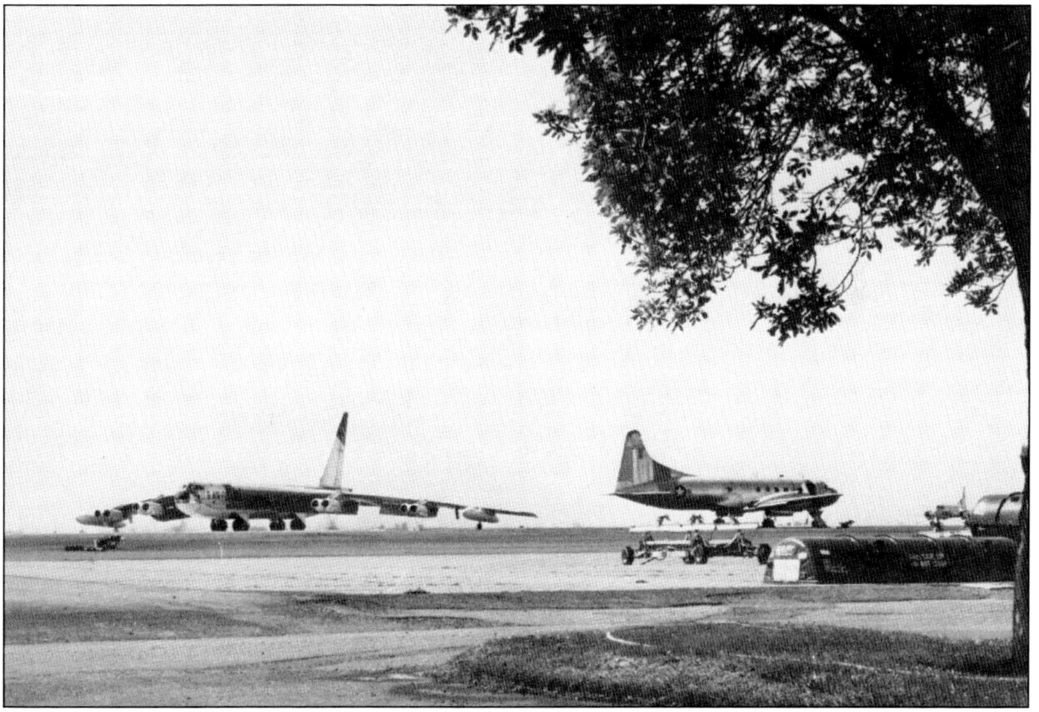

Perhaps the two most recognizable aircraft of Mather's Cold War existence, the B-52 (left) and T-29, are shown in this 1968 photograph. The T-29 was dropped as Mather's primary trainer in the mid-1970s, replaced by the jet-powered T-43. Concurrently, the Pentagon established undergraduate navigator training for all service branches at Mather. After nearly three decades at Mather, the 320th's B-52s were disbursed into other SAC wings in 1989. (SPL.)

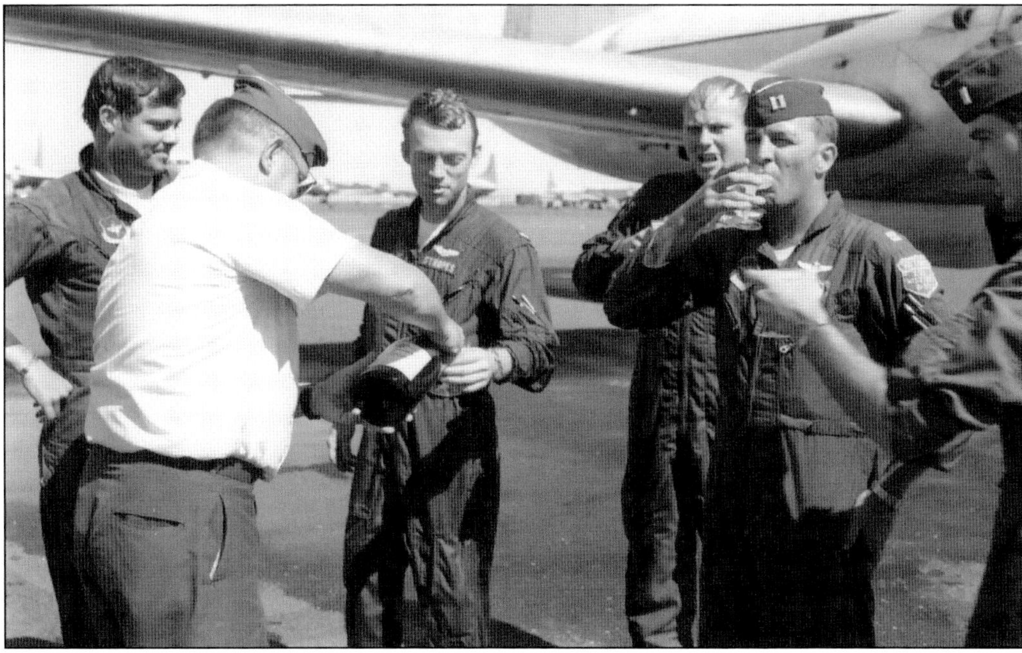

In this 1972 photograph, a group of relieved celebrates their graduation from navigator bombardier training at Mather Field. The 28-week curriculum exposed students to the fundamentals of radar navigation bombing through classroom instruction, equipment simulator practice, and T-29D aircraft missions. Although B-52-oriented, the flexibility of the training readied graduates to seamlessly adapt to other bombardment aircraft. A T-29D flying classroom sits in the background. (SPL.)

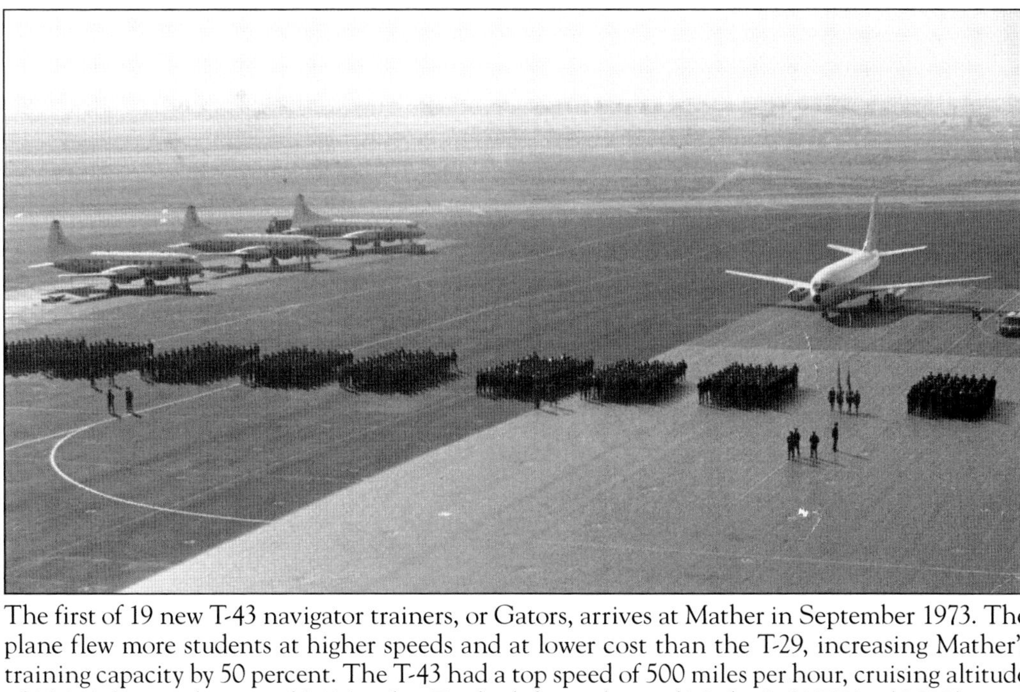

The first of 19 new T-43 navigator trainers, or Gators, arrives at Mather in September 1973. The plane flew more students at higher speeds and at lower cost than the T-29, increasing Mather's training capacity by 50 percent. The T-43 had a top speed of 500 miles per hour, cruising altitude of 35,000 feet, and range of 3,100 miles. To the left are three of Mather's 56 T-29s. (CSH.)

This 1973 photograph shows navigation instructor Capt. Joe Novich checking the sextant of a new Boeing T-43A navigator trainer. Five sextant ports, geared to celestial navigation training, were spaced overhead along the T-43A's fuselage. Each plane could also accommodate up to 12 trainees, who were required to complete 21 flight missions in the T-43A and 20 missions in a ground simulator. (CSH.)

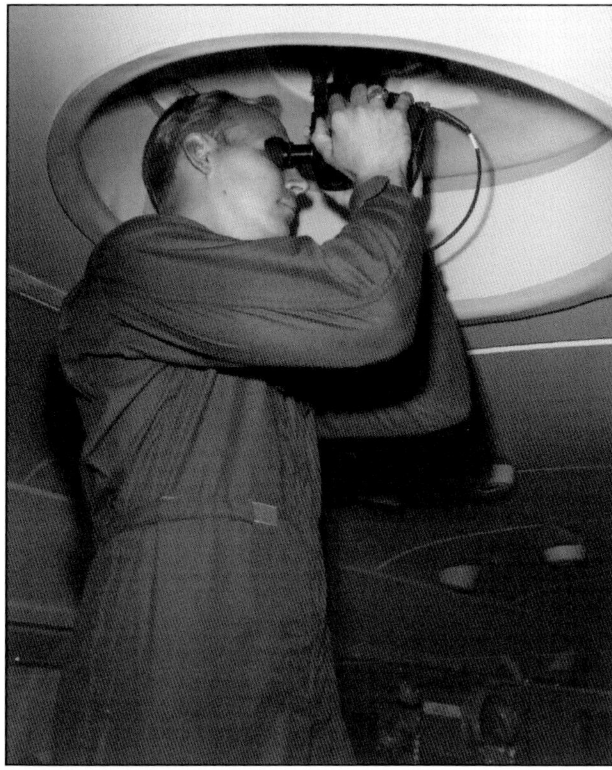

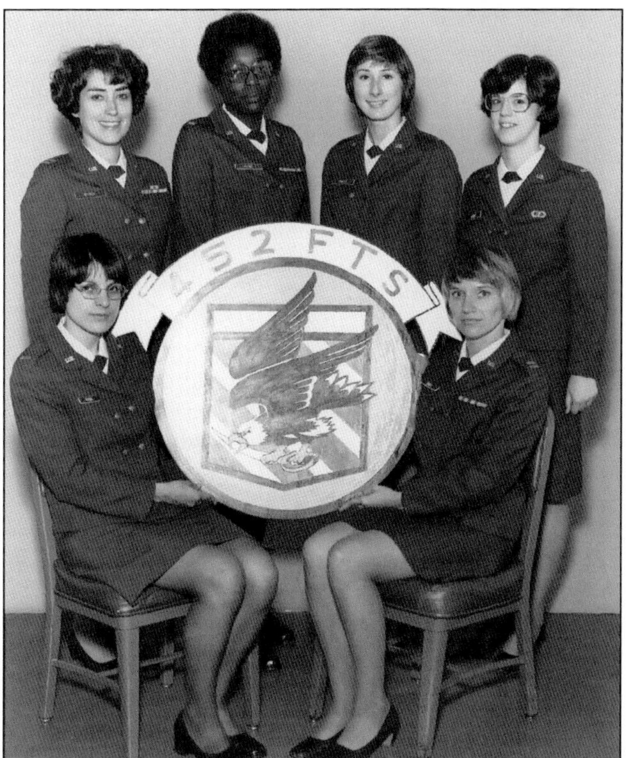

Shown in October 1977 and holding the insignia of the 452nd Flight Test Squadron is Mather Field's first graduating class of female navigators. By 1980, Mather had trained all 12 of the Air Force's female navigators with an eye on tripling that number soon thereafter. In the early 1980s, KC-135 tankers, EC-135 reconnaissance planes, WC-135 weather craft, and C-141 transports were the most common placements for female navigation officers. (CSH.)

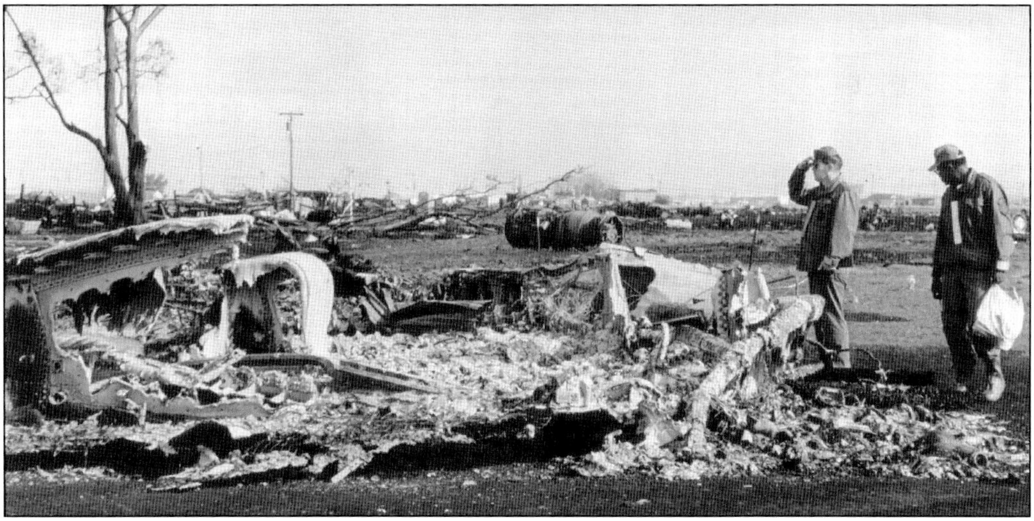

On the morning of December 16, 1982, a B-52G bomber practicing quick takeoffs (also known as minimum interval takeoffs, or MITOs) from runway 221 careened into a pasture located just to the southwest of the base. All nine crew members were killed in the conflagration that left a 400-yard swath of destruction. By December 18, an 11-member investigative team from North Dakota's Grand Forks Air Base was dispatched. (CSH.)

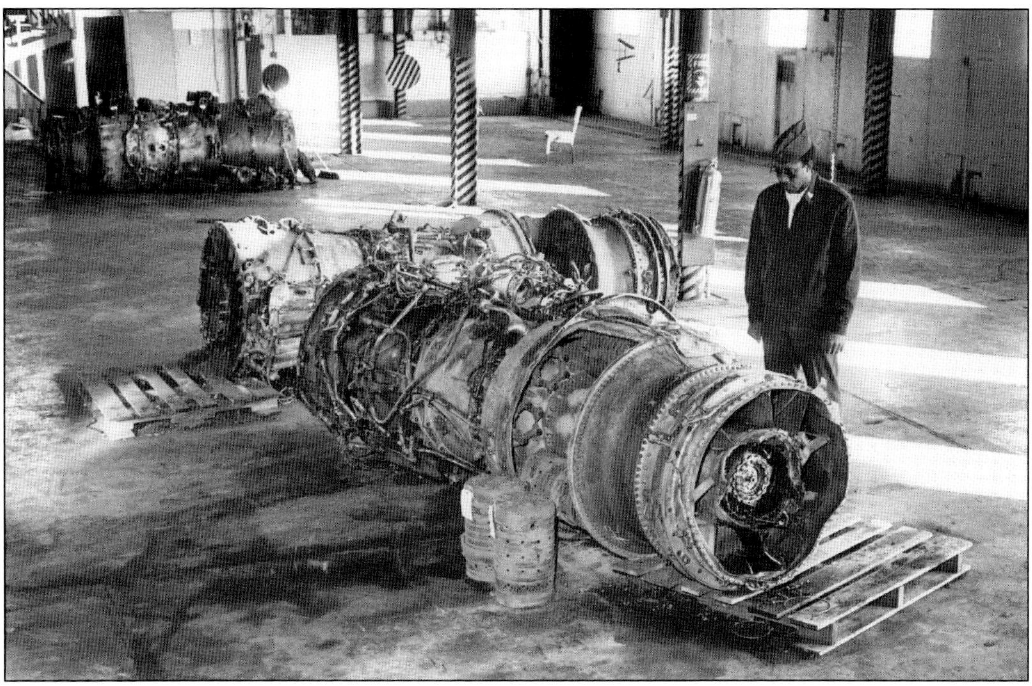

A February 1983 report on the B-52G's demise revealed no structural, engine, or maintenance problems. However, because Air Force regulations forbade the exact cause's release, questions lingered. At the behest of Congressman Robert Matsui, the Air Force revealed the crash to have resulted from the felled craft's effort to avoid the lead plane's jet wash. In this image, Mather TSgt. Nathaniel Tall inspects two of the plane's charred engines. (CSH.)

In 1987, the intersection of Happy Lane and Kiefer Road proved an ideal perch for viewing a B-52G tear its way westward. Despite the allure, the noise created by the 2,000 monthly flights of trainers, bombers, and tankers prompted the base, as early as April 1977, to alter flight patterns, veering ships by 15 degrees to the south and away from the sprawling residential sections west of Mather. (CSH.)

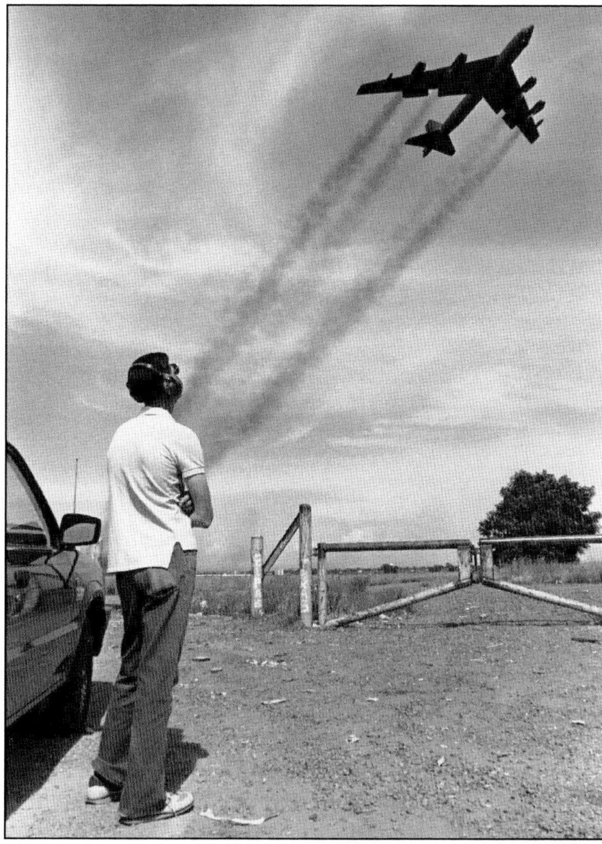

Pictured in 1987 are TSgt. John Halsey and his falcon Jenny. To minimize bird strikes, Jenny was charged with keeping birds off Mather's flight line. She joined a lengthy peerage of Mather working birds, starting in 1918 with Lt. W.D. Parrott's 81 homing pigeons, used to transport data to observation posts countywide. One pigeon, named Determination, set a speed record, flying from Sacramento to Mather in six minutes. (CSH.)

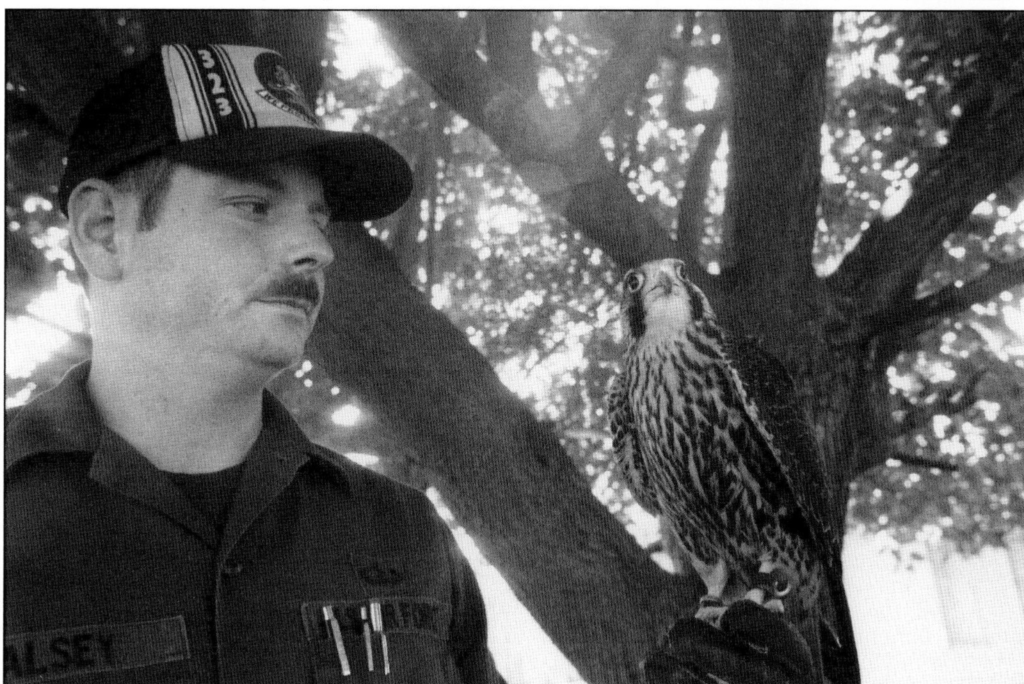

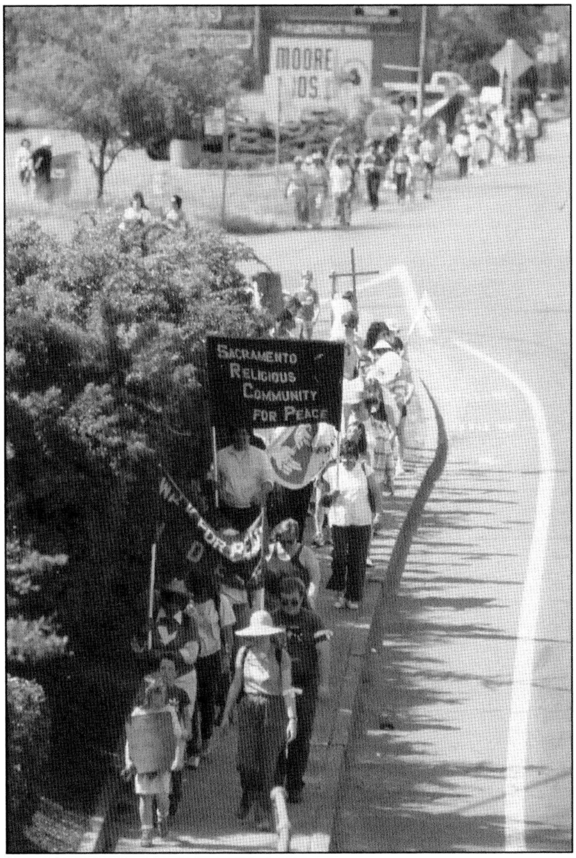

Protest held a near-constant presence during Mather's nuclear-age experience. Since January 1960, the base had operated as one of the Strategic Air Command's alert pads, mandating Mather's 320th Bombardment Wing to be on 24-hour attack readiness for the delivery of nuclear ordnance. Pictured at left is a procession of marchers making its way along Folsom Boulevard toward Mather. The fifth annual Walk for Peace, sponsored by the Sacramento Religious Community for Peace, covered 13 miles. Mather's nuclear arsenal was removed in October 1988, shifting the duties of its 14 B-52Gs to conventional bombing, aerial mine-laying, and maritime surveillance. Below, a 1982 photograph shows protestors outside Mather's front gate. A few participants hold a banner announcing the World Peace March and its support of the second United Nations special session on disarmament. (Both, CSH.)

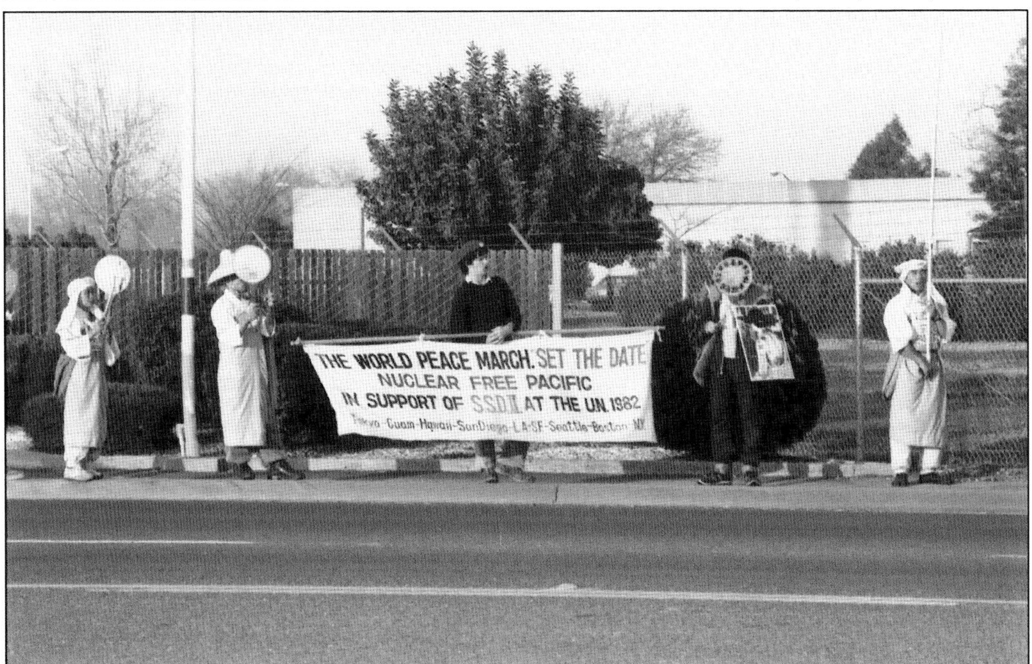

Six

Closure and Renewal by James Scott

A drive around 2011's Mather leaves the historian feeling a bit cheated. Where gaggles of JN-4s once sputtered about a dusty flight line, jet-powered commercial cargo carriers now cook atop a blackened tarmac. The venerable base headquarters remains, but all-weather siding now covers its original frame, and linoleum floors have been replaced by carpeting. Dorms that once billeted nervous navigation neophytes now operate as Mather Community Campus, a nationally recognized transitional housing program.

Mather's September 1993 closure lives in paradox. As an outpost of deterrence, it excelled at making "Peace its Profession," so much so that a well-earned peace dividend also begged a reapportionment of resources for a nation in gradual stand-down from the Cold War. In January 1987, the Air Force conceded Mather a "base of marginal utility," a comment preceding 1988's Base Realignment and Closure Act, which made the base one of 17 installations, nationwide, slated for closure. Congressmen Robert Matsui and Vic Fazio ensured Mather strong advocacy, challenging Pentagon assertions well into the eleventh hour.

Within 10 years, however, Mather was flourishing, having morphed into a business, medical, and air-transport hub attracting nearly $405 million in investment and selling many of its commercial lots. Central to this was May 1995's transference of aviation facilities to the Sacramento County Airport System, highlighted by the opening of the Mather Airport where, in 2006, airborne cargo carriers processed nearly 169.6 million pounds of freight. Although Mather's 4,500 new jobs fell short of the 8,000 existing prior to closure, the future looks bright with Commerce Park standing as both an international model for base repurposing and an exemplum of interagency cooperation.

In the mid-1990s, Sacramento activist Marilyn Evans was tabbed by Sacramento County to head a grassroots effort to promote and protect Mather's historical and environmental integrity. Born were the Friends of Mather Regional Park and, for Evans, an abiding affection for a space she envisioned to one day flower into a semirural version of Golden Gate Park. The group also committed itself to observing and honoring the collective memory of those who, for over 75 years, made Mather so indispensable to the nation's defense.

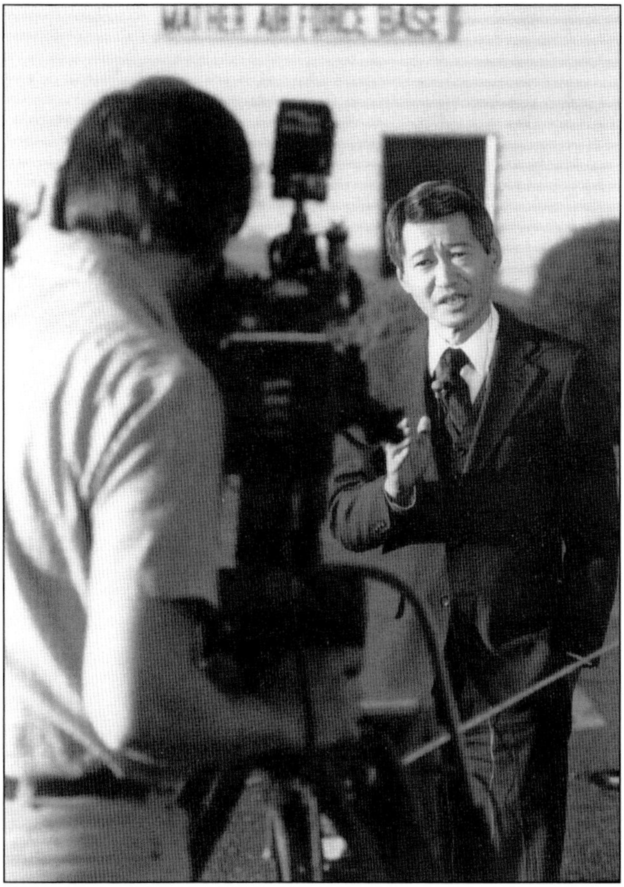

US representative Robert Matsui is pictured during a March 1987 fact-finding tour at Mather vis-à-vis an Air Force–initiated study on the feasibility of closing Mather, a move that the congressman opposed. Matsui came to be one of Mather's most ardent champions, contending that eliminating the base's navigation school would undercut the Air Force's conventional fighting strength and add to an already perilous reliance on nuclear weapons. (CSH.)

One of the first to fall victim to Mather's incremental closure was hydraulics mechanic Bill Buelow, standing near a C-37 trainer in November 1989. At that time, he became one of 64 civil servants and 228 uniformed personnel to be liquidated in favor of Texas-based contractor Serv-Air. This made Mather the seventh Air Training Command base to abdicate its maintenance needs to a civilian firm. (CSH.)

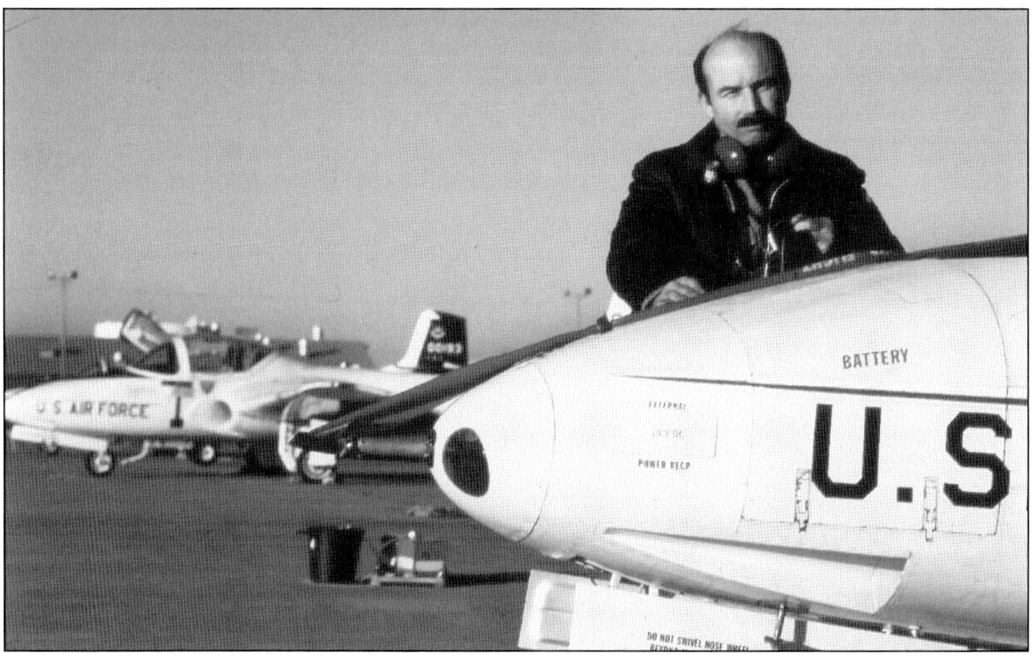

Mather graduated its first class of navigators on November 15, 1941, and its last on April 19, 1993. That final ceremony's program is pictured here. The group was composed of 51 officers—mostly Americans, but consisting also of Germans and Italians. They would ascend to navigator, electronic warfare, and weapon systems officer posts in B-52 bombers, Panavia Tornado and F-15E fighters, C-130 transports, and various other ships. (Marilyn Evans.)

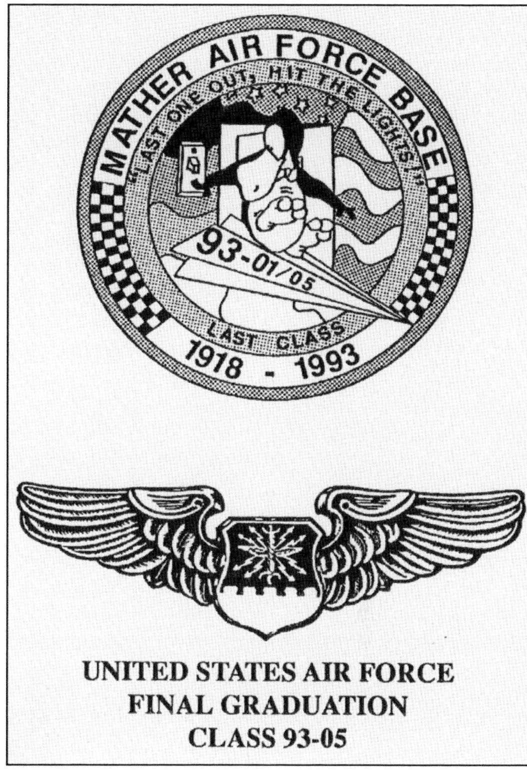

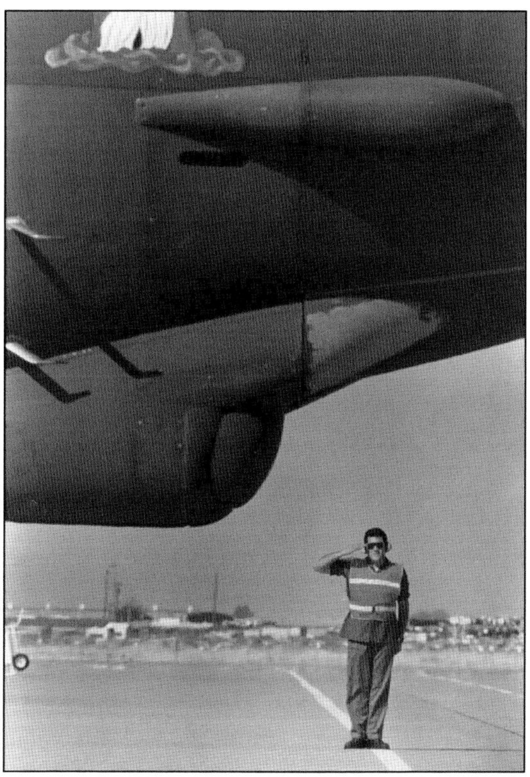

Pictured in July 1989, SrA. Jose Jimenez salutes *Eldership*, the last of Mather's long and proud peerage of B-52s. This particular ship was built by Boeing in 1957 and flew combat missions over Vietnam in 1972 and 1973. As of 2011, *Eldership* is on display near the entrance to Offutt Air Force Base in Omaha, Nebraska. Mather's entire 320th Bombardment Wing was officially deactivated on October 1, 1989. (CSH.)

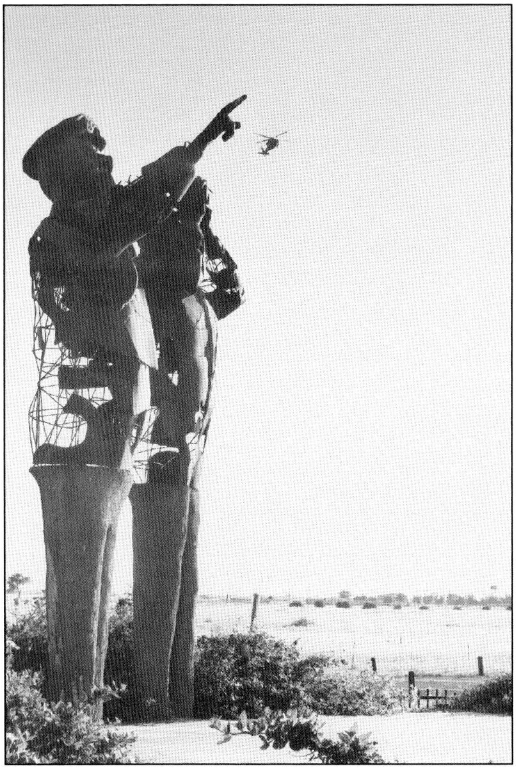

Standing 18 feet high, *The Navigators* search for ever-steady Polaris. The sculpture was created by artist Darrell Fleener and dedicated in 2003 under the auspices of the Friends of Mather Regional Park. The elder navigator's finger forms a sundial on the platform below. The accompanying plaque reads, "To their skill to set the course, to their duty to complete the mission, to their dedication to bring their crew home safe again." (SPL.)

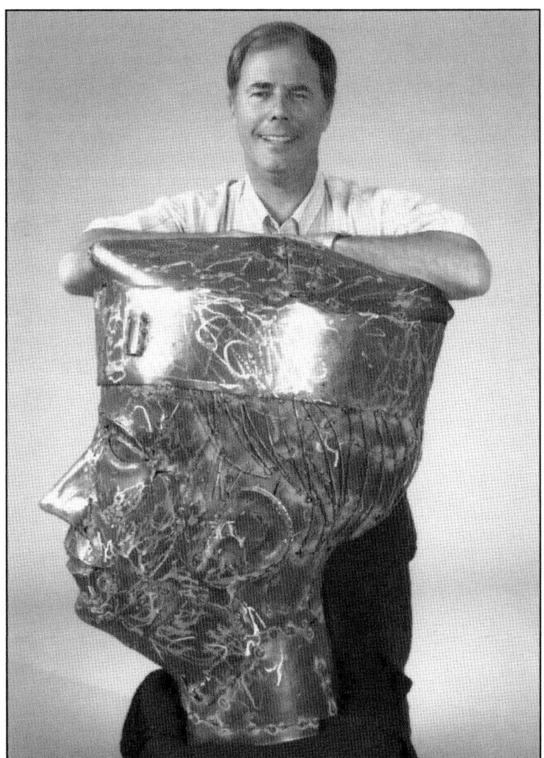

Resting on the bust of one of *The Navigators* is Darrell Fleener. A veteran of the Air Force, Fleener's association with Mather, where he worked as a civilian artist in the graphics division for 15 years, spanned three decades. He is responsible for no less than 20 base murals and served as the curator of Mather's Silver Wings Museum until its closure in 1993. (Marilyn Evans.)

Seen in the image on the right and twisting itself skyward, with Mather's erstwhile headquarters in the background, is a sculpture dedicated to the spirit of flight. Commissioned for $45,000, it was created in 1998 by Northern California artist Dan Dykes and marks both the old and new entrance (at the same spot) to Mather. The so-called Mather Field Entry Sculpture was funded by a grant from the Economic Development Administration of the Federal Bureau of Commerce. Set within a compass rose, the piece is ringed by several historical comments, attributable to aviation and aerospace luminaries like John Glenn, Charles Lindbergh, and Wernher von Braun. Also included and pictured below is the mantra of Mather's "tenacious tenant," the Strategic Air Command: Peace is our profession. (Both, SPL.)

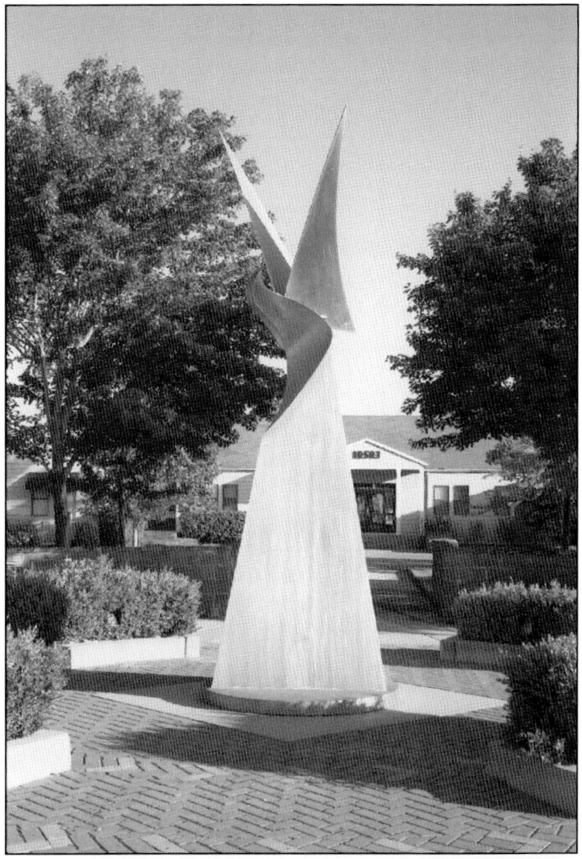

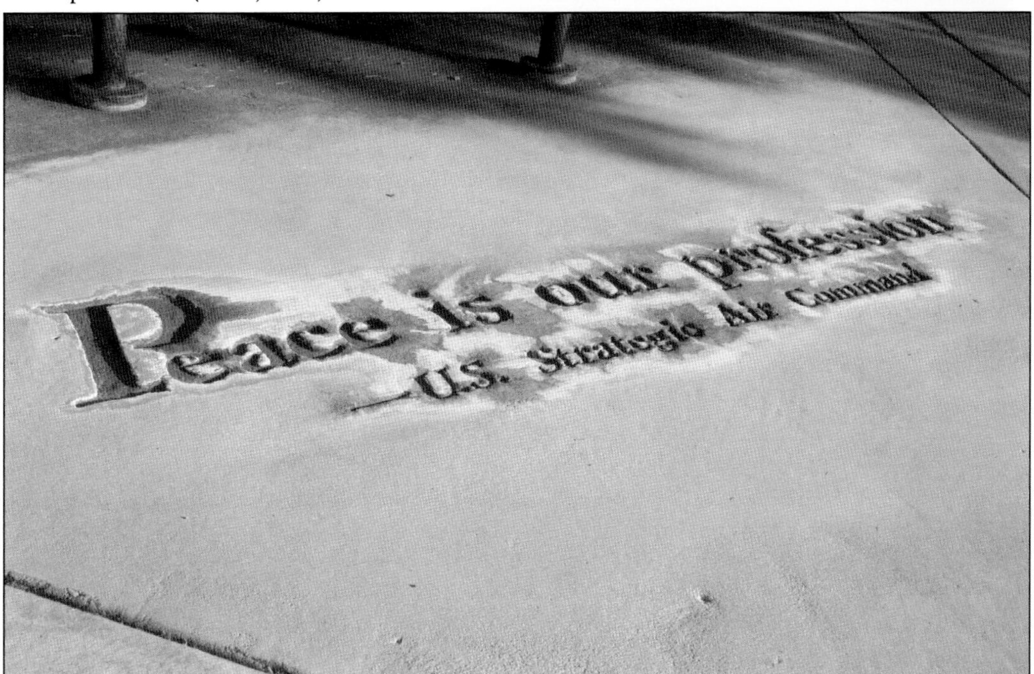

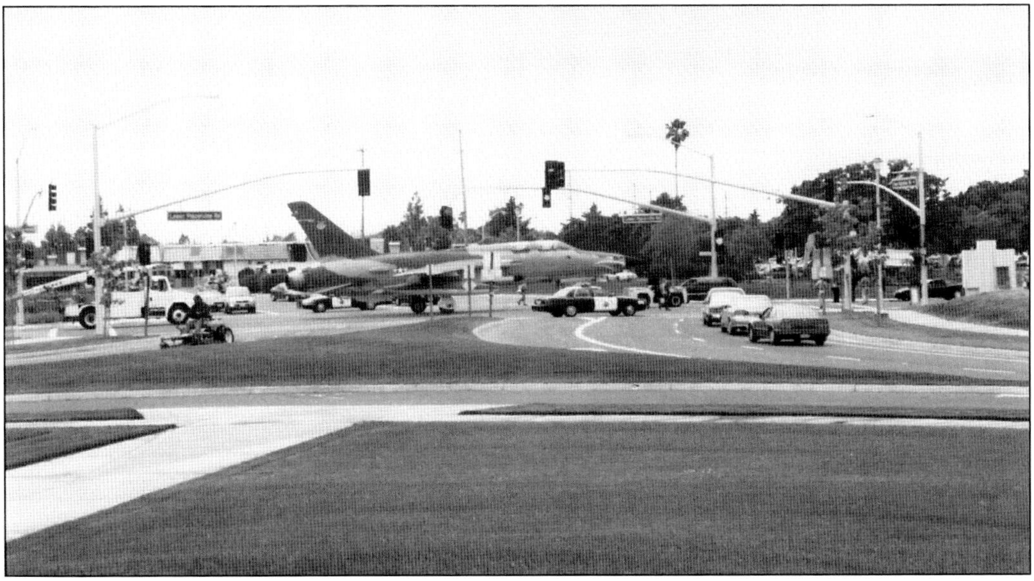

Above and bordering on the surreal in May 2000 is an F-105G Wild Weasel being shepherded down Lower Placerville Road toward its new aerie at Mather's Veterans Affairs (VA) Medical Center. The plane's migration was a team effort, utilizing the might of public and private sectors. Below, a satisfied group poses before the F-105G after its migration from the Mather tarmac to the hospital's southern grounds. The plane's primary steward, Marilyn Evans, stands fourth from the left. As founder of the Friends of Mather Regional Park and mother of a Mather-trained officer, Evans well understood the plane's importance: "[It] has a story, a history here. The navigation officers who sat in the back seat were trained here." (Both, Marilyn Evans.)

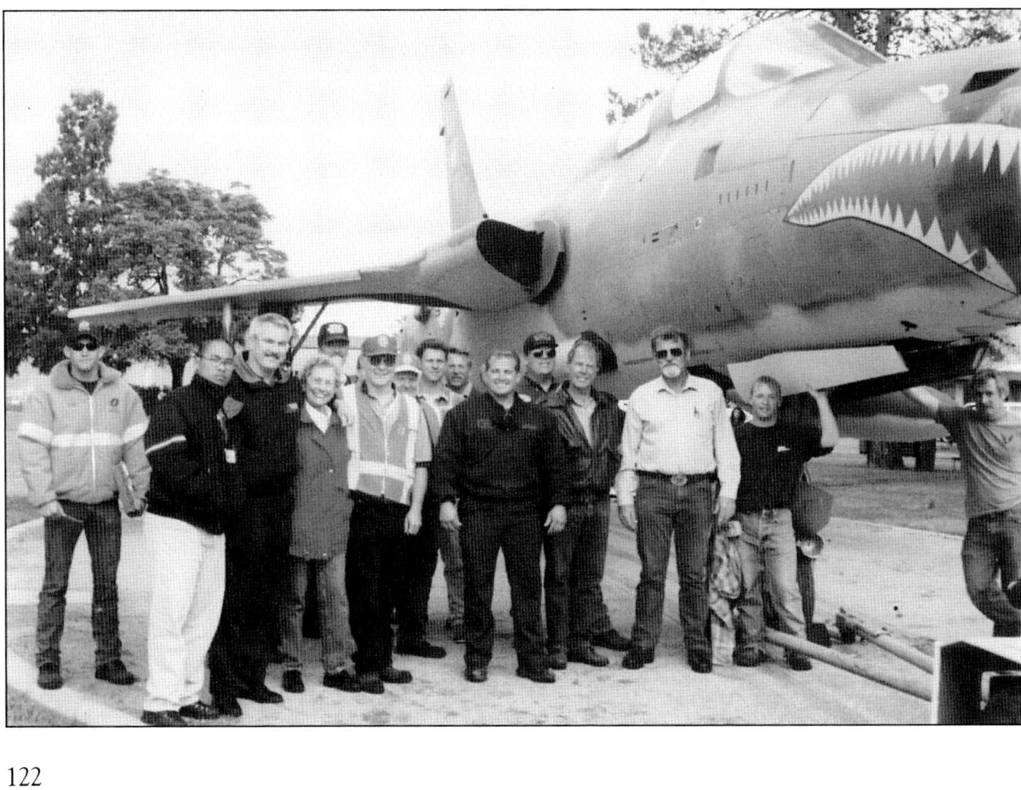

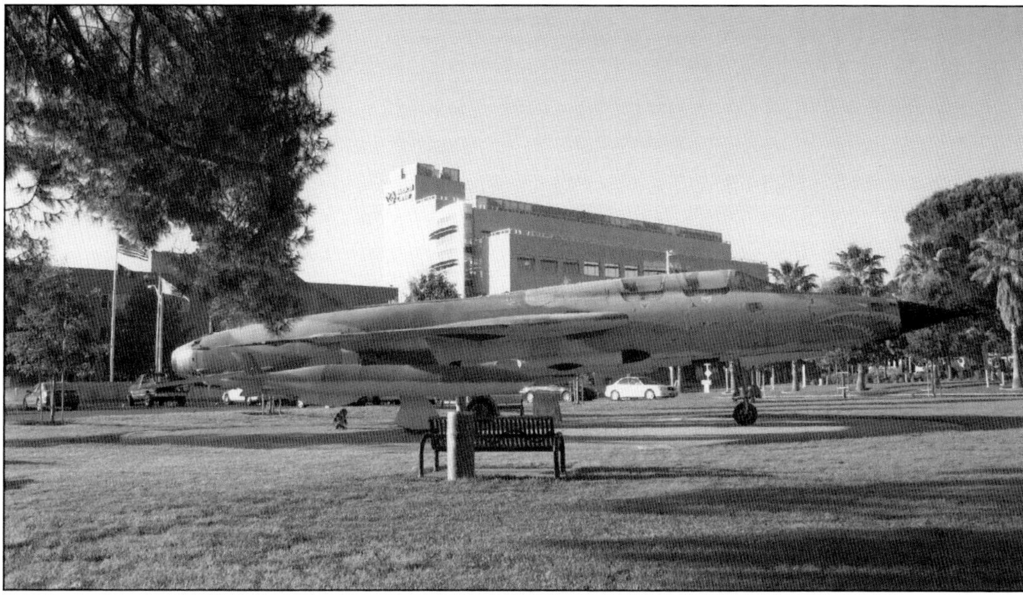

Pictured in 2011, the F-105G sits on permanent display before the VA Medical Center. During the Vietnam War, many Thunderchiefs were retrofitted into Wild Weasels and charged with destroying surface-to-air missile and radar-tracking sites. Starting in 1996, the Friends of Mather Regional Park launched a campaign to purchase and maintain the artifact. Successfully achieving as much, the plane was dedicated on May 21, 2000. After the VA's 1998 acquisition of the Mather Community Hospital, a series of additions followed, with the newest portion, a $39.5 million inpatient tower, opening in June 2003 with research facilities, operating rooms, and 55 beds. To the photograph's left is a vestige of Mather's past, the base hospital built in the 1960s. Below, a child plays inside the afterburner of a plane that once flew combat missions over North Vietnam. (Both, SPL.)

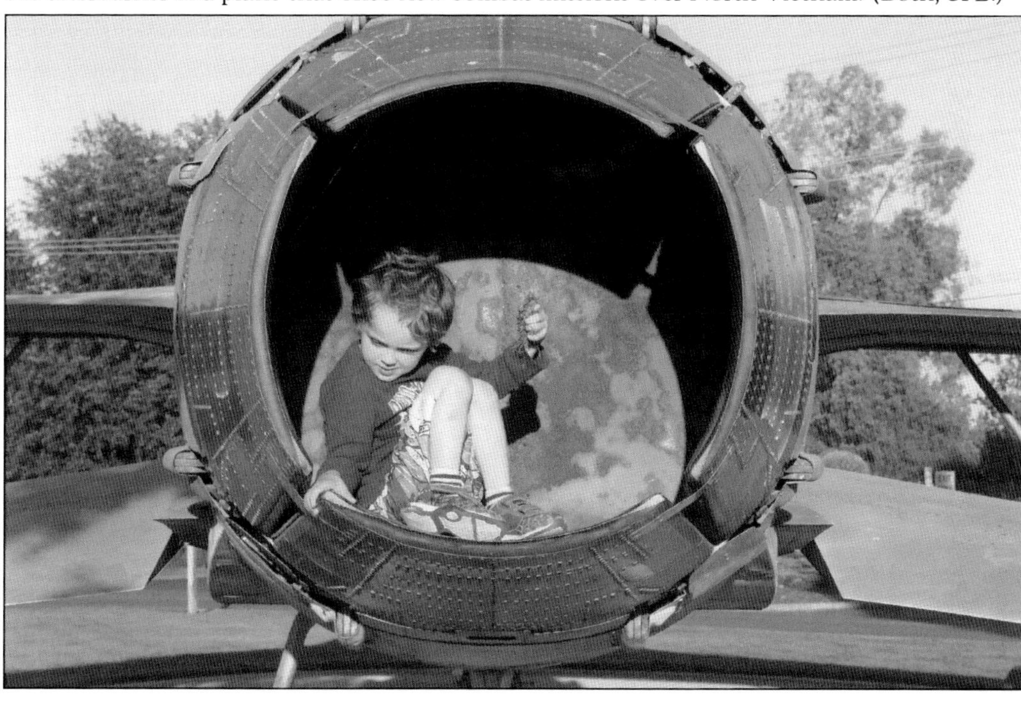

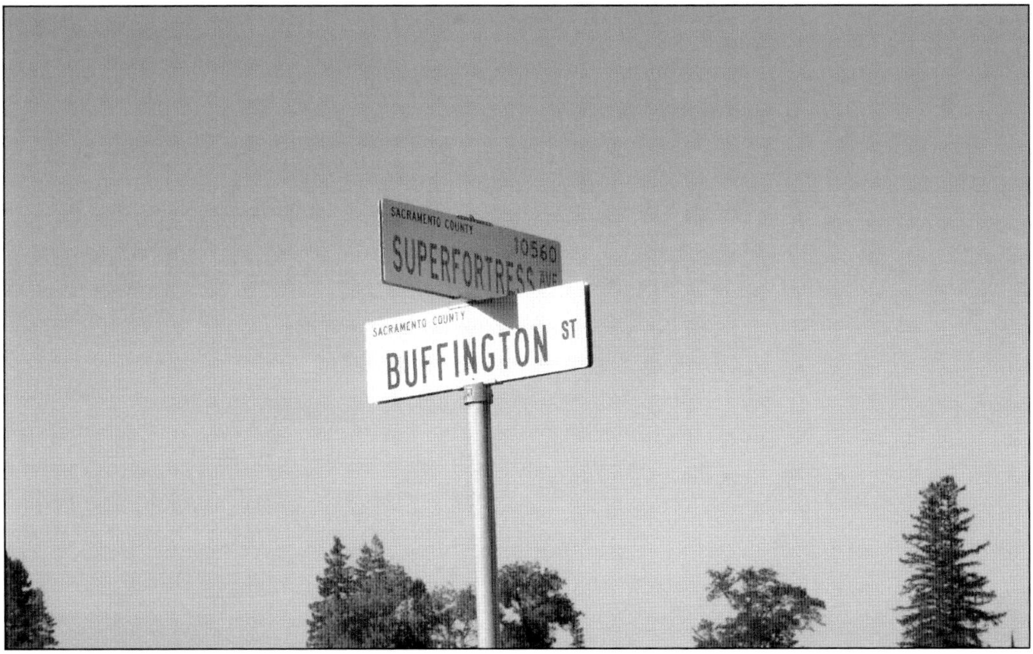

Street signage eulogizes two influential chapters in the Mather story. Lt. John Buffington made Mather's inaugural flight in June 1918, piloting a Sacramento-built JN-4 and what the *Sacramento Bee* likened to "a great bird, graceful and responding to the most delicate touch." The B-29 Superfortress's silvery-riveted scales were commonplace at Mather from 1945 to 1949. Over 3,000 B-29 crewmen died in the Pacific, many passing through Mather en route. (SPL.)

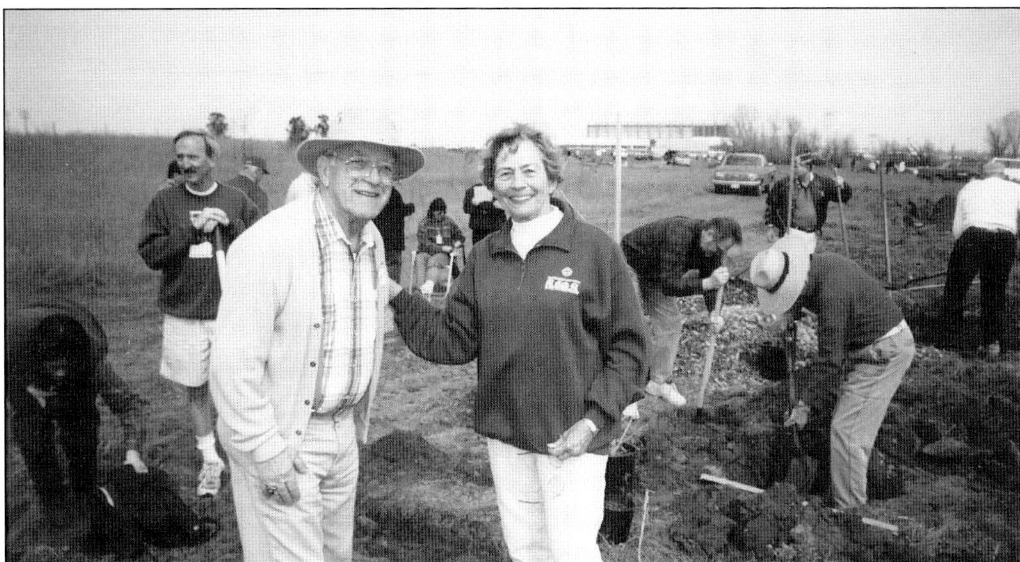

In the foreground of this April 1999 photograph stand longtime Sacramento tree advocate Austin Carroll (left) and Mather activist Marilyn Evans. Organized by the Sacramento Tree Foundation, the pictured tree-planting event sought to populate a section of the 1,500-acre park. As of 2010 and under mounting budget pressure, Sacramento County has studied the possibility of a mixed-purpose status for a portion of the park. (Marilyn Evans.)

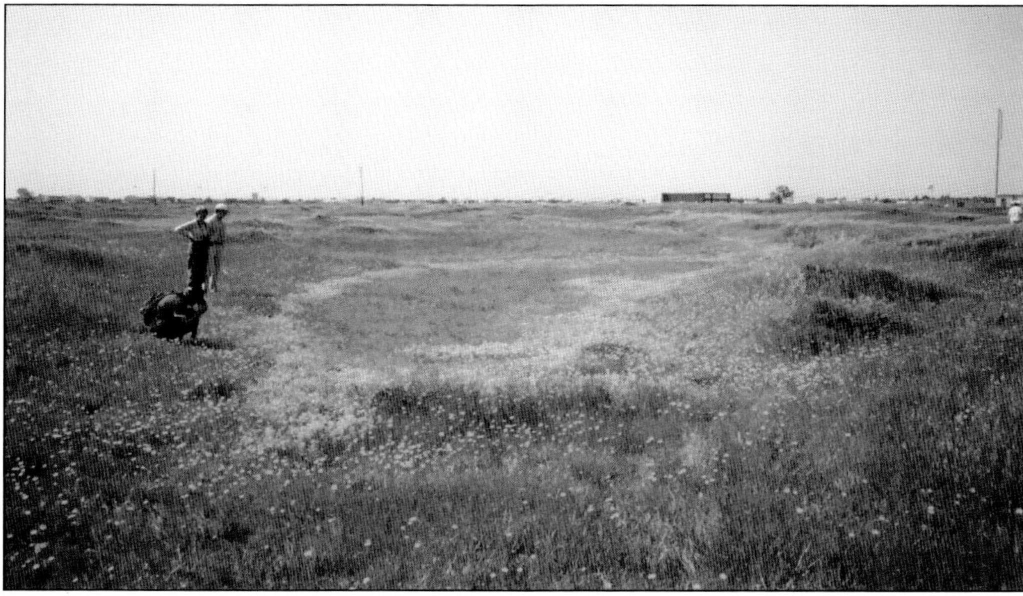

Pictured in 1998, nature enthusiasts take in Mather's exquisite collection of vernal pools. The wetlands fill up in the winter and dry down in the spring and summer, providing habitat for an abundance of flora and fauna that, simply put, can live nowhere else. Sustained by California's unique combination of hardpan soils and Mediterranean climate, Mather's pools comprise part of the mere 10 percent that remain in California. (Marilyn Evans.)

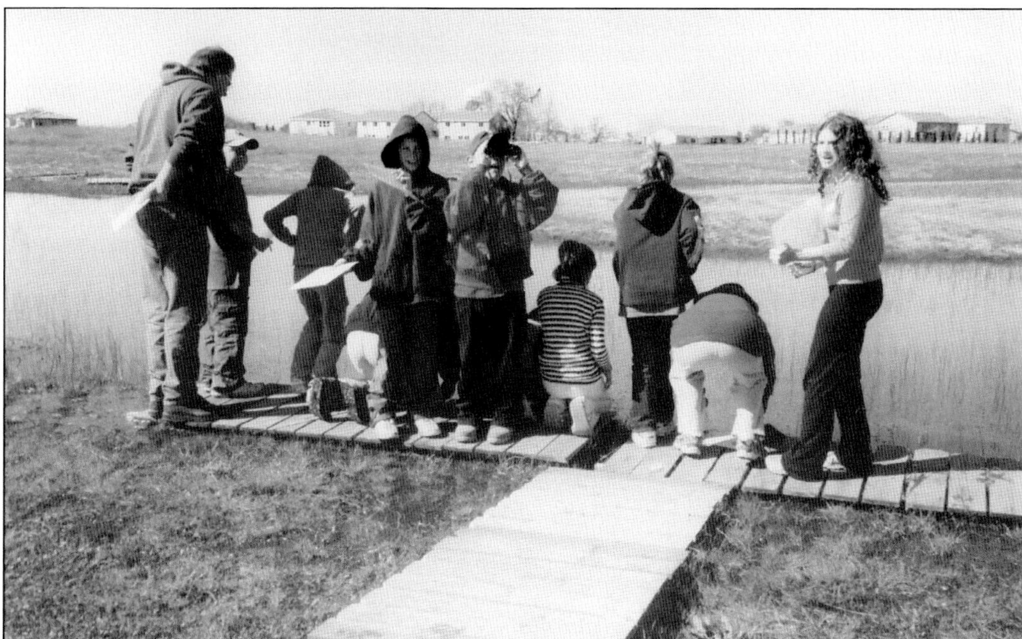

As captured in this 1999 photograph, children participate in the Splash Elementary Program. Founded in 1999 by local biologist Eva Butler, Splash has stood as a nonprofit venture to provide stewardship for and public education on many of Sacramento's native habitats, particularly vernal pools. The program's foundational beliefs are that nature inspires learning and that properly educated children will become advocates for nature. (Marilyn Evans.)

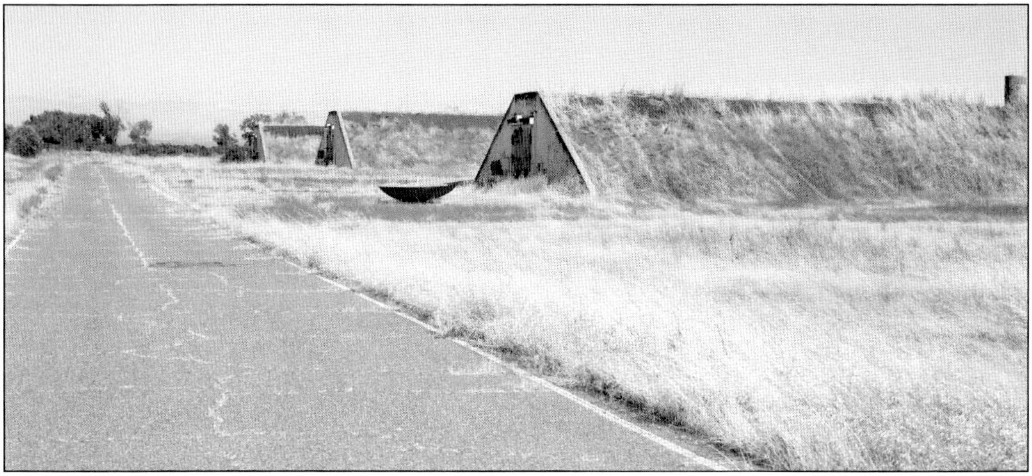

A sequence of concrete bunkers near the eastern edge of Mather's weapons-storage area is pictured above in July 2011. It is here that the base's highest-profile nuclear ordnance, the standoff-oriented AGM-28 Hound Dog missile, was stored. Newer air-launched cruise missiles were also kept here following the Hound Dog's late-1970s scrapping. Prior to their 1988 removal, Mather possessed a speculated 60 short-range nuclear attack missiles and 150 nuclear bombs. Two decades later and in stark contrast, county officials, in the spirit of repurposing, were approached with ideas ranging from the academic to the downright curious. One concept with more than a bit of traction relates to a future college campus, while another sought the use of the bunkers for wine storage. Pictured below in 2000 is an unsettling reminder of Cold War protocol. (Above, SPL; below, Gerald Ward.)

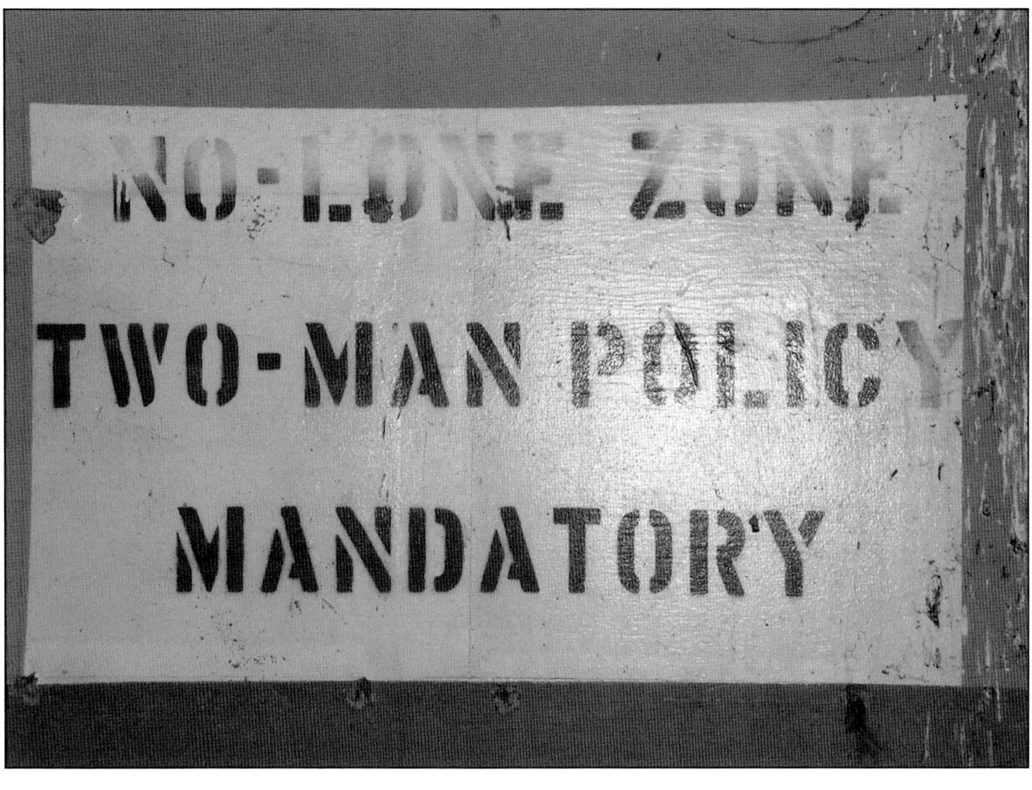

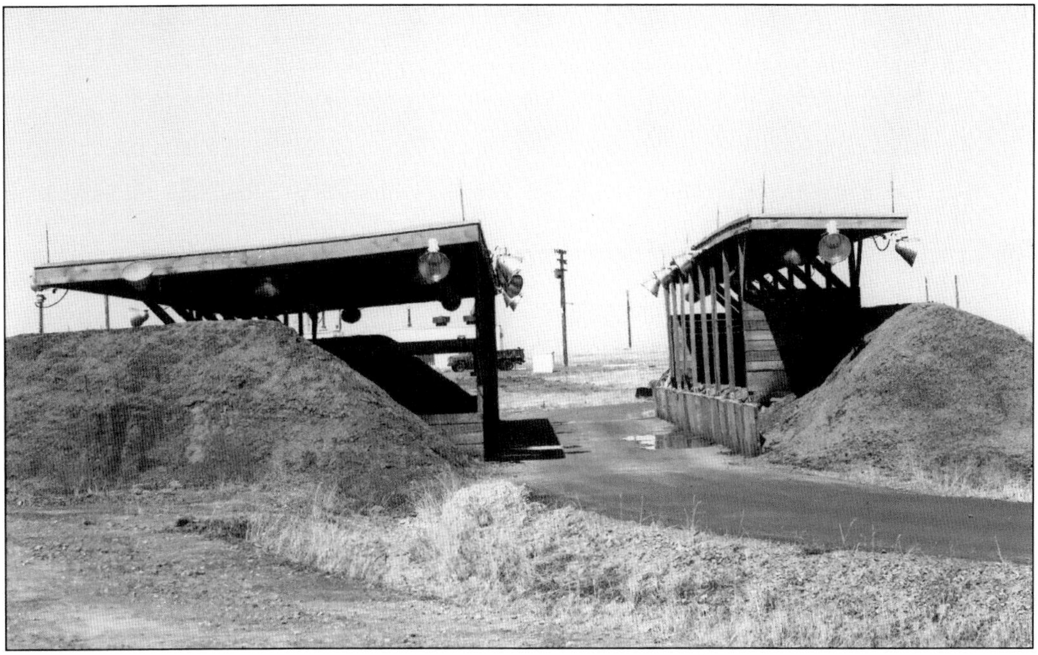

Shown above in October 1967 is building 18090, a shelter within the conventional weapons section of Mather's weapons-storage area. At that time, Mather's 14 B-52Gs were the only base aircraft carrying weapons. Forty-four years later in July 2011, the same bomb-storage shelter (below) sits, not guarded by an M-16–toting security police squadron but by an army of western fence lizards and a legion of spent spray-paint canisters. Again, contrasts dominate a spot once at the forefront of nuclear war and now, for the time being, left for nature to both repossess and repopulate. (Above, CSH; below, SPL.)

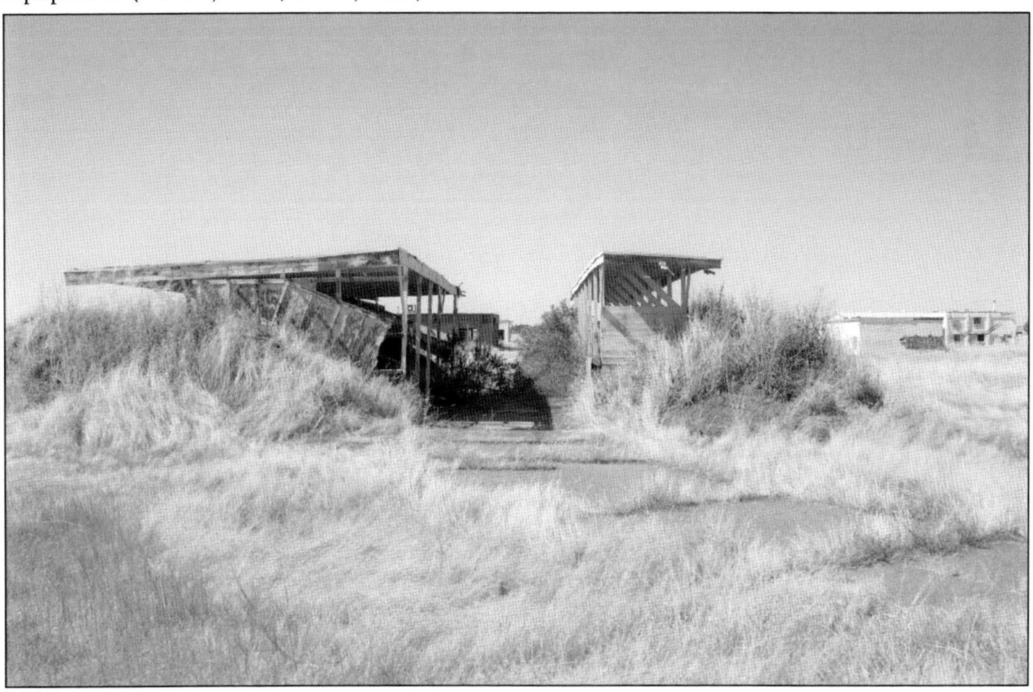

DISCOVER THOUSANDS OF LOCAL HISTORY BOOKS
FEATURING MILLIONS OF VINTAGE IMAGES

Arcadia Publishing, the leading local history publisher in the United States, is committed to making history accessible and meaningful through publishing books that celebrate and preserve the heritage of America's people and places.

Find more books like this at
www.arcadiapublishing.com

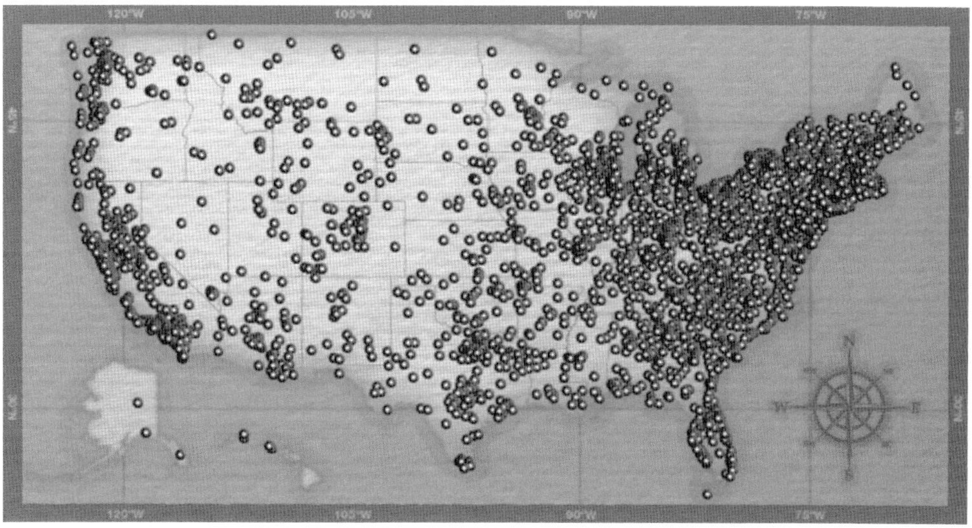

Search for your hometown history, your old stomping grounds, and even your favorite sports team.

Consistent with our mission to preserve history on a local level, this book was printed in South Carolina on American-made paper and manufactured entirely in the United States. Products carrying the accredited Forest Stewardship Council (FSC) label are printed on 100 percent FSC-certified paper.

MADE IN THE USA